COMPREHENSION SHOULDN'T BE SILENT

FROM STRATEGY INSTRUCTION TO STUDENT INDEPENDENCE

Michelle J. Kelley
Nicki Clausen-Grace

INTERNATIONAL
Reading Association
800 BARKSDALE ROAD, PO BOX 8139
NEWARK, DE 19714-8139, USA
www.reading.org

The International Reading Association attempts, through its publications, to provide a forum for a wide spectrum of opinions on reading. This policy permits divergent viewpoints without implying the endorsement of the Association.

Executive Editor, Books   Corinne M. Mooney
Developmental Editor   Charlene M. Nichols
Developmental Editor   Tori Mello Bachman
Developmental Editor   Stacey Lynn Sharp
Editorial Production Manager   Shannon T. Fortner
Design and Composition Manager   Anette Schuetz

Project Editors   Tori Mello Bachman and Christina Lambert

Cover   Design and Illustrations, Thomson Digital; Photograph, © Corbis

Library of Congress Cataloging-in-Publication Data

Kelley, Michelle.

  Comprehension shouldn't be silent : from strategy instruction to student independence / Michelle J. Kelley, Nicki Clausen-Grace.

      p. cm.

  Includes bibliographical references and index.

  ISBN-13: 978-0-87207-620-4

  1. Reading (Elementary) 2. Reading comprehension. 3. Children--Books and reading. I. Clausen-Grace, Nicki. II. Title.

  LB1573.K44 2007

  372.47--dc22   2007024505

CONTENTS

Part III
Metacognitive Strategy Units

Michelle J. Kelley is an assistant professor in reading at the University of Central Florida (UCF), Orlando, Florida, USA, where she teaches preservice teachers and graduate students in the Teaching and Learning Principles Department. Her role also includes mentoring and providing professional development to educators.

Michelle's teaching career began in West Gardiner, Maine, USA, where she completed her MA in Literacy Education from the University of Southern Maine, Portland, Maine, USA while teaching fifth graders. She later moved to Central Florida, where she taught for nine years before becoming a literacy specialist for the intermediate grades. Upon receiving an EdD in Educational Leadership from the University of Florida, Gainesville, Florida, USA, Michelle worked for the Florida Literacy and Reading Excellence Center (FLaRE) as a professional developer.

Michelle has worked extensively in urban and suburban schools. Her research area is comprehension, and she has devoted a great deal of time to the role of independent reading in terms of engagement, motivation, self-efficacy, and metacognition. Her articles have appeared in *The Reading Teacher* and *Voices From the Middle,* and she reviews professional materials for *Curriculum Connections*. She has authored several children's books as well, including *Just Like Me*; *Rules, Rules, Rules*; *Different Places, Different Words*; and *Job*. She has been recognized with several Disney Teacherrific awards and received numerous grants to facilitate literacy. Michelle is actively involved in the Florida Reading Association, serving on the Board of Directors as the Family Literacy Chair.

Michelle and her husband, Shaun, have two children, Tyler and Heather. Michelle enjoys crossword puzzles, reading, traveling, and cooking. She can be reached at mkelley@mail.ucf.edu.

Nicki Clausen-Grace is a teacher, author, consultant, and staff developer. She teaches fourth grade at Carillon Elementary School in Oviedo, Florida, USA, and is an adjunct instructor of literature at the University of Central Florida, Orlando, Florida, USA. As a consultant, she speaks on a variety of literacy topics, including reading engagement, content area reading, literature/text circles, word study, and comprehension strategies.

As a columnist for *Central Florida Family,* Nicki authored more than 50 articles on local schools and other education topics. She has published articles on parenting and reading, as well. She regularly reviews children's books and professional materials for

School Library Journal and *Curriculum Connections*. She has written three children's books: *Please Say Please, Haircuts Don't Hurt,* and *What Can You Make?*

Born and raised in Missouri, USA, Nicki earned her undergraduate degree in Elementary Education from the University of South Florida, Tampa, Florida, USA, and her Masters in Elementary Education from the Lockheed Martin/UCF Academy of Science and Math at the University of Central Florida, Orlando, Florida, USA. She has won numerous Disney Innovative Teaching Practices and Teacheriffic awards and attained National Board Certification as a Middle Childhood Generalist in 1999.

Nicki lives in Florida with her husband, Jeff, and their children, Brad and Alexandra. Both she and her husband teach at their neighborhood school, which their daughter attends. When she is not working, Nicki likes to cook, read, and spend time outdoors with her family. She can be reached at njgrace@bellsouth.net.

> *Every year our class visits a simulated medieval village. We walk through a string of artisan cottages and learn from docents dressed in period costumes. Despite the occasional waft of country music intruding on the fantasy, one room never fails to amaze. It's the one where they take raw cotton, spin it into yarn, and then weave it into fabric. The woman in this room doesn't have to speak with a fake accent to impress—we all press forward to watch her nimble fingers deftly maneuver a skein of yarn through the web of string. She pulls on the frame with a clack and one more tiny row is completed. We gaze at the plain looking garments hung in the room beyond with new appreciation. Someone made that fabric. By hand.*

For most of us the idea of weaving a cloth fine enough to make into clothing is a daunting one indeed. But, like anything else, the art of weaving can be learned if broken into smaller, more manageable bits.

While the act of weaving isn't simple, it is easy compared to the process of reading. In fact, learning to read is so complex that many of us forget the intricacies of how we read, we just do it. For most teachers who teach children beyond the primary grades, the idea of teaching a child to read from scratch is intimidating. Fortunately, our students are usually on their way to becoming readers when we get them, and many are fluent. Unfortunately, many come with a view of reading as a purely mechanical act, something they do just at school. These students can read most of the words on a page, but they haven't yet learned how reading can help them lead a richer, more meaningful life. They haven't yet escaped into a text. And, just as importantly, many students do not know how to repair meaning when it breaks down.

Our task is to take all of these readers, whatever their strengths and needs are, and help them gain a deeper understanding of what they read. We must indoctrinate them into the world of thoughtful literacy. To do this, we may still need to work on the mechanics of reading with some and stimulate a motivation to read with others. But to improve comprehension, all readers will need the intricate act of making meaning to be broken down into smaller, more explicit steps.

Who We Are and Why We Wrote This Book

In December of 2003, Nicki, then a third-grade teacher, and Michelle, an assistant professor, collaborated on some key issues in Nicki's class. There were a couple of groups of students Nicki felt she wasn't reaching. The first was what she called her "fake" readers, or disengaged readers—those who would consistently read the words in a section of text without making meaning. Their abilities to read and comprehend ranged from near the top of her class, to the bottom. When asked to read either for work or pleasure, their comprehension reflected a universal lack of engagement with the text. The second group was made up of her highest readers, many of whom came to her reading and comprehending texts up to two grade levels above. Nicki really wanted to move them purposefully forward, to give them the more advanced skills they needed to comprehend a wide variety of texts. Widespread among both groups was a general lack of metacognitive awareness, or a lack of knowledge of the thought processes they use as they read.

Michelle was further interested in finding out to what extent elementary-age students could metacognate. She knew that nonfiction exposure was integral to later success in school and life. Therefore she wanted students to work with both fiction and nonfiction texts as we helped them become strategic and reflective readers.

In addition, we both recognized that independent reading was important to this process but were concerned about students' lack of engagement. We were committed to providing students with time to read books of their choice, but we had both experienced students who avoided reading. Some students chose inappropriate books and others pretended to read, but really their eyes just passed by print without any of the students thinking about what they were reading. We hoped that in our quest to find out more about students' metacognitive awareness, we would also discover how to engage our fake readers and purposefully accelerate our highest readers.

Our data suggested that students would benefit from direct strategy instruction. Both of us had a lot of experience teaching strategies, but we felt our instruction and the professional resources devoted to strategy instruction fell short of creating independent strategy users. We found that the students tended to use the strategies during lessons, but many times failed to carry the skill use to independence. We thought if students developed strategy self-improvement plans and implemented them during independent reading, they might begin to internalize the lessons being taught during direct instruction while reading.

Unfortunately, the first plans were disappointing. Our higher achieving students used teacher lingo to please us, while other students' plans reflected a total lack of understanding. We quickly realized we had "put the cart before the horse"—students did not fully understand the intricacies of each strategy, how and why they were using a strategy, or how to employ the strategy to better comprehend, and therefore they were unable to write meaningful plans.

We decided to start over with metacognitive units of study instead. We felt if we could demonstrate for students how we as expert readers use a strategy with a variety of texts, then supported them while they practiced using the strategy, over time they would gain the ability to write a plan for using the strategy independently—our ultimate goal.

Our first unit was about predicting. We spent a few weeks researching the strategy, and we observed the reading and thinking habits of students, ourselves, and our families to determine how predicting takes place and how it helps support engagement. Because we wanted students to be metacognitive, we felt we needed to break the strategy into components to help them notice their strategy use as well as improve upon it. The predicting components became the basis for all the lessons we taught, from the first think-aloud to the conferences during independent reading.

We also orchestrated a structured independent reading block and named it R⁵, which stands for Read, Relax, Reflect, Respond, and Rap. R⁵ is a time for students to read for pleasure and for us to observe and coach their strategy use. We designed the process to help engage the fake readers and provide a time for all students to use their strategy plans with support. R⁵ became the students' favorite time of day, and it helped us take strategy lessons to the next level—independence.

What emerged from this first unit was a pattern of instruction, which we named the Metacognitive Teaching Framework, or the MTF. We realized this framework provided scaffolding for students and for us as teachers. By implementing the MTF—and through a tremendous amount of reflection—we were able to make our thinking and students' thinking visible. Integral to the effectiveness of the MTF was creating a community of learners who engaged in meaningful talk centered on strategies and learning. By developing a common language and encouraging talk throughout the MTF, students moved forward in their desire and abilities to comprehend what they read.

This Book's Organization

This book supports many of the professional resources available on teaching strategies. Where it differs, however, is the level of specificity it offers teachers and students. The MTF, including strategy components, self-assessment goal-setting plans, and R⁵, can be used to help your students take what they learn in strategy lessons to the highest level of integration, which is independent use. If you haven't yet used strategy units, this book supplies a basis for doing so. These strategy units work especially well when you integrate reading with content area studies, which results in a deeper understanding of both content and reading strategies.

This book is divided into three sections. The first section provides an overview of the MTF, how to create an environment to support the MTF, and the various teaching structures employed throughout the MTF. The second section contains a more in-depth description of how we nurture and promote conversations about books, specifically through literature circles, textbook circles, and R⁵. The third section describes the strategy units you can use to make each strategy more accessible to students. It includes student samples, transcripts of classroom dialogue, activities to engage students and reinforce component use, and self-assessment goal-setting plans for each strategy.

In chapter 1 we share our rationale for explicitly teaching reading strategies to develop metacognitive readers. We also provide brief definitions of terms, concepts, and structures we use throughout the book. Then, we outline the MTF used to teach each strategy, including how to create an environment that nurtures metacognition. In chapter 2 we help you get started by sharing daily, weekly, and yearly plans for implementation. Chapter 3 explains literature circles, textbook circles, and other structures to promote discussion, and chapter 4 provides a detailed look at R⁵. Chapters 5 through 9 describe the five metacognitive strategy units to use to facilitate students' learning. Throughout the book, you'll read classroom transcripts and view student samples and quotes to help clarify key points. Appendix A provides a matrix to help you identify activities for teaching metacognitive strategies, and Appendix B holds numerous reproducibles to help you put the strategies to use right away.

This book would not be possible without the work of a number of literacy pioneers. We were highly influenced by the work of Ellin Oliver Keene and Susan Zimmermann in *Mosaic of Thought: Teaching Comprehension in a Reader's Workshop* (1997). And as we read Cris Tovani's *I Read, But I Don't Get It: Comprehension Strategies for Adolescent Readers* (2000) and Debbie Miller's *Reading With Meaning: Teaching Comprehension in the Primary Grades* (2002), we were compelled to look deeper at our own comprehension process. Harvey Daniels's *Literature Circles: Voice and Choice in Book Clubs & Reading Groups* (2002) guided us in our evolution of literature circles and as we developed textbook circles to help our students engage more with their content. With a foundation of these inspirational books, we researched, developed, and adjusted instruction to make strategy use more explicit and accessible to our students.

This book is the chronicle of our journey toward a classroom in which every child thinks deeply and purposefully about what he or she is reading and how he or she is reading it. It explains how to empower children with the language and skills to make their thinking visible—and ultimately improve their reading comprehension and engagement. We hope that what we have presented in this book makes as much of a difference in the reading lives of you and your students as it has in ours.

Acknowledgments

This book would not have been possible without the foresight of Chris Watson, who placed Michelle's son, Tyler, in Nicki's third-grade classroom in 2003. The journey we have taken has resulted in tremendous professional growth for both of us. We could not have traveled this path without all three groups of Nicki's students. They helped us to develop and evolve the Metacognitive Teaching Framework into its current format. In addition, we would especially like to thank Katy Hanbury for her transcription assistance when interviewing students.

We also owe thanks to our families, who have been flexible as our work has taken us across the country and tied us to our respective computers. Our husbands, Shaun and Jeff, have become good friends, perhaps out of survival (or not), and have been supportive and lighthearted through the writing process. Our children have been patient as we type away during the wee hours and during our multiple daily phone calls.

Thank you also to our editors Corinne Mooney, Tori Bachman, and Christina Lambert. Tori's attention to details and cross-checking were exactly what we needed because we were so close to the content and could not always see how to clarify our message. Without her, our manuscript wouldn't have been as comprehensible and consistent. Worse yet, it may have turned out to be a Lifetime network original movie.

PART I

The Metacognitive Teaching Framework in Your Classroom

Teaching reading comprehension strategies has become commonplace in many classrooms. Publishers offer teachers a potpourri of resources to support strategy instruction. But simply teaching strategies is not enough. Students often fail to transfer this knowledge to independent application. The Metacognitive Teaching Framework (MTF) provides a vehicle for you to gradually release responsibility for strategy application to students through a consistent series of learning structures that rely on the use of discussion to help make thinking visible and take the silence out of reading.

The chapters in this section explain the specifics of the MTF, including how classroom environment and teaching practices can enhance metacognition. We have also included a detailed account of how to launch the MTF during the first six weeks of the school year. Laying this foundation pays off as children are then completely ready to improve their use of metacognitive reading strategies. More importantly, as students advance through the MTF, they begin to apply those strategies in all of their reading.

CHAPTER 1

Introducing the Metacognitive Teaching Framework

If you left us in a room with a bag of fresh-picked cotton, and all the materials necessary to weave a fine cloth, then came back in three days, you probably wouldn't be surprised to find us much as you left us. We might have thought to comb the cotton and remove debris. We might even have been able to twist a little of it into a thick, but weak facsimile of yarn. But there is little hope that you would come back to find us busy at work, nothing to be heard but the clack of the loom and the whir of the spinner. Even the threat of being unclothed in an impending bitter winter would not be enough to yield fabric from our unskilled fingers.

For us to be able to make a cohesive cloth, we would need to be taught the weaving process step by step. We would need to watch a proficient weaver, then attempt to mimic her movements while she held our hands in the correct position. We'd need her to watch over our shoulder and instruct us as we tried it out on our own. And as we gained skill, we'd still need that expert to oversee our work and make suggestions along the way. After all these experiences, we might finally be ready to weave a decent cloth completely on our own.

The Importance of Metacognitive Awareness

In many trades, the process described in the vignette is called apprenticing; in teaching we call this scaffolding, and the Metacognitive Teaching Framework (MTF) is based on this simple but effective concept. If we were to weave a cloth—had spent days stringing the loom, preparing the cotton, and begun weaving—it would be devastating to let a mistake go unnoticed for very long. No doubt we would have to carefully cut out the offending yarn and go about the meticulous chore of repairing it. If we didn't notice the misstep, our end product would be flawed. What's more, if we made error after error, our cloth might not even be usable in the end.

Being aware of mistakes and self-correcting is essential for effective reading. Flavell (1987) defines metacognition as active monitoring and regulation of cognitive processes. *The Literacy Dictionary* (Harris & Hodges, 1995) describes metacognition as "an awareness and knowledge of one's mental processes such that one can monitor, regulate and direct them toward a desired end; self-mediation" (p. 153). Students who effectively self-monitor take the time to stop and correct miscues and any misunderstandings that occur as they read. They read for meaning, and when this breaks down they notice and repair meaning.

While most researchers agree that metacognition is an important part of how readers make meaning of texts, we find that the majority focus on only one part of that definition, the self-monitoring aspect. We agree wholeheartedly that self-monitoring is a vital part of what good readers do, but we think there is a lot of untapped potential in students' regulation and control of cognitive processes as they read. Just being aware of mistakes isn't enough; to become advanced readers, students need to have quick access to a variety of strategies to assist them as they tackle more complicated texts.

In order for students to notice their errors and then repair their mistakes, they must be reflective on their performance (Bransford, Brown, & Cocking, 2000), yet most children cannot reflect on something they do not know much about. We learned this early on when we asked students to self-assess their use of strategies and then write a plan on how they could improve strategy use. They were unsuccessful. Not only was reflection a new concept, but students also lacked knowledge of strategies. In addition, many were unaware that they used strategies while reading.

Assessing Metacognitive Awareness

"Metacognition is crucial to effective thinking and problem solving and is one of the hallmarks of expertise in specific areas of knowledge and skills" (Pellegrino, Chudowsky, & Glaser, 2001, p. 4), but you cannot assume that students are metacognitive just because they are good comprehenders. There are a variety of existing tools that can assist you in assessing metacognitive awareness. We have used the Developmental Reading Assessment (DRA) 4–8 as pre- and postperformance tasks (Beaver & Carter, 2000), and we have adapted some well-known inventories and interview formats to best reflect what we want to know about children's metacognitive abilities (see the Attitude and Metacognitive Survey in Appendix B, page 186). We describe how to use these in chapter 2.

Perkins (1992), referring to his work with Swartz, distinguished four levels of metacognitive knowledge that can assist you in determining to what extent readers understand and use strategies:

1. Tacit learners/readers—Readers who lack awareness of their thinking as they read

2. Aware learners/readers—Readers who know when meaning breaks down but do not have the strategies to repair meaning

3. Strategic learners/readers—Readers who know when meaning breaks down and are able to use a strategy or strategies to fix meaning

4. Reflective learners/readers—Readers who reflect on their reading and intentionally apply a strategy, not only when meaning is lost but also to deepen understanding

Our lofty goal is to create reflective learners/readers who are engaged in their learning and reading. Therefore, using these assessments is critical because metacognition is usually hard to see; it's an internal conversation. We want to have students make their thinking external so we can direct instruction based on what they know and what they don't know. For them to do this, they must learn to talk about the cognitive processes that occur as they read.

Successful Metacognitive Teaching Practices

The good news is that metacognition can be taught (Pellegrino, Chudowsky, & Glaser, 2001). Perkins (1995) identifies three types of intelligence: (1) *neural*, what we are born with; (2) *experiential*, which includes the specialized knowledge we acquire via immersion; and (3) *reflective*, which combines knowledge, understanding, and strategic ability. It is this reflective intelligence that we can manipulate. Perkins suggests that reflective intelligence is increased through instruction that nurtures metacognition and develops strategies and attitudes that result in thoughtful thinking. But because metacognition occurs in one's head, the teacher must employ techniques to make thinking visible. And, although direct teaching in a strategy is necessary, instruction must also include class discussions, peer interactions, and coaching, with the goal being self-regulation and independence (Bransford et al., 2000). In addition, research has demonstrated that metacognitive activities must be integrated into subject matter to increase the degree to which students will transfer their new learning to other settings (White & Frederickson, 1998). The MTF builds upon this research.

An Overview of the Metacognitive Teaching Framework

The MTF is an apprenticeship comprehension model that allows you, the teacher, to introduce a strategy by first modeling its use (see Figure 1). Although the MTF is cyclical in nature, we have separated it into four phases (Think-Aloud, Refining Strategy Use, Letting Strategy Use Gel, and Self-Assessment and Goal Setting). The time spent in each phase will differ depending on your students' needs and your instructional goals. We have focused on five cognitive strategies: predicting, connecting, questioning, visualizing, and summarizing.

Each cognitive strategy unit is launched during a think-aloud, where you, an expert reader, stop to identify the mental strategies you are using as you read (Wilhelm, 2001). The mental strategies you model are the components that make up the particular strategy being taught. For example, in the prediction unit, one of the components is using the title, subtitle, or chapter heading to predict what you are going to read. During the think-aloud you would talk out loud, demonstrating how you use the title, subtitle, or chapter heading to predict what you are going to read. This continues as you explicitly model how you use other strategy components.

Gradually, in subsequent whole-group lessons, the responsibility is passed from teacher to student (Graves & Graves, 2003; Pearson & Gallagher, 1983) as students join in and help you identify strategy use. Students use the strategy components and then

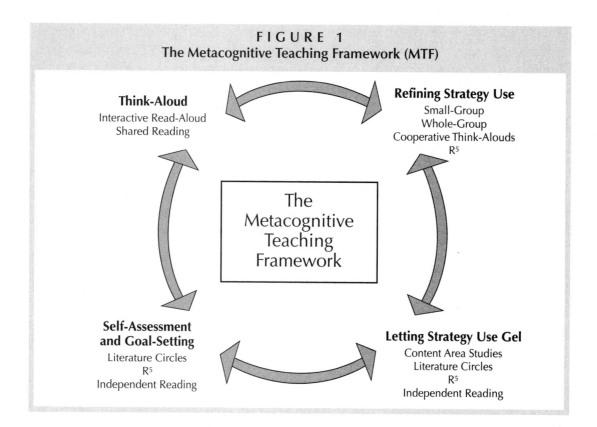

FIGURE 1
The Metacognitive Teaching Framework (MTF)

Think-Aloud
Interactive Read-Aloud
Shared Reading

Refining Strategy Use
Small-Group
Whole-Group
Cooperative Think-Alouds
R^5

The Metacognitive Teaching Framework

Self-Assessment and Goal-Setting
Literature Circles
R^5
Independent Reading

Letting Strategy Use Gel
Content Area Studies
Literature Circles
R^5
Independent Reading

refine their strategy use through a series of whole-group and small-group guided reading lessons. Once strategy use has begun to gel, the majority of the mental work shifts to the students, with you and peers serving as coaches during literature/textbook circles and our structured independent reading block, called Read, Relax, Reflect, Respond, and Rap (R^5).

Then, after several weeks immersed in the strategy unit, each student self-reflects and writes a plan based on one component of the strategy that he or she would like to improve upon. During R^5, the teacher provides support through on-the-spot coaching and reading conferences, designed to monitor students' use of their metacognitive strategy goals as they are reading independently.

How the MTF Differs From Other Reading Comprehension Models

Although many comprehension programs include work in the areas of predicting, connecting, questioning, visualizing, and summarizing, the focus is sometimes on an activity, not necessarily the strategy. Even programs that concentrate on the strategy sometimes fail to support students to independence, such as that provided during R^5. The teaching of comprehension strategies alone does not promote thoughtful literacy.

In one widely used basal series, a fifth-grade teacher's edition includes 6 prereading, 30 during-reading, and 12 postreading activities for only 14 pages of text. Many of these activities are mundane. The tasks are primarily designed to assess understanding; rarely is there any discussion of strategy use and application while reading. Allington (2006) refers to these as assign-and-assess materials because there is little to no instruction provided by the teacher, and students are left to self-discover useful comprehension strategies. Although there are valuable tasks included, they can easily be lost as the teacher sifts through and chooses instructional activities.

Teaching reading comprehension strategies is not enough. It is always important to explicitly tell students the goals of an activity or strategy. Even with a well-established learning structure such as K–W–L (What you Know, Want to Know, and what you Learned) (Ogle, 1986) teachers must take the time to focus students on learning goals and desired outcomes. Otherwise, many students just fill in information without really thinking, just to finish the assignment and make the teacher happy. K–W–L is a great strategy because students activate prior knowledge, make connections, set a purpose for reading, question what they are going to read, answer questions posed, and summarize what they have learned. However, without a clearly stated purpose, is it realistic to think students will apply a K–W–L—or the thinking process behind a K–W–L—independently?

The goal of teaching is to shape students into independent, self-reliant learners. The goal of comprehension instruction should be "on the development of transferable strategies" that promote the "independent use of effective thinking while reading" (Allington, 2006, p. 120). Teachers model, scaffold, and guide students in the use of strategies, such as K–W–L, but the question remains: How do we ensure students apply these strategies independently? Even programs that focus on one strategy at a time fail to break each strategy into fundamental components that students practice and apply independently. This is what led us to develop the MTF. We wanted children to become thoughtful readers who can repair meaning when it breaks down and who can apply strategies adeptly. This book provides the background knowledge for each strategy that can support students as they use strategies independently and take them to new depths of reading comprehension.

The MTF is crafted to support students as they gain a deeper understanding of what, how, and when they predict, connect, question, visualize, and summarize, but it goes far beyond that. The framework allows you to help students improve comprehension by first defining, then recognizing, and finally purposefully applying various strategy components. To help students break down a strategy into smaller steps, we've identified several components for each strategy. We've designed a tally sheet of the components, related think sheets to support small- and whole-group strategy instruction, and a self-assessment/goal-setting sheet to ensure independence during R⁵ and other reading times.

Developing a Common Language

Just as the craft of weaving has a specialized vocabulary associated with it, so does the act of developing metacognitive readers. What follows is a listing of terms, concepts, and learning structures that you will read throughout this book. We will delve into these more deeply in each strategy chapter.

Cognitive Strategies

In this book, we refer to five strategies that readers use to help them make meaning as they read. The strategies should be posted in your classroom so students can easily use them to frame their thinking as they read and discuss texts (see Figure 2). We have observed that teaching students to use a range of strategies more deeply influences and enhances their comprehension of text (Keene & Zimmermann, 1997). Our definitions for these strategies are as follows:

Predicting. Readers use clues from the text and their own background knowledge to forecast what will happen or what information the text will contain. While reading, students confirm, reject, and adjust their thinking based on what they're reading (Beers, 2003), textual evidence, and their own experiences.

Making Connections. Readers relate something in the text to something they've experienced, read about, or seen through other media. Lay the groundwork by having students notice three general forms of connections—text-to-self, text-to-text, and text-to-world connections (Keene & Zimmermann, 1997)—then delve deeply to help students understand just how these connections help them understand texts.

Questioning. Readers ask questions and read on for answers to help them comprehend the text as they read. Questions are posed before, during, and after reading to help students actively wonder about and interrogate a text (Daniels & Zemelman, 2004).

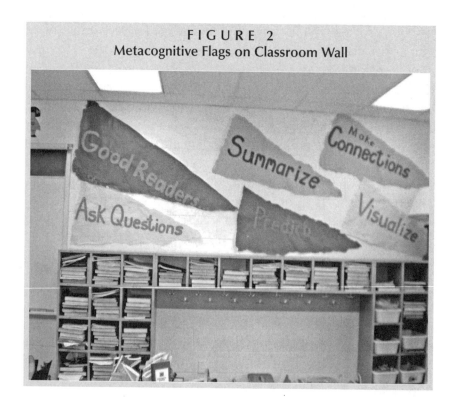

FIGURE 2
Metacognitive Flags on Classroom Wall

Visualizing. Readers can use their senses to experience something in the text vicariously. When students visualize they evoke images while reading, including being able to picture, smell, taste, hear, or feel something in the text (Keene & Zimmermann, 1997; Wilhelm, 2001).

Summarizing. Readers are able to glean the essence of the text and report only the most essential parts (Keene & Zimmermann, 1997), identifying the main idea and supporting details from the text being read.

Strategy Components

As previously mentioned, for each strategy, we've identified fundamental components that represent all the ways a reader might use a particular strategy. We list them on the tally charts students use, and we use them as a basis for think-alouds and strategy lessons. Also, these components serve as the foundation for the self-assessment goal-setting plans students write to help them more effectively use each strategy. The components can provide a road map for both you and your students to notice the strategies they use effectively and identify skills they need to improve as they read.

Timeline and Structures for Teaching

Each strategy is taught over the course of a unit, and each unit can last up to six weeks. Although it is possible to complete all of the units within one school year, benefits can also be reaped by choosing to focus on only those strategies for which your students demonstrate a need. You can determine students' needs by using an assessment tool to evaluate metacognitive awareness, such as those described in chapter 2.

Each strategy is taught throughout an integrated literacy block, using a variety of proven instructional structures. You can employ these methods to scaffold strategy use depending upon student needs. At first this will be direct and explicit instruction, but as students become more skilled in each strategy, you will release this responsibility to them (Graves & Graves, 2003). The structures used to teach each strategy include the following:

Think-Aloud. Traditionally, the teacher reads a piece of text to students, pausing to verbally model the thought processes of a skilled reader as he or she interacts with a text (Wilhelm, 2001). In the MTF, you describe your use of strategy components as you read a text. Most think-alouds should be highly focused, explicit, and well planned so that both you and your students know what they are supposed to glean from the experience. If the students aren't oriented to the fact that you are modeling your thinking, that you have a specific learning goal in mind for them, and that they have a responsibility to take that skill and use it in their own reading, then the results may be random at best. This is further illustrated later in this chapter and in the strategy chapters where you will read transcripts of Nicki doing a think-aloud on each strategy with her students.

Shared Reading and Cooperative Think-Aloud. When you do a think-aloud as a shared reading you should also communicate your thought processes as you move through a text. Students more actively participate in shared reading, though, because they have access to the same text you are using as you model. Students may be able to jump in and share their own thinking as they read along. This evolves into cooperative think-alouds as the students begin to take ownership of strategy components. Cooperative think-aloud continues throughout a strategy unit as students often work in pairs sharing their thinking as they work through chunks of texts in a variety of subjects.

Interactive Read-Aloud. We believe that read-aloud should be a part of every school day. In contrast to think-aloud, in a read-aloud you read to students for the sheer pleasure of bonding over a well-written piece of text. Spontaneous learning occurs as students continue to learn the language of texts, gain an appreciation for a variety of genres, authors, and titles, and discuss with interest their thoughts on what is being read.

While daily read-aloud provides many opportunities for impromptu think-alouds, these should be done judiciously so as not to interrupt the flow of the reading. At times you may pause at significant points, invite discussion, or ask for student comments (Fountas & Pinnell, 2001). We recommend you include only one or two strategy quips per read-aloud session, as the focus of the read-aloud is primarily on enjoyment.

Guided Reading. Guided reading is when you work with a small group on specific skills, using a text at the students' instructional reading levels (Fountas & Pinnell, 2001). You should purposefully guide students' learning by helping them navigate the text. In the MTF, guided reading is used to help students more deeply understand strategy components using an appropriately leveled text. Each guided-reading group might focus on the same strategy component, but the level of scaffolding and text will vary depending on the needs of each group. Again, like the previous structures, there is a lot of social interaction to promote engagement in each strategy and more importantly to enhance comprehension.

Literature Circles and Textbook Circles. The hallmarks of traditional literature circles are student-selected texts and student-driven discussions about those texts. The purpose is for students to read and enjoy a text they are interested in, and then, deepen their understanding of what is being read through a student-led peer discussion. Your role in literature circles is to teach students how to think about what they are reading and how to have a quality conversation about a text. You should group circle members according to text selection and group dynamics. You also must select an appealing, discussion-inspiring set of texts for students to choose from and coach students as they engage in the process (Daniels, 2002).

Textbook circles also feature student-led discussions but may involve a teacher-selected text such as a section in a content textbook, article, or student periodical. The groups for textbook circles aren't organized according to text selection, but rather to facilitate peer scaffolding of the content in the text.

Literature circles and textbook circles provide opportunities for peer-supported application of the strategies students are learning. Chapter 3 explains the role of discussion as it relates to the MTF, especially during literature circles and textbook circles, by providing recommendations for promoting and implementing talk with and among your students.

R⁵. Read, Relax, Reflect, Respond, and Rap, or R⁵, is a structured independent reading time that allows students to practice their reading strategies independently, with the added benefit of teacher and peer scaffolding (Kelley & Clausen-Grace, 2006). The time is broken into three phases: Read and Relax, Reflect and Respond, and Rap. During the Read and Relax portion of R⁵, students read independently while you record what they are reading on a "status of the class" log. Students continue reading as you confer with one or two individually. During conferences you can evaluate a student's metacognitive strategy use, provide support and counseling in strategy use, and monitor the student's reading habits.

During Reflect and Respond students think about any strategies they used while reading, then record their thoughts, book title, and pages read on an individual log. What follows is Rap, when students share their strategy use with a partner and then partners share their discussions with the whole group, as you facilitate the discussion. We believe reading is a social process and readers create meaning through these interactions (Durkin, 1993; Rosenblatt, 1978). Both literature circles and R⁵ promote this interaction and further support readers as they become independent strategy users. R⁵ is further described in chapter 4.

Independent Reading. Independent reading is not the same as R⁵. When we refer to independent reading, we are talking about those times that students read without any sort of scaffolding. This usually occurs when they have completed work early or when they read at home for pleasure. Ultimately, our goal is that students apply the strategies when they read independently and as needed when learning.

Digging Deeper Into
the Metacognitive Teaching Framework

Think-Aloud

A strategy unit is kicked off with a preplanned think-aloud, which is broken into three distinct phases:

1. Introducing, explaining, and defining strategy components

2. Noticing and applying strategy components

3. Clarifying strategy purpose

You can teach these phases during one session or break instruction into as many sessions as needed to ensure students aren't overwhelmed by the number and complexity of the components.

Phase 1: Introducing, Explaining, and Defining Strategy Components. Hang a poster-size laminated class tally chart at the front of the room (see Figure 3) to show

FIGURE 3
Predicting Tally Sheet—Class Sample

Think Aloud: This Prediction Uses...	Tally
title/chapter headings.	~~IIII~~ ~~IIII~~ III
the front and back cover.	~~IIII~~ II
pictures and captions.	~~IIII~~ IIII
questions that might be answered as I read.	~~IIII~~ II
what I already know about the topic.	~~IIII~~ II
what I know about the genre or series.	~~IIII~~ I
what I know about text structure.	~~IIII~~
what has happened so far in the book.	~~IIII~~ ~~IIII~~ ~~IIII~~ ~~IIII~~
meaningful connections.	IIII

students a list of the components for the strategy being taught. Each student should keep a personal copy of the components on an individual tally sheet (see Appendix B), which becomes a personal data collection device and mirrors the class chart. Students will later use this to document their application of strategy components as they read. As the unit progresses and they begin to notice their use of strategy components, students begin to record on this sheet by putting down tally marks that represent the components they are using.

Prior to the think-aloud, students read through the list of components on the class tally chart and briefly discuss with a partner what they think each component means. Then, in a whole-class lesson, you explain and define each strategy component on the tally sheet, providing examples from specific texts the class has read to illustrate or demonstrate what each component means and how to apply it when reading.

Phase 2: Noticing and Applying the Strategy Components. After students have been introduced to the strategy and its components, it is time for you to model component use as you read aloud. Prior to this point, you will have preselected a text and thought about places where you will pause to share your use of components. (One technique we have used successfully is putting sticky notes right in the text where we will stop to talk about our mental processing.) A student assistant uses a water-based marker to tally strategy use on the class chart during the think-aloud lesson. At the start, you may be the only one in the room identifying components from the tally sheet, but usually by the end of the lesson students will be ready to jump in and tell which component is being modeled. During tallying, you can clarify student thinking as students attempt to use and identify components.

This is an important phase of the think-aloud and the MTF as students often mimic or give the appearance of strategy use at this point. Because students are making approximations of strategy use, their attempts must be celebrated, but you should redirect any missteps. At this phase you want to be clear and direct to avoid misconceptions. Begin noting the components students seem to be confused about so that in follow-up lessons you can address these components more thoroughly to refine strategy use.

Phase 3: Clarifying Strategy Purpose. The third phase of the think-aloud is when you wrap up the introduction lesson (or lessons) by restating the purpose of the think-aloud and clarifying the strategy's purpose.

Refining Strategy Use

Display the class chart prominently in the classroom and refer to it continually as you and students identify and record strategy use during subsequent whole-group lessons over the next few weeks. As previously mentioned, students individually collect data of their strategy use on their personal tally sheets, giving them a basis for completing the self-assessment/goal-setting sheet toward the end of the unit.

You may do another whole-group, shared-reading lesson to help students become familiar with the strategy components, or you may be ready to pull them into small groups for some up-close practice and modeling. The lessons in this book are not text specific so you can use basals, trade books, content area texts, or supplementary materials such as periodicals for think-aloud, shared reading and other whole- and small-group lessons.

Lessons occur during shared reading, when you ask students to bring their tally sheets to the reading area. During shared reading you should pause to think aloud and ask students to identify the component being modeled. This instruction also occurs during strategic whole-group lessons, which are designed to teach one specific component in more depth. One example from the unit on prediction is a lesson on text organization and structure in which students work with partners to analyze the organization and structure of question-and-answer books (see chapter 5, page 94, Expository Text Investigation). This helps students understand the component of using "what I know about text organization and structure" to predict.

Most lessons can be done in both small groups and whole groups, depending on the needs of the class. Because many of the components may be new concepts, a combination of both is usually needed to ensure understanding. In each of the strategy chapters, we have included think sheets for use in guided reading and whole-group lessons. These can help focus learning on the desired strategy.

Letting Strategy Use Gel

At first students will identify strategy use on a superficial level. For example, a student may predict that a book is about hurricanes based on its title, but may not pull in background knowledge and coordinate other information, such as the cover photograph and summary in order to make a more detailed prediction about the book's content. Because the purpose of the MTF is to move students beyond simply noticing strategy use into purposeful and then automatic application, it is important to give them time and support as they work toward these ends. As students gain familiarity with strategy components, encourage them to use their tally sheets and notice when they use various components during content area reading, independent reading, and guided reading. Continue to guide students in more structured whole- and small-group lessons. The extra time to notice and reflect on strategy use leads to a richer, fuller understanding.

Self-Assessment and Goal-Setting

After several weeks of collecting personal data on their tally sheets and becoming more comfortable with strategy use, students are ready to reflect on their use of the various strategy components. In a whole-group lesson, guide students through the process of looking at their completed tally sheets and noticing which components they use a lot and which components they hardly use. On the self-assessment/goal-setting sheet, students check off what they do well and highlight components they need to work on. With your guidance, they choose one area to enhance and then write a workable, multistep plan to improve in that area.

At this point, teacher scaffolding is minimized. Remind students to use their plans when reading during R^5, literature circles, and (for those who still need more teacher support) small-group work. You and student peers serve as coaches, weaving discourse on strategy throughout the day. Each strategy chapter in Part III of this book describes self-assessment and goal-setting in more depth.

Benefits of Using the Metacognitive Teaching Framework

The MTF has some distinct advantages for both teacher and students:

- It promotes discussion. Every aspect of the MTF encourages and often scaffolds meaningful talk centered on text.

- It makes strategy use explicit to teachers and students. The MTF breaks down each strategy into well-defined components, allowing teachers to teach thoroughly.

- It provides a routine that helps students make connections and helps the teacher be more efficient. Students quickly understand that the phases of the MTF are part of a learning sequence that can be applied to each of the strategies, and they begin to anticipate the tally sheets, think-alouds, and other structures and tools for learning used in the MTF.

- It provides a common language for discussing metacognition. Students begin to use framework and strategy vocabulary in their discussions and written reflections.

- It scaffolds think-aloud for teachers and students. Although think-aloud is a well-known structure, it is often implemented haphazardly. The MTF offers a structure and a purpose to the think-aloud process.

- It develops reflective intelligence. The use of the tally sheet and the self-assessment and goal-setting process leads students through reflection. In addition, students are reflecting every time they engage in R^5.

- It is inquiry-based. The teacher and students become co-researchers as they learn about and apply each strategy with different texts.

- It uses best practices in literacy instruction. The structures used during the MTF are those that have been identified in research as assisting in the development of effective readers.

- It is not text-dependent. You can use literature, trade books, basals, student periodicals, or even content area textbooks to teach strategies in the context of the MTF.

- It helps *all* readers to comprehend better. Below, on, and above grade-level readers have all demonstrated growth when exposed to the MTF.

- It develops a bonded community of literacy learners. The structure and the language of the MTF foster the development of a culture that focuses on reading and learning.

The Importance of Classroom Environment

You should be thoughtful about the atmosphere you create. Effective teachers know their students, create a supportive climate, and establish relationships that enhance learning (Stronge, 2002). And although most of your school day is spent interacting with students about academics, teachers who create opportunities for social interaction cultivate a positive, caring learning environment (Good & Brophy, 1997). Engaging students in purposeful talk within a nurturing environment builds trust and respect. In addition, teachers who demonstrate enthusiasm for learning contribute to student motivation and promote student achievement (Darling-Hammond, 2000).

FIGURE 4
Reading and Relaxing on Classroom Couch

The Classroom Layout

The physical layout of a classroom should be inviting. You want a place earmarked for coming together as a community of readers and writers. This area should include places where students feel relaxed and comfortable enough to enjoy reading. You might have a couch, a chair, large pillows, and even lawn chairs available for students to use while they read (see Figure 4). Some students will be happy sitting at desks while others may find their own niche against a file cabinet or wall. The classroom walls should demonstrate a passion for books with posters, book jackets, student responses to reading, and so forth. You might have your recent reads or new purchases prominently displayed to entice students. Wherever students do choose to read, you want the space to cry, "We are serious about reading and writing in this room!"

The Classroom Library

Access and appeal are important. If the classroom library is used exclusively for independent reading it is recommended that the teacher have 10–12 titles per student

FIGURE 5
Series and Authors You Need to Know

	Developing Readers	Advancing Readers
Adventure		Among the Hidden Brian Books On the Run
Fantasy	Geronimo Stilton Magic Tree House Ricky Ricotta Secrets of Droon Spiderwick Chronicles	Artemis Fowl The Chronicles of Narnia Left Behind A Series of Unfortunate Events The Seventh Tower
Historical Fiction		American Girls Dear America My America
Humor	Captain Underpants Hank the Cowdog	Rotten School Wayside School
Mysteries	A to Z Mysteries Cam Jansen Encyclopedia Brown Ghosthunters Mostly Ghostly Woodland Mysteries	Goosebumps Nightmare Room Sammy Keyes
Realistic Fiction	Bailey School Kids Junie B. Jones Nate the Great	Abby Hayes The Baby-Sitters Club Boxcar Children Judy Moody Ramona Books
Authors	Judy Blume Beverly Cleary Lois Lowry Garth Nix Louis Sachar	Matt Christopher Kate DiCamillo Carl Hiaasen Will Hobbs Gordan Korman Gary Paulsen Jerry Spinelli

(Neumann, 2000). If you use the library to support content area studies, guided reading, shared reading, and read-aloud, the library size should range from 1,500–2,000 titles (Reutzel & Fawson, 2002). In addition, these books should range in levels and genres. You want to include series books in your collection. Series such as A to Z Mysteries, The Baby-Sitters Club, A Series of Unfortunate Events, On the Run, and The Seventh Tower hook readers through compelling characters and story development, which serve as a support for readers, especially reluctant readers, as they devour a series. You'll also want to include titles from the most loved children's and young adult authors including Gary Paulsen, Carl Hiaasen, and Kate DiCamillo. And be sure to stock your own favorites! Figure 5 lists some series and authors with which you should make yourself familiar.

Be picky—a library full of boring or unattractive titles isn't going to tempt anyone. Make sure the books in your classroom library are appealing. You might use a group of students to weed out books with torn or unappealing covers and have them organize the classroom library to make it accessible to students. Books should be at eye level and below. Books should be categorized by author, genre, series, or reading levels. You might even have the class determine how the books should be organized, which can familiarize students with what's available and instill a sense of ownership in the classroom library (Kelley & Clausen-Grace, 2006).

Sources for identifying good titles include newspaper or magazine reviews, the Children's Books section of *The Reading Teacher*, trade publications such as *School Library Journal* or *Curriculum Connections*, the shelves of your local library or bookstore, and the advice of fellow teachers and students. There are also several online resources for finding good books:

- www.sunlink.ucf.edu—This site, Sunlink, has much to offer teachers, parents, and students. The bar located on the left-hand side of the main page, "Book Lists," contains some of the best links you will ever click on regarding books.

- www.ala.org/ala/alsc—This American Library Association (ALA) website provides a plethora of information for teachers. To find great books click on the Great Websites for Kids link located on the left-hand side. Once there, the authors and illustrators and children's book award links are most helpful if you are trying to identify books to purchase for your classroom library.

- www.nsta.org/ostbc—The National Science Teachers Association (NTSA) website offers a list of Outstanding Science Trade Books for Children annotated and organized under the eight science content standards.

- downloads.ncss.org/notable—Each year the National Council for the Social Studies (NCSS) creates a bibliography of books for grades K–8 organized under the 10 social studies standards. You can access the previous year's annotations for free, but if you want this year's list you must be a member.

- www.kidsread.com—Our most recent find, Kidsread, is amazing! It gives you a teaser for the newest books by your favorite authors and from your favorite series, as well as interviews and other goodies. It has many quality links, but if you click the "Series" button at the top of the page, you get an A to Z annotated list of the most popular series that may grab your students' attention.

- www.hbook.com—The Horn Book Magazine website offers an extensive searchable database of children's and young adult titles.

Creating a Culture of Avid Readers

Although too much manipulation of students can have unintended consequences, no one can argue with a few well-intentioned ploys in the name of literacy! As the head reading cheerleader, you should lead impromptu book pep rallies on a regular basis. Enthusiastically talk about the winning qualities of your favorite new kids' titles, or walk into the room with a bookstore bag full of selections chosen to appeal to your stu-

FIGURE 6
Students Engrossed in New Book Selections

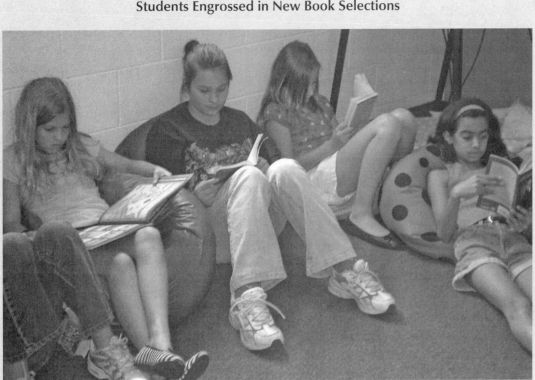

dents. Create a little competitive tension where kids are vying for the first chance at a book endorsed by you. One way to do this is to designate a special place in your classroom where you put new books after completing a book talk. Kids will naturally congregate in this area every chance they get to look over the new titles and snag up the one that appeals to them (see Figure 6).

For your most reluctant readers, use the information on their Interest and Wide Reading Inventories (see Appendix B, page 187) to choose new books you are sure they will like. Do a book talk as described below, then let these children have the first shot at reading the book. Or, write little notes and put the book on the students' desks so they see it when they first come in. They won't be able to wait to dig into their new treasure.

Most importantly, show your students that you value books and reading. Share interesting clips from your magazines or the newspaper. Tell them of the interesting plot twists or characters in the books you read for pleasure. Show them your enthusiasm—it is contagious!

Book talks are a way to hook even the most reluctant readers. By giving students just a taste of what a book is about, usually by sharing a compelling passage from the book, you will create some anticipation over the text. Students will want to read your copy of the book, check out a copy from the library, or go home and beg their parents to buy them a copy. If you carefully write or select a book talk based on what your students are interested in, you will ensure they eagerly anticipate their next read.

FIGURE 7
Books and Authors I Want to Read—Student Sample

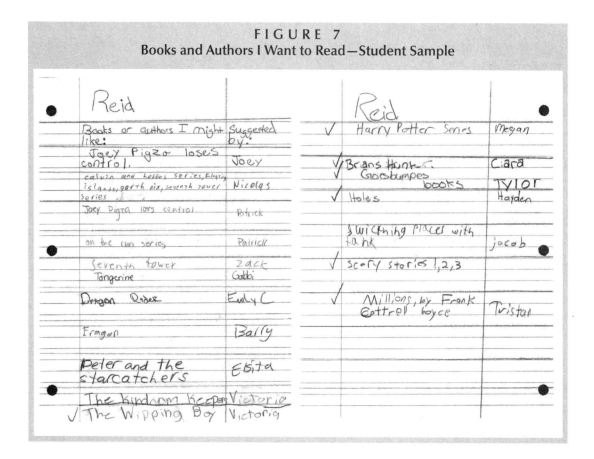

Furthermore, having students create their own book talks can give them another purpose for at-home reading and promotes the reading–writing connection. Book talks range in formality, from the formally prepared graded report to the quick quip about a new book in the classroom collection to the snippets heard about each book during the Rap portion of R^5. Be careful, though—you'll want book talks only on those books that can deliver—in other words, those books in which students are interested and that are written on an attainable reading level. Your students *will* want to read the books you share. If they are consistently disappointed because the books are too difficult or just not that good, they will either lose faith in you, or they'll lose interest in reading for pleasure.

As students become more excited about reading on their own time, invite them to keep track of books they want to read on a list of in their R^5 folders. This will allow quick access to the next title when they finish a book (see Figure 7).

Final Thoughts

Although the MTF methods were used by the authors in third- and fourth-grade classes, many primary, middle, and high school teachers have adapted the framework with a high degree of success. The critical ingredient of the MTF is discussion. It permeates the day as we talk purposefully about our reading, thinking, and learning. Because the

MTF is used day after day, across content areas, and in a variety of contexts, students develop a habit of thinking deeply. After working through the first unit, both teacher and students begin to anticipate the support the framework provides for subsequent strategy units.

In the next chapter you will read about how to launch the MTF with suggested daily, weekly, and yearly plans. We'll help you set the stage for teaching metacognition and elaborate on how to teach various aspects of the framework.

CHAPTER 2

Laying the Foundation for the Metacognitive Teaching Framework

Powerful silence envelops the classroom as students read and try to identify the different ways they are predicting. No one has ever asked them to be this specific before. They must focus intently on their thinking. In a few weeks, there will be an excited chatter as kids volunteer to share loquaciously their prediction strategies. They will be transformed into mighty metacognitive readers—able to notice each nuance of thought as they process what they read. It isn't magic that transforms them. It is the careful planning and gentle leadership of a reflective teacher who guides them.

The Importance of Planning Instruction

Although you can employ strategy-based lessons in your reading block without much long-range planning, you will need to plan ahead for success if you want to use appropriate scaffolding every step of the way. Effective teachers prioritize instruction by providing students with consistency and organization (Wang, Haertel, & Walberg, 1993) and establishing procedures and routines early in the year. Furthermore, effective teachers systematically develop objectives and activities that "reflect higher-level and lower-level cognitive skills as appropriate for the content and the students" (Stronge, 2002, p. 39).

In this chapter we share sample daily, weekly, and yearly schedules for implementation and suggestions to prime students for success during the first six weeks of the school year. This chapter will also describe how to create a caring classroom environment that nurtures thoughtful discussion and metacognitive awareness.

Yearly and Monthly Plan

Although we provide a suggested yearly plan for those who wish to teach all the strategy units in a school year, by no means is this the only approach. Also keep in mind that while we highlight the strategies of predicting, questioning, visualizing, connecting, and summarizing, the Metacognitive Teaching Framework (MTF) can be used to improve the teaching of any other strategy units you wish to teach.

Take a look at Figure 8, which shows our suggested yearly plan for the MTF. Notice the school year is broken into six units of study, each lasting about six weeks. The first six weeks are spent building a community of readers and writers and teaching the learning

FIGURE 8
Sample Yearly Plan for Metacognitive Teaching Framework: Cognitive Units of Study

Six-Week Period	Unit Focus
September–Mid-October	*Laying the Foundation* • Define: Self-Monitoring, metacognition • Identify: Strategies (names and general understanding of the five strategies) • Whole- and small-group lessons: Text features, genre, general text structures (narrative vs. expository) • Establish: Community, class rules, daily routines, R^5, literature circles, writer's workshop • Assess: Reading interests, habits, abilities Reading conference focus: Intervention (choosing the right level of text based on personal interests, extracting students who are stuck in a genre or series)
Mid-October–End of November	*Prediction Unit* • Define: Prediction components using tally sheets • Identify: Strategy use by teacher, students • Whole- and small-group lessons: Text features, vocabulary activities, genre, expository text structures, anticipation guides • Reconfirm: Purposes and processes for think-aloud and small-group work • Refining: R^5, literature circles • Assess: Students self-assess and set goals for prediction at the end of this unit • Reading conference focus: Refining prediction goal plans, monitoring independent reading
December–Mid-January	*Questioning Unit* • Define: Questioning components using tally sheets • Identify: Strategy use by teacher, students Whole- and small-group lessons: Categorizing questions, using text features to question, questioning the textbook • Refining: R^5, literature circles Assess: Students self-assess and set goals for questioning at the end of this unit • Reading conference focus: Checking to see if students are using prediction plans, refining questioning goal plans, monitoring independent reading
Mid-January–February	*Summarizing Unit* • Define: Summarizing components using tally sheets • Identify: Strategy use by teacher, students • Whole- and small-group lessons: Concept-definition sort, write a better heading, summing up by chunking and rereading, vocabulary lessons, anticipation guides • Refining: R^5, literature circles • Assess: Students self-assess and set goals for summarizing at the end of this unit • Reading conference focus: Checking to see if students are using questioning plans, refining summarizing goal plans, monitoring independent reading

(continued)

FIGURE 8
Sample Yearly Plan for Metacognitive Teaching Framework: Cognitive Units of Study
(continued)

Six-Week Period	Unit Focus
March–Mid-April	*Making Connections Unit* • Define: Connecting components using tally sheets • Identify: Strategy use by teacher, students • Whole- and small-group lessons: Connections continuum, story map • Refining: R^5, literature circles • Assess: Students self-assess and set goals for connecting at the end of this unit • Reading conference focus: Checking to see if students are using summarizing plans, refining connecting goal plans, monitoring independent reading
Mid-April–End of May	*Visualizing Unit* • Define: Visualizing components using tally sheets • Identify: Strategy use by teacher, students • Whole- and small-group lessons: Visualizing think-pair-share, visualization continuum, anticipation guide extension, character quilt, draw to remember • Refining: R^5, literature circles Assess: Students self-assess and goal set for visualizing at the end of this unit • Reading conference focus: Checking to see if students are using connecting plans, refining visualizing goal plans, monitoring independent reading, helping students generate individual reading lists for summer

structures associated with the MTF. Introduce students to the concept of metacognition at this time by having them notice how and why they clarify.

After setting the stage through the introductory unit, the order of implementation is not set in stone, but, because the prediction unit front-loads a lot of the skills and processes needed for the other units, prediction should be the first strategy unit presented. Other than that, you can differentiate the progression of units based on your students' needs and your specific goals for instruction. Figure 9 shows a completed integrated month-by-month planning sheet, and Appendix B contains a reproducible planning sheet (see page 184) to assist you in implementation and to allow you to adapt the schedule based on your students' needs.

Daily Schedules

The MTF addresses all areas of literacy instruction, with the exception of writer's workshop, fluency and spelling/phonics. The first sample daily schedule shows how these things fit in with the MTF to provide a comprehensive reading program. Specific skills

FIGURE 9
MTF Integrated Month-by-Month Planning Sheet

Time Frame	Metacognitive Focus	Activities	Texts for Think-Aloud, Shared Reading, Read-Aloud, and Small-Group Instruction	Writing Project
August–Mid-September	Define metacognition, self-monitoring, clarifying	Establish routines for R⁵, literature circles, Words Their Way, Soar to Success, writer's workshop, common language	*Night in the County, The Writer's Notebook*, iOpeners, basals, science and social studies texts	Personal narrative
Mid-September–End of October	Prediction, with a special focus on text structure and features	Introduce metacognitive tally sheet, prediction indicators, prediction self-assessment and goal-setting sheet	Q-and-A books, animal rescue heroes, cut-apart books, basals, science and social studies texts	Q-and-A books
November–Mid-December	Making connections	Introduce metacognitive tally sheet, making connections indicators, making connections self-assessment and goal-setting sheet	Bermuda Triangle, Donner Party, Sally Ride biography, basals, science and social studies texts	Biography of Florida explorer
January–Mid-February	Questioning	Introduce metacognitive tally sheet, questioning indicators, questioning self-assessment and goal-setting sheet	Weekly readers, student essay samples, science and social studies texts	Expository and narrative essays
Mid-February–End of March	Visualizing	Introduce metacognitive tally sheet, visualizing indicators, visualizing self-assessment and goal-setting sheet	*The Seventh Tower: The Fall*, basals, *Joy* chapters, science and social studies texts	Fantasy/science fiction story with common theme: We have used up one of our vital natural resources
April–Mid-May	Summarizing	Introduce metacognitive tally sheet, summarizing indicators, summarizing self-assessment and goal-setting sheet	*A Guide to Rocks and Gems*, science and social studies texts.	Whole-class reference book on rocks

like inferring, determining author's purpose, and cause and effect are embedded within the framework, as is vocabulary development.

It should be noted that in the literacy block schedule shown in Figure 10, science and social studies are completely integrated, with the exception of an inquiry lab each Wednesday. Whole-group lessons on fluency are alternated weekly with whole-group lessons on word study. Word study is also taught in small, developmentally leveled groups on a weekly basis. Whole- and small-group lessons on metacognition are taught during the morning 10:00–10:30 and 10:30–11:15 time blocks, with some flexibility to expand either and retract the other, as the need arises.

The second daily schedule (see Figure 11) reflects a 90-minute reading block. Fluency is taught in minilessons during whole- or small-group lessons, depending on student needs. Word study is taught during small-group time. Both fluency and word study are reinforced in centers and with homework. Writer's workshop is done later in the day. As in the daily schedule in Figure 10, the time allotted to whole-group and small-group lessons can be reconfigured as needed on a day-by-day basis.

In both models, strategy instruction with an emphasis on metacognition is woven throughout the instructional block, sometimes through clearly articulated planning and sometimes through unscheduled teachable moments.

FIGURE 10
Sample Daily Schedule A: Literacy Block

	Monday	Tuesday	Wednesday	Thursday	Friday
8:45 a.m.–9:15 a.m. Writer's Workshop					
9:15 a.m.–9:30 a.m. Fluency/Word Study					
9:30 a.m.–10:00 a.m. Choice Reading	R⁵	Literature Circles	Literature Circles	R⁵	R⁵
10:00 a.m.–10:30 a.m. Whole-Group Lesson					
10:30 a.m.–11:15 a.m. Small-Group Lessons					
10:30 a.m.–11:15 a.m. Literacy Centers	Fluency	Vocabulary	Comprehension	Words Their Way (Word Study)	Make-Up Day
Special Areas: Art, Music, P.E., Computers					
Noon–12:20 p.m. Read-Aloud					

FIGURE 11

90-Minute Reading Block Daily Schedule

	Monday	Tuesday	Wednesday	Thursday	Friday
9:45 a.m.–10:15 a.m. Whole-Group Lesson					
10:15 a.m.–10:45 a.m. Small-Group Lessons					
10:15 a.m.–10:45 a.m. Literacy Centers	Fluency	Vocabulary	Comprehension	Words Their Way (Word Study)	Make-Up Day
10:45 a.m.–11:15 a.m. Choice Reading	R⁵	Literature Circles	Literature Circles	R⁵	R⁵
Special Areas: Art, Music, P.E., Computers					
Noon–12:20 p.m. Read-Aloud					

Introductory Unit—A Week-by-Week Guide to Establishing the MTF

In the next section we explicitly describe the six-week introductory unit, which you can use to build your students' comfort with the MTF. Activities are organized by week. We indicate where activities with corresponding lesson plans appear within the chapter.

Activities for Week 1

- Establish an emotionally safe, discussion-rich environment through cooperative learning and other activities (class meetings, interview a friend, etc.).
- Have students work in cooperative groups to develop class rules.
- Set aside an unstructured time for students to read independently so you can observe and note students who can and cannot engage with a text, and identify fake or disengaged readers (see page 28).
- Assess reading comprehension, metacognitive awareness, and students' ability to self-assess and set goals (see page 29).
- Assess students' interests and reading preferences using an inventory (see page 29).
- Begin a read-aloud.
- Brainstorm what it means to have a discussion, practice discussing a topic of interest (this is elaborated on in chapter 3).

The first week of school is challenging enough, but these activities will help you begin to get to know your students and will help you establish the norms and expectations you have for your classroom.

Identifying Fake or Disengaged Readers

Before you launch Read, Relax, Reflect, Respond, Rap (R[5]) you want to find those readers in your classroom who are having difficulty engaging. In addition, you want to begin talking to your students about why independent reading is important and to say that you take this time seriously.

Activity. During the first week observe your students reading. The Silent Reading Behaviors Observation Checklist (see Appendix B, page 185) is used to note off-task behaviors students are exhibiting during independent reading. Once you identify a student not reading, write down the student's name on the form. This checklist can help as you identify those readers who have difficulty engaging. Use the columns to the right to tally each off-task behavior for each student. The three categories we focus on during this time are "out of seat," "looking around, flipping pages, not reading," and "talking." Use the notes section for any specific observations. Total the number of off-task behaviors to give you a quick snapshot of each student's ability to engage.

After one session you will quickly begin to identify fake or disengaged readers. And no matter how hard it is for you to delay interventions, wait a few sessions before you say something to each student. When you have collected enough data from observations you might want to try a series of questions with your whole class such as these:

- What do you think I was doing while you were reading?
- If I were looking for kids not reading what would I notice?

When we have asked these questions of our students, we have been amazed to learn that not only did they know what we were doing, they could also identify what behaviors we were looking for. Ironically, many of the disengaged readers were the students who told us what they were doing that constituted disengagement. The italicized text below shows a few of these students' responses:

Teacher: What do you think I was doing while you were reading?

Students: *Talking.*
Watching us to see what we were doing.
Maybe thinking about a video you could create for teachers to decide who was reading and who was not reading.

Teacher: If I were looking for kids not reading what would I notice?

Students: *Just flipping pages of the book.*
Not looking at the book, just looking around.
Talking.
Staring at the book.

Students: *Walking around the classroom.*
              Getting different books.
              Just looking at the pictures.

Wrapping it up. Kids are smart. They know what a disengaged reader is, and yet many of them still cannot or do not engage in silent reading time. A follow-up question could be, Who had trouble focusing? And although not many students will be honest right then, you will be surprised by some of the hands that go up. Some students have gotten so good at faking it that in your observations they appeared to be reading yet they self-report they have a hard time engaging. Chapter 4 offers you further support on working with fake or disengaged readers.

Assessing Students' Comprehension and Metacognitive Awareness

During the first few weeks of school you will want to determine your students' independent and instructional reading levels. This assessment can take more than a week but in order to match students to text they can read, this is crucial (Allington, 2006). Knowing students' comprehension level will also help you determine texts for small-group instruction.

Activity. The instrument we use to determine levels is the Developmental Reading Assessment (DRA), grades 4–8, published by Pearson Learning (Beaver & Carter, 2000). This assessment gives us individual data on wide reading, self-assessment and goal-setting, fluency, prediction, summary writing, literal comprehension, interpretation, reflection, and metacognitive awareness. But, any informal reading inventory can help you determine a student's reading level. We have developed an Attitude and Metacognitive Survey (see Appendix B, page 186) to assist those of you who do not have access to the DRA 4–8. Depending upon students' writing skills you may want to do this as an interview to ensure that their responses were not cut short because they did not want to write.

Wrapping it up. This is something you will want to use at the beginning of the year and at the end of the year in order to evaluate your effectiveness and determine student growth in these areas. After establishing students' reading levels and the degree to which they metacognate you will next want to find out about their interests.

Inventorying to Learn Interests and Find Out What Students Know

Matching children to books is critical to having a successful independent reading block. We developed an Interest and Wide Reading Inventory (Clausen-Grace & Kelley, 2007) to help us guide students in choosing appropriate books based on their interests (see Figure 12 and Appendix B, page 187, for a reproducible). The survey assesses students' outside interests, reading tastes, awareness of genre, and the breadth of their reading experiences, and it

FIGURE 12
Interest and Wide Reading Inventory—Student Sample

1. If you could be anything in the world when you grow up, what would you be? Why? _____
   A vet I like animals a lot

2. What are your hobbies? Soccer

3. If you could travel anywhere at all, where would you go? California

4. What do you like to do with your friends? Play with dogs

5. What is your favorite television show? Why? Fear Factor, looks fun

6. What is your favorite animal? Horse

7. What do you do when you have time to do what you want? Phone

8. What subject or subjects do you like best in school? Reading

9. What is the title of the last book you read? Black Beaty

10. What are you reading right now? Mary Kate and Ashly

11. Put an X in the box that tells how you feel about reading each of the following:

Type of Text	I like it a lot.	I like it a little.	I don't like it.	I haven't tried it yet but would like to.	I don't know what it is.
Magazines			X		
Biography			X		
Science		X			
History			X		
Historical Fiction			X		
Adventure					
Romance					X
Sports	X				
Comic Books			X		
Mysteries			X		
Science Fiction/Fantasy		X			
Realistic Fiction		X			
Horror	X				
Poetry			X		
Short Stories		X			
Picture Books	X				

should be given during the first week of school, or at least sometime at the beginning of the school year. The survey helps you bond and connect with your students, and their responses can help you plan appropriate minilessons related to genre study. Many students have misconceptions about genre. There can be a heavy emphasis on narrative text in the primary grades, and some children are not aware that other types of books exist (Duke, 2004). This survey gives you some idea of what students know and don't know about different genres. Furthermore, it can guide you in selecting books for students to read.

McCall's teacher used her inventory to make book suggestions and to broaden her reading experience. Because McCall likes animals a lot and had previously read *Black Beauty,* her teacher's first suggestion was *Dog to the Rescue II: Seventeen More True Tales of Dog Heroism* (Sanderson, 1995). Next, her teacher suggested a nonfiction book on horses. Another suggestion was *A Dog's Life: Autobiography of a Stray* (Martin, 2005). In this way, her teacher was able to gently move McCall into short stories, non-fiction, and a fictionalized autobiography, expanding her genre circle with topics that appealed to her.

Activities for Week 2

- Set up writer's workshop or the writing program you use.
- Define metacognition and introduce the metacognitive flags (see Figure 2, page 8) and the strategies they list: predicting, connecting, questioning, visualizing, and summarizing.
- Teach the structure and set expectations for R^5 and begin implementation (see chapter 4 for more specific guidance).
- Introduce think-aloud by explicitly telling students what you are doing (modeling your thinking) and what you want them to get from it.
- Use think-aloud to introduce the concept of clarifying when reading (see below).
- Have students notice and share when they clarify, such as when they pause to repair meaning when it breaks down.

During week 2 you will be introducing a lot of vocabulary terms. This is just the beginning of the students' journey through the MTF, but this may be the most important week as they begin to realize they are metacognitive or they need to be metacognitive.

Introducing the Concept of Clarifying Using Think-Aloud

The relationship between metacognition and clarifying is significant. One of the reasons we want students to develop metacognitive awareness is so they will have a repertoire of strategies they can use when they need to clarify something they are reading and that they will actually use those strategies to clear up confusions. Many disengaged readers are not aware that they (not the teacher) must do something when they do not understand a text. They will either keep reading and ignore their confusions or appeal to the teacher to help them. The goal when teaching clarification is to get students to contemplate and then correct confusions while they are reading (Beers, 2003).

Activity. One way to introduce students to the concept of clarifying is through think-aloud, and it's especially important to familiarize students with think-aloud because this is a structure used frequently in the MTF. You will want to identify a text to read and intentionally identify with sticky notes or highlighting tape placed in the text where you will share your confusions out loud. Consider demonstrating the following:

- Rereading
- Reading ahead
- Using text features or picture supports

- Breaking down a word into parts
- Accessing background knowledge

These demonstrations should be done so students can see the text. You may want to use a big book, an overhead projector, or provide students with a copy of the text you will be sharing. The transcription below shows the teacher introducing clarifying through think-aloud using the big book *Wild Weather* (Berger, 1993). It is early in the year and her class is still developing the stamina for a teacher-directed lesson, so she has selected only two pages of text for today's lesson:

Teacher: I am going to model my thinking when I read something and I need to clarify. Your responsibility is to know what it means to clarify and to notice today when you do it. So notice when you are reading if you have to go back and clarify. Who knows what it means to clarify?

Student: To predict.

Teacher: It does not exactly mean that...can you share what you were thinking?

Student: Like if a storm was just about over I would clarify.

Teacher: OK, you are talking about modifying your prediction, or confirming your prediction. What does clarifying mean in general?

Student: When you don't know a word and you figure it out.

Teacher: Yes, that is one thing you might want to clear up, a word. So if you do not know how to pronounce a word or you do not know what a word means you want to figure that out. What else?

Student: Sometimes it can mean predicting.

Teacher: Not exactly. Let me go ahead and tell you. And after I tell you I want you to be able to tell it back to me. I want you to listen. Clarifying is when something doesn't make sense and you pause to make it make sense. You can clarify in a conversation if you feel like you do not understand what someone is saying or you think you understand them but it doesn't make sense. Or you can clarify when you read. Today we are focusing on clarifying when we read. [Begins reading the text] "Hurricanes are hug, swirling storms that can form over the ocean." I am going to stop there. That does not make sense. Hug. I am going to reread that word. Oh, I see, h-u-g-e, I didn't see the *e*. Now I need to go back and read the entire sentence. It says, "Hurricanes are huge, swirling storms that can form over the ocean. The entire hurricane may cover an area as big as the state of Georgia."

Teacher: Wait! I have been to Georgia. That doesn't make sense to me, it is a big state. I need to reread. [She reads the text again] Yes, it says that and now I see a picture. It does look really big. What did I do?

Student: You reread and looked at the picture.

Teacher:	[Continues to read] "When such storms form in the Pacific Ocean, they are called typoons." I've never heard of a "typoon." I need look at the word more closely. *Typhoons*. I am going to break this word into chunks: "oons" like in the word *loon* or *moon*; "ty" like in the word *type*, and "ph," like *phone*, the "ph" makes an "f" sound. Typhoons. I've heard of typhoons and I have been to Typhoon Lagoon. That makes sense now. [She finishes reading the text] OK, how did I clarify today?
Student:	You fixed words.
Teacher:	What else?
Student:	You always reread.
Teacher:	Yes, when you fix up your mistake or confusion you need to reread the part where you had a problem. Did I do anything else?
Student:	You used pictures and what you know about Typhoon Lagoon.
Teacher:	Today when you read during R^5 I want you to notice when you need to clarify and what you do to clarify. This is what you will discuss with your partner after reading.

Wrapping it up. After the think-aloud, have students read and practice noticing when they clarify. Next have them share with a partner while you walk around the room to listen in on conversations. If you notice students did not clarify while reading or recognize when they clarified, you will need to do some follow-up lessons on clarifying, including creating a class chart with how to clarify something when reading. Some classes will catch on very quickly, while others will require more patience and repeated lessons. It is best not to begin a strategy unit until your students understand why and how to clarify.

Activities for Week 3

- Continue writer's workshop, read-aloud, and R^5.
- Have students notice and share when they clarify during R^5 and direct reading instruction (both whole and small group).
- Establish literacy centers and expectations for all during small-group work.
- Review the difference between fiction and nonfiction texts.
- Teach students to distinguish between narrative and expository genres (see page 34).
- Begin noticing and identifying nonfiction text features (see page 35).

Now that students have been introduced to the vocabulary of metacognition and they have begun to explore when and how they clarify when reading, it is time to add the language of literacy to their repertoire; specifically you will explore genre and text features.

The following activities will provide a strong foundation for your students as they progress into each strategy unit. You will use the scaffolding model of the MTF with each activity, begin the whole-group lesson with guided practice, and then do a similar activity using a different text in small, leveled groups. Some groups may need more than one session before being ready to move into peer-supported use and monitored independence.

Distinguishing Between Narrative and Expository Texts

Most children are taught to distinguish between fiction and nonfiction early in their school careers. As kids progress through school those genre lessons expand to include fairy tales, folk tales, realistic fiction, mystery, biography, and informational text. All of these are valuable lessons, but children need to know more about the various ways these genres are organized. In chapter 5, we'll really dig into the organizational characteristics of the various texts through expository text investigations. In this particular lesson, however, you will lay the groundwork by helping students understand the two major forms of writing they will first encounter in school: narrative and expository.

It is important to remember that the terms *narrative* and *expository* refer to the format and other organizational characteristics of text, not to whether a piece is fiction or nonfiction. Narrative texts refer to stories, or a set of events and experiences (Harris & Hodges, 1995) written to entertain or provide a literary experience. They can be true or untrue and, typically, have a beginning, middle, and end. They are always meant to be read from beginning to end. Expository texts are those that present information, intended to inform, explain, describe, or persuade (Harris & Hodges, 1995). Again they can be true or untrue, but the organizational format often enables the reader to find specific information without reading the entire text. They rely heavily on text features and can have multiple jump-in points, or places where the reader can enter the text to ascertain information. While many expository texts also have a beginning, middle, and end, these take the form of an introduction, the promised information, and sometimes a conclusion. Others, such as dictionaries or encyclopedias, are meant to be accessed as needed, with a limited context.

Activity. For this lesson you need a stack of texts that span both narrative and expository structures, as well as fiction and nonfiction. Well-known stories such as The Three Little Pigs and Little Red Riding Hood are excellent choices for modeling narrative text structure. For expository text you can pull alphabet books, question-and-answer books, newspapers, and just about any Dorling Kindersley (DK) publication. Make sure your stacks include nonfiction narratives, such as biographies, and fictional expository texts, such as *The Dragonology Handbook: A Practical Course in Dragons* (Drake, 2005) or the *Disney Princess Essential Guide* (Bray-Moffatt, 2003). After defining *narrative* and *expository* and posting the definitions on chart paper or the chalkboard, show students examples of each type of text. Focus on the difference in format, not content.

After sharing some examples of narrative and expository texts, put students in groups and give each group a few narrative and expository titles. Have groups flip through each book to determine whether it is narrative or expository. Students can divide titles into two stacks (narrative and expository) or they can place a sticky note on the text and write whether it is narrative or expository. Be sure to walk around, as students might have some questions and disagreements at this point.

Wrapping it up. Have groups share each title, whether they determined it was narrative or expository, and why. Let the other groups comment and give a thumbs-up or thumbs-down to indicate whether they agree or disagree. Once the class has agreed on where a title fits, have a student write the title under the appropriate heading on the class chart. Next, ask students to describe the characteristics of each type of book. Summarize for them by pointing out that narrative books tend to have different characteristics than expository books.

Use this structure in small groups for kids who need extra support. Be sure to allow students access to these titles after the lesson, as you have already sneakily introduced a collection of books they might want to read.

Noticing and Identifying Nonfiction Text Features

So many of the texts we ask our older learners to read rely heavily on text features to support comprehension, yet many students either ignore text features entirely or skim over without ever noticing what the features contribute to the main idea of a piece (Spencer, 2003). If we want kids to be wide readers we must teach them how to read a variety of text types. Start the process here with an introductory lesson on text features.

This week you have reviewed the difference between fiction and nonfiction with your students and helped them further distinguish between the narrative and expository structures these two types of texts take. Remind your students that expository texts have many more graphic elements such as pictures and captions, cross-sections, tables, timelines, inset photos, and maps, and show them examples of these. It is not necessary to show an example of every possible text feature—they'll soon begin asking you to define a wide variety of features they encounter.

Activity. Group students into pairs, and give each pair a Text Feature Hunt handout (see Figure 13 and Appendix B, page 188) and two different expository texts such as a science or social studies textbook, a trade book, or periodical such as *Weekly Reader.* Have the partners hunt through each text to find an example of the various features, then record the page number where they found each feature. They need to record only one or two examples for each. Be sure to circulate to help pairs identify what they find.

Wrapping it up. Ask pairs to share some of the features they found and ask if students have questions about any of the features. Invite students to share something they learned from one of the text features. Because this is the first lesson on features, you do not need to go into great depth here. The focus is on getting students to notice and recognize text features. We will get more in depth in subsequent lessons. At the end of the lesson, challenge students to notice text features in all they read. Use this structure in small, guided-reading groups this week. It will give the kids more practice and help you see where they might need help.

FIGURE 13
Text Feature Hunt—Student Sample

Name _____   Date 5/3/04

Directions: Using the texts you have been given, identify which text features your books have and which text features they do not have. Place a "no" in a box if the text feature is not in the book. Write a page number if the book has the text feature. You need to give only one page number for each text feature. For example, if there are several photos in a book just put one of the page numbers (where the photo appears) in the box.

Title of Text	Table of Contents	Page Numbers	Pictures/ Captions	Cutaways/ Cross Sections	Maps	Diagrams	Glossary	Boldface	Index
Peculiar Plants	#1	#1-21	#3	NO	NO	#13	#20	#14	Back cover #21
Scientists at Work	#1	#1-21	#2	NO	NO	no	#20	#2	Back cover #21

Activities for Week 4

- Continue writer's workshop, read-aloud, and R⁵.
- Create an interactive text feature wall (see below).
- Broaden lessons on text features to include using them to aid comprehension (previewing, predicting, and learning from text features) (see page 38).
- Begin small-group work (guided reading) to help students better understand what has been taught in think-aloud and other whole-group lessons.

Creating an Interactive Text Feature Wall

As students become more familiar with text features, they will begin to see them everywhere they look—and they will want to show others the interesting and unique features they find. The interactive text feature wall gives students a forum for sharing their finds and exposes them to new text features. Once the categories are established, it becomes a low-maintenance independent literacy center that serves as a visual support to students as they begin to write their own nonfiction.

Activity. Tell students that they are going to make a large mural of all the different types of text features. Have them brainstorm an exhaustive list of all of the features they know. You may want to let them flip through a variety of texts to jog their memories. As students share, record each feature on a sentence strip.

FIGURE 14
Interactive Text Feature Wall

Once they have run out of ideas, ask students which features will take up the most room on the chart. The amount of space needed is influenced by both how common the feature is and how much space it takes up. For example, pictures and captions are very commonly found in a variety of texts, and they can be relatively large so the section for that heading would need to be big. Although italic print is common in certain types of texts, it isn't as widely used and it doesn't take up much space so the section for italics would be smaller.

After the group has decided which headings need the most room, make a chart (the bigger, the better) with boxes drawn for each type of text feature (see Figure 14). You can tape the sentence-strip headings at the top of each box.

Provide a stack of magazines, student newspapers, and other consumable print sources along with scissors, glue sticks, and tape. If you have access to a scanner, let kids scan pages from their textbooks to be used. Instruct students to search for various features and then cut them out and affix them to the mural. This center can stay in place for at least a few weeks, but display it for as long thereafter as you like—kids will refer to it throughout the year for support as they use more text features in their own nonfiction writing.

Wrapping it up. As students place text features on the wall, they will often seek verification or clarification from classmates or from you. Your role at this point is just to help them clear up any confusion and to provide encouragement.

Previewing, Predicting, and Learning From Text Features

Last week you awakened your students to the world of text features around them. It is likely that they are excitedly raising their hands or coming up to you to share interesting features they have found as they read. This is a good start, but we don't want students to get stuck in the identifying stage. We want to quickly move them into reading and using text features to support comprehension. In this learning sequence, students start on the cover of a book or periodical and read each feature, then pause to summarize what they learned from reading the feature. These summaries will help students make strong predictions about the content they will read.

Activity. Use a shared nonfiction text to model this strategy through think-aloud. With a copy of the Previewing, Predicting, and Learning From Text Features worksheet (see Figure 15 and Appendix B, page 189) on the overhead projector, write the text's title in the appropriate space. Next, explain that the title usually tells us what a text is about and write that in the column headed "What this text feature does." In the column headed "What I learned from reading this feature," you will write something like "Based on the title, I think this text will be about...." Continue through the first few pages, including the table of contents, to model how the learning structure works.

Now have students work in pairs using the Previewing, Predicting, and Learning From Text Features worksheet to preview a nonfiction text. They need only to look through a few pages to get the idea. Make sure you walk around and help clear up any confusion students may have as they work. It is not uncommon for kids to mistakenly assume the second and third columns are asking for the same information, so be sure to monitor.

Wrapping it up. After pairs complete their work, pull everyone back together for a whole-group share. Go through the features students recorded and what they learned from each. Next, ask what they believe this section of text will be about. Point out that they have already read and thought about nearly half of the selection, just by reading the text features. Allow students to read the section of text they previewed, then discuss as a whole group to confirm, refine, or reject predictions they made.

Be sure to take this learning structure to small groups and use again where you can closely monitor and guide. Some groups may need to use it a couple of times.

Activities for Week 5

- Continue writer's workshop, read-aloud, and R^5.
- Introduce the text feature walk structure (see page 40).
- Begin formal literature circles training (see chapter 3 for further guidance).
- Continue to add to the interactive text feature wall.

Text Feature & Page	What does the text feature do?	What I learned from reading the text feature...
Bold #6	The Word is inport-ent /glossary Tells what it is about	forest is inportent.
Sub title #6	Tells what the pic-Sher is.	It tells us about the forest.
Photoy and capsh-ion. #6	Tells parts of a pic-Sher.	Ponderoso pines are in the forest.
label diagram #6		It Tells the forest layers in th g.c.
Picter and capshion#7	Tells what the Picture is.	
bold #8	Tells a inportent Word.	flowers in the forest.
Photoy and capshion #8,9	Tells what a Pic-ure is.	Shelter is importen-t.
Picture and Capshion #10,11,12,13	Tells what a Picwa is.	A Jay and deer are in the forest. horses, coctus, flowers, mouse, Snake, sheep live in the Desert.

Text Feature & Page	What does the text feature do?	What I learned from reading the text feature...
Bold #10,11	inportent words/ glossary	desert, moisture ond evaporates.
lable diagram#10	Tells parts of the Picture	Shows desert layer
Sub heading#10	Tells what it is about	Tells about the desert.

Text Feature Walk

Just as a primary teacher uses a picture walk to preview and predict a story with students, so should teachers of older kids use the text feature walk to help students set a purpose for what they will read. If students get in the habit of previewing their selection's text features before they read the main body of text, they will automatically obtain background information, including important vocabulary. Once proficient, students will use this structure before they read during content area studies as well as literature circles, textbook circles, and R[5].

The text feature walk can be an extremely powerful structure for English-language learners (ELL) if you strategically pair students of varying levels together. Text that may have been inaccessible to an ELL student can become accessible because of the rich discussion that occurs during the text feature walk.

Activity. You may want to have a big book or transparencies of the text you are using in this think-aloud so that you can point to the features you are referring to as you model. Begin as you did with the last lesson by reading the title and looking at the cover to make predictions. Next, read the back cover and predict/confirm/revise what the text is about. Continue this process with the table of contents and first few pages. Let students jump in and help you predict as they are ready, but be sure not to overdo this lesson by covering too much text. You simply want students to understand how a text feature walk works.

Have students work in pairs to do a text feature walk. Point out that the goal is not only to preview, but also to discuss any background knowledge they may have about the topics they see in the text features. Have students walk through the front and back cover, table of contents, and a small section of text. If you are using a vocabulary-rich and feature-rich text, such as a science textbook, it is enough to have them walk through just a few pages. Roam the room to monitor students' conversations and clear up confusions.

You don't need to have students read the body of the text on this day—if time or student focus does not permit, let them read it the next day. This will make the reading go more quickly and you will have provided a lot of support to your lower readers, which will make it easier for them to read the text.

Wrapping it up. Bring students back for a whole-group sharing session. Ask if they had any interesting discussions about the text and what they learned about the topic from the activity. Ask them to estimate how much of the information in the text they think they read during the text feature walk.

Continue to use this structure in your small-reading groups for a few weeks. After that, have students use it with peers during literature circles and textbook circles. Make sure you continue to monitor and help polish this teaching tool. Students will need a few reminders and minilessons to help them refine the process and get the most out of it. Your time is worth it—of all the lessons introduced in the past few weeks, this one has the most potential to support you students long after they leave your classroom.

Activities for Week 6

Wow! You have been busy establishing rules and procedures, getting to know your students, and laying the foundation for the MTF. Take a week to polish the rough spots on the following structures, which should be in place: writer's workshop, read-aloud, think-aloud, R^5, literature circles, small-group reading, and independent literacy centers. And take a moment to celebrate—the most difficult work is behind you!

Final Thoughts

Through unit 1, laying the foundation, you have introduced and begun to implement most of the structures in the MTF. You have established routines for success and have engaged students in many lessons that will give them the background knowledge to be successful in the strategy units. The first six weeks take a lot of energy and planning, but the payoff is well worth your effort: Students are transformed from passive readers into active readers who willingly and skillfully discuss what they have read and how they read it.

Chapter 3 describes how to promote discussion throughout the school day, especially during literature circles and textbook circles.

PART II

Encouraging Talk About Books

E ven though a strong research base has identified talk as a common feature of effective classrooms, many classrooms remain silent. However, highly effective teachers engage their students in quality conversations. This purposeful talk should pervade the school day, but many students are not skilled in talking about books or their own cognitive processes.

In Part II we delve deeper into the structures of literature circles, textbook circles, and Read, Relax, Reflect, Respond, and Rap (R^5), which are put to work in the Metacognitive Teaching Framework (MTF). It is during these routines that students hone metacognitive skills and demonstrate their thinking out loud. You can use these structures to coach, monitor, and facilitate students' independent use of strategies.

Cultivating Conversations: From Literature Circles to Textbook Circles

> It is the first week of school and students are working in cooperative groups to formulate classroom rules. Five minutes into the exercise, one group is still arguing about who will speak first while another group completed the task three minutes ago. A third group appears to be doing a better job. They are sitting calmly, taking turns speaking, and sharing ideas. As you listen in, you notice that as students in this group share, they explain their own ideas but never respond to the thoughts of those who go before them. Furthermore, they are almost too calm. The animated exchange of ideas that characterizes a true discussion is conspicuously absent.

How Discussion Fits Into the Metacognitive Teaching Framework

Discussion is a vital factor at every stage of the Metacognitive Teaching Framework (MTF). From teacher-led discussions during shared reading/think-alouds, to small guided groups using reciprocal teaching, to the Rap portion of Read, Relax, Reflect, Respond, and Rap (R^5) and discussion in literature circles, the MTF relies heavily on fully engaged student discussion. If we want students to be completely successful in all of these structures, then we must first teach them how to have a real discussion about an assigned topic.

Throughout the MTF, we require students to engage in real discussions about what they have read and how they have read it. Nowhere is discussion more important than during literature and textbook circles. During these structures you, the teacher, must feel confident that quality conversations are happening. You must know that even without your tutelage, students are engaging in the task at hand in a meaningful way. In order for high-quality, genuine discussions to occur, we need to first train students how to engage in them.

Teaching Students to Discuss Effectively

When we first started teaching, we thought our lot in life was to try and keep kids from talking all day. How ironic that we now spend time trying to teach them how to talk more effectively—and more often! Students come to us with a wide variety of discussion deficits. For instance, some are shy and would prefer to sit quietly while others monopolize the conversation. Some like to talk and talk—with no concern, if anyone else is listening. Others understand the polite rules of conversation—speak in turn, sit quietly when it is not your turn, look at the speaker—but they fail to fully engage, resulting in a glorified sharing session rather than a true discussion. All of these students can learn to have real discussions about the things we want them to discuss, it just takes a little concentrated effort.

Langer and Close (2001) recommend four ways teachers can scaffold discussion: tapping understanding, seeking clarification, inviting participation, and orchestrating discussion. Any or all of these may need to be explicitly modeled depending upon your students and what they are discussing. In this chapter we will describe how Nicki does this with her students and offer you suggestions for developing meaningful discussion with your students.

A good way to begin teaching students about discussion is to spend lunchtime with them or eavesdrop during recess. Listen to what they talk about when they are outside the constraints of the classroom. For example, one year, Nicki overheard students avidly discussing their favorite roller coasters. Even kids who didn't make a peep in class were excitedly describing their favorite rides. The next day, she introduced the idea that she wanted this same kind of enthusiasm and genuine participation in classroom discussions. She asked her students what a real conversation looks like, and steered them away from the "hands folded on lap, taking turns, looking at the speaker" mode by reminding them of how they looked, acted, and felt during the lunchroom discussion on roller coasters. Next, she strategically placed students in groups of three and four to ensure a range of verbal skills and compatible personalities. She assigned groups the task of authentically discussing their favorite theme park rides. Students discussed for 10 minutes, then assessed the quality of their conversations. They agreed that a good conversation would have full participation. It would include students reacting to and building off of one another's ideas. Students also agreed that people engaged in a real conversation would look interested. They might break off into a quick side discussion about the topic, then find their way back to the main thread. Students decided that a successful conversation would remain true to the topic.

Students responded well to this assignment, actively participating and quickly recognizing areas of weakness in discussions. Later, students used the ideas they talked about to write a piece on their favorite theme park rides.

After students are comfortable discussing a topic they are naturally interested in, you can steer them to use these same skills when talking about more academic topics. These early, assigned discussions should be followed with students self-assessing the quality of the conversation using the same criteria they developed during the first discussion.

What Are Literature Circles?

Many educators claim they are incorporating literature circles, but they really are not. Harvey Daniels (2002), the father of literature circles, laments,

Today, it seems that any time you gather a group of students together for any activity involving reading, you can go right ahead and call it literature circles. It doesn't matter if the teacher has picked the story, if the book is a basal (or a science textbook!), if the teacher is running the discussion, if the kids have no voice—it's just cool to call it a literature circle. There are even traditional round-robin reading groups being called literature circles, even if this activity is about as antithetical to the lit circle idea as you could imagine. (p. 12)

Daniels (2002) identifies 11 key points that he describes as the key ingredients of literature circles.

1. Reading material is chosen by students.
2. The groups are small, temporary, and based on book selection.
3. Each group reads a different book.
4. Groups meet on a predictable and regular schedule.
5. Written or drawn notes are used by students to guide their discussion.
6. Discussion topics come from the students.
7. The discussions are characterized by natural conversations about the book.
8. The teacher does not belong to the group but serves as a facilitator.
9. Teacher observation and student self-evaluation are the evaluation techniques employed.
10. The atmosphere should be fun and playful.
11. Readers share what they have read with classmates when they have finished and then form new groups based on text selection.

There are probably as many different ways to do literature circles as there are teachers doing them, but for us two major criteria distinguish this learning structure: (1) Students get to choose the texts they read and (2) students lead the discussion.

The Importance of Literature Circles

In recent years, research has linked literature circles to gains in student achievement (Daniels, 2002). Students involved in peer-led discussions made more gains on reading comprehension than those in control groups (Klingner, Vaughn, & Schumann, 1998). Literature circles are the perfect opportunity for students to practice strategies taught "not in drills or worksheets, but in real conversations about real books" (Daniels, 2002, p. 38). Critical thinking is strengthened by the discussions that occur in these small groups (Gambrell & Almasi, 1996).

Furthermore, literature circles are formed on the premise of collaborative learning. The predictable student-led structure allows for shared leadership among students and invites diverse points of view. Because groups are not based on friendship, but on text, students who do not normally converse with one another have the opportunity to communicate, which widens the classroom community (Daniels, 2002). Literature circles support Vygotsky's (1978) theories of social interaction. While students are engaged in literature circles they construct their understanding of the text through interactions with peers and the teacher, as well as sharing what interests them about the books they have read (Stien & Beed, 2004).

Problems With Literature Circles

As with almost any structure, roadblocks are inevitable. Problems you may encounter when implementing literature circles include the following:

1. Students are not prepared and do not know how to prepare for the discussion. Some will assume that because this is not a teacher-led activity they don't have to put in as much effort. Others will not know what to do to prepare for a literature discussion. During the training phase you can model how you take notes and prepare for discussion. You can also emphasize the importance of being a contributing group member.

2. Students do not know how to participate in a discussion. Because many of students' classroom experiences so far may have involved the teacher talking rather than the students, they may not know how to hold a productive academic discussion. Again, training and practice in effective discussion techniques are vital.

3. Students' conversations are superficial or contrived. As with anything students are learning to do, their first attempts are likely to be approximations. They will mimic what they believe to be good conversational habits but may not pay much attention to the quality of what they discuss. You can monitor and coach during discussions. Also, be sure to recap after a literature circle session and highlight what went well with groups and what could be improved.

4. Students find the reading material unappealing. You must actively seek out high-quality texts that meet your criteria and student interests.

5. Students may not be involved in the conversations. Reminding students before they begin that a good conversation will include all members and then asking them what went well during the recap will help draw in reluctant contributors. Also, the Literature Circles Bookmark (see templates in Appendix B, pages 191–192) provides conversation starters to help less verbal students jump into the conversation in a meaningful way.

6. Students digress. Just as in adult book clubs, sometimes the conversation flows off topic. Teach students how to notice this and bring conversation back on track. The Literature Circles Bookmarks include "conversation continuers" for bringing the conversation back on topic.

7. Students are off task. This is where teacher and student monitoring come in. Let group members know that they should invite off-task peers back into the discussion. If that doesn't work, let them know that you are available to correct off-task behavior if group members cannot self-monitor. And remember, if students are engaged in talking about a great book, they won't be off task.

How Do Literature Circles Fit Into the Metacognitive Teaching Framework?

The ways we train students to lead literature circles overlap with the work we do in the MTF. This training is the students' first formal introduction to the metacognitive strategies and enriches discussions during read-aloud, R⁵, and other reading lessons. To teach students to comprehend, we teach them to connect, visualize, predict, question, and summarize. To prepare them for literature circles, we teach them to predict, connect, question, visualize, and summarize. We also teach students how to recognize and capture the author's craft as they read. We show them how to refer back to the text to support their thoughts as they discuss, and to rely on one another to help clarify things they did not understand. Perhaps most importantly, we teach students how pleasurable it can be to bond over a good book in a nurturing literary environment.

As students progress in a strategy unit from teacher-led think-alouds to small-group and paired work, their proficiency in using the strategy increases. For example, in the Prediction unit, students begin to stretch the ways and depth with which they predict. This is evident in work done with the teacher as well as peer-supported work. R⁵ and literature circles give students the chance to continue honing their new skills on self-selected texts. With literature circles, students have the added benefit of peers supporting their comprehension. Group members also help students to develop more thoughtful responses to the text.

Getting Started

Once you've laid the groundwork with training in discussion, students are primed and ready to move into literature circles training. After trying many versions of literature circle training, we have settled on a streamlined process that first introduces then capitalizes on strategy training done throughout each metacognitive strategy unit (introduced in chapters 5 through 9).

After introducing the goals, use the Literature Circles Training Template (see Figure 16 and Appendix B, page 190, for a reproducible) to help students practice thinking about a shared text using the metacognitive strategies on the template. Depending on the students' maturity and ability, you could train them in one or more strategies per day, followed by a session of using all the strategies together with a text (see Figure 17).

To introduce the concept of literature circles, it is helpful to focus on your goals. For our purposes, the goals are to read and enjoy a good book and have a meaningful discussion about the text. By focusing on these goals, students aren't as likely to focus on less important things such as making sure their notes are Pulitzer Prize–quality or having the correct number of sticky notes affixed to their pages. The first goal is (in our opinion) the most important and doesn't require a lot of teaching for students to understand. The second goal is best illuminated with a quick brainstorm of what a meaningful discussion is. The transcript beginning on page 51 illustrates Nicki introducing literature circles to her class:

FIGURE 16
Literature Circles Training Template

Strategy	How I used this strategy...	Page number where I used this strategy
Connecting: I connected something in the text to something I've read about, seen, or experienced myself.	I have a connection because We have had a hurricane coming to Florida	page 3
Predicting: I used what I have read or what I know to make a prediction about the text.	I predict that the weather forecasters will find out where the hurricane is going.	page 5
Questioning: I have a question about what I am reading or about ideas the text made me think about.	I'm wondering if hurricane Mitch will get stronger when it hits land. Where will hurricane Mitch will hit?	page 6
Visualizing: I can see a clear picture of something in the text. Hint: you can write a description or draw a picture of what you see.	I can see a clear picture of something in the people geting ready for the hurricane by boarding their houses and moving out because of the waves and tide	page 7
Clarifying: I clarify vocabulary, an idea, or concept, or what has happened in the book.	I claisfyed cay.	
Writer's craft: I notice something unique or remarkable about the way the author wrote this text. Hint: This could include special words or phrases that really speak to you.	I like how the author discribed Baily and how he acted. I also like the name of the soup.	page 8

FIGURE 17
Suggested Timeline for Literature Circles Training

Day 1 Introduce the concept of literature circles, the Literature Circles Training Template, and connecting. Practice discussing connections. Recap and clarify.	**Day 2** Introduce predicting. Practice discussing predictions using a shared text. Recap and clarify.	**Day 3** Introduce questioning. Practice discussing questions using a shared text. Recap and clarify.	**Day 4** Introduce visualizing. Practice discussing visualizations using a shared text. Recap and clarify.
Day 5 Introduce clarifying. Practice discussing clarifications using a shared text. Recap and clarify.	**Day 6** Introduce the concept of the writer's craft and practice discussing comments about writer's craft using a shared text. Recap and clarify.	**Day 7** Introduce the literature circles bookmarks. Practice using these to stimulate discussion of a shared text. Recap and clarify.	**Day 8** Introduce the titles offered for the first cycle of literature circles. Have students preview and choose their books. Set up a routine and guidelines for each literature circle session.

Teacher: In a literature circle you read the same book as others and you discuss the book together. In our classroom we will have textbook circles and literature circles. With textbook circles everyone will read the same text. Usually this is a section from the science or social studies textbook. In literature circles I will provide you with books that you can choose from.

There are two goals for literature circles [writes on the board]:

1. Read and enjoy a good book.
2. Have a meaningful discussion about the book you read.

Which word do you think is really important in the second goal?

Andrew: *Meaningful.*

Teacher: Yes! What is meaningful in terms of a discussion about your book?

Hunter: Stuff important to the story or main idea.

Teacher: Good! What else?

Brian: Maybe what happened in the book.

Teacher: Right, something important to the plot.

Jessica: A part which was sad or made you feel a certain way.

Teacher: What do we call that?

Taylor: A connection.

Teacher: OK, a connection to an emotion.

Autumn: A question about what you're reading.

Teacher:	Yes.
Aaron:	You might talk about what you think the book is going to be about.
Teacher:	Right, a prediction.
Ashlyn:	If you didn't understand something you could ask your group.
Teacher:	What do you call that?
Ashlyn:	Clarifying.
Teacher:	Exactly.
Casey:	You could share a visualization.
Teacher:	Yes, what you visualized. You could talk about it using details or maybe even draw a picture and show it to your group.
Joshua:	Visualize what you think might happen next.
TJ:	You could, like, draw a picture of your prediction and ask your group what they think.
Teacher:	Great idea! During the literature circle I want you to enjoy the book, I want you to be involved in the conversation, and I want you to learn something.

After this introduction to the process, you will want to focus on one strategy at a time, building time for defining, practicing, and clarifying what each strategy entails. We teach one strategy per day when working with intermediate students. Each strategy lesson follows a predictable pattern:

1. The teacher introduces the strategy using the blurb on the template and examples.

2. The teacher assigns a short piece of text for students to read and practice strategy use. Students are told to write at least one example of how they used the strategy being practiced on the appropriate block of the template.

3. Students read and take notes.

4. The teacher leads a class discussion of how and where students used the strategy, making sure to clarify as needed.

As students progress through the strategies, the talk evolves from the whole class simply sharing strategy use to discussions of text based on strategy use and, finally, to small-group discussions of strategy use. This way, you can help students understand that literature circles are more than just reading, taking notes, and listening quietly as their group members share. You can reinforce groups who are doing a good job of discussing and work with those who need more support. The following transcript demonstrates Nicki training students to connect:

Teacher:	We will officially start literature circles next week. This week I am going to introduce each strategy you might use during a literature circle and I am going to have you practice the strategy. We are going to use the book *Hurricane.* Today we'll work on connections. We're going to use a training

	template to help us. [She has passed out the sheet and book, now goes over the first row on connecting] Open the book to page 3. While you read page 3, I want you to make a connection.
Ru:	What if you don't have a connection?
Teacher:	This is a practice time, so I want you to try and force yourself to connect. [Students read and fill out the first row of the Literature Circles Training Template]
Teacher:	OK, let's begin sharing our connections.
Brian:	I made a connection from Hurricane Katrina and how the trees hit homes.
Teacher:	What in the text made you make that connection?
Brian:	[He holds up the book and shows the picture] Right here.
Hunter:	[Not written on his sheet] We had a 20-foot tree fall near our house.
Autumn:	I made a connection because it reminded me of Hurricane Katrina on the news and in the newspaper.
Teacher:	Remember, your connections need to be more specific.
Morgan:	I could connect when it said that the hurricane had a lot of fury because when Hurricane Charlie hit here it had a lot of fury, too.
Teacher:	That was terrific. She even used vocabulary from that page in her connection.

The other strategies are similarly introduced. After groups have met and you have circulated the room to monitor discussion, hold a debriefing to clarify strategy use and student participation and roles. This debriefing time allows you to correct misunderstanding and reinforce the behaviors you desire. The following transcript shows how Nicki facilitated a debriefing on a group's discussion of author's craft:

Teacher:	Let's start with some celebrations. What I noticed when I walked around was that every group was having a conversation and talking about the text. So that is a celebration. Let's talk about what went well in your groups.
Teacher:	Morgan, what went well?
Morgan:	We were able to talk about the beginning or if we didn't relate to it or we were off track...or we didn't get something, we were able to clarify why she wrote that in there.
Teacher:	I heard that group questioning choices the author made, and that is good. I don't think everybody in that group loves the writing style of this author so far, so let's hear what Victoria has to say. She's in the same group.
Victoria:	I think it really went well, because everybody was in the conversation. Nobody was just sitting there.
Teacher:	Did Prerna contribute?
Victoria:	Yes, she contributed a lot.
Teacher:	Not just when Mrs. Grace was around?

Victoria:	No.
Teacher:	Brian, you were in that group. What else went well in your group?
Brian:	Everything went well, but I didn't like how the author put us in the middle of the story instead of in the beginning. And I think by the end of the story I'll know the whole thing, and I think the chapters...there shouldn't be just a lot of headings.
Teacher:	I heard you guys talking a lot about the writer's craft in that group. It wasn't all complimentary. They didn't all love the way the author wrote. They weren't just talking about what they liked. They were also talking very specifically about how Sharon Creech wrote that book. So that was a really good thing. And I think I heard Brian saying if you kept on reading it will make more sense, because he thinks she is starting you in the middle, and it will probably go to the beginning.
Teacher:	I think everybody did a great job today. Some of our conversations weren't just about writer's craft, but even so everything we discussed was about the text. So that was fabulous. You guys are gifted conversationalists. That means you're good talkers, which sometimes I like. Sometimes I don't. We will do this again on Monday.

Tools of Talk

After students have practiced taking notes and thinking about each of the various ways we discuss literature, they can graduate to Literature Circle Bookmarks (see templates in Appendix B, pages 191–192). On one side these show conversation starters designed to lead students to discuss their use of strategies and writer's craft, and the reverse side shows conversation continuers to scaffold students as they work to build on one another's ideas. Students find these bookmarks to be helpful as they move from the training template to less scaffolded note-taking.

Other important tools include sticky notes or spiral notebooks for taking notes as students read. We like to give students a choice of sticky notes or spirals because the students really seem to have a preference here. Some of them like sticky notes because they can place them right in the text where they had the thought, while others prefer to have all their notes in a central location. Students continue using the bookmarks and other tools throughout the year.

Textbook Circles: Assigned Texts

If you are like most teachers, you are often pressed for time. Lesson planning is a constant exercise in prioritization, and it can be difficult to cover the prescribed content in a meaningful way. Once students are adept at discussing their self-selected texts in literature circles, they can transfer these skills to assigned texts. As long as you take a little time to build interest in the subject and help students notice and pronounce text-critical vocabulary, peer-led textbook circles can be very effective.

It is important to distinguish literature circles from textbook circles. Unlike literature circles, in textbook circles students form temporary small groups and work through a piece of content area text identified by the teacher. The goal of textbook circles still includes having a quality discussion, and we hope students enjoy the process, but an added purpose is enhanced comprehension through peer scaffolding. You could use the textbook, but textbook circles could also center on informational text such as *Weekly Reader*, newspaper articles, or other periodicals. Because most of students' reading beyond the elementary school is going to be informational text (Kristo & Bamford, 2004), using this structure with this type of text makes sense.

Before assigning a textbook or periodical, you should consider a few factors. First and foremost, is the content of the text interesting and accessible enough to engage students without a teacher-directed lesson? Is the text written well with related visual supports? Students shouldn't be required to cover large amounts of content-rich material in student-led groups. Pick the section of text that really gets at what you want them to learn—don't let students think this is about "covering" a certain number of pages or getting through the textbook.

Also, you need to be strategic about how the groups are formed. Ideally, you would have at least one student in each group who has some related background knowledge to share with peers. Again, groups should not be made up entirely of reticent speakers. You also want a range of reading abilities so the struggling readers have added peer support. So a prototypical group would have at least one strong reader, at least one child with background knowledge on the topic, one or two verbal kids, and one or two lower level readers.

Prior to turning groups loose to predict, read, and discuss, it is helpful to get students ready mentally by using activities such as Word Alert! (see page 91), Anticipation Guides (see page 86), and a student-led Text Feature Walk (see page 40). These activities help students set a purpose for the reading, facilitate engagement, and build background for the reading. After setting students up to be successful, you can release a little control and let them continue the process in the same manner they have used for literature circles.

With assigned texts especially, your role as mentor and coach remains crucial. It can be much easier for students to get off track if they are not interested in the material or are not getting enough support. Make sure to circulate and monitor comprehension and engagement. Students may still need help with vocabulary or pronunciation in a content area text. Walking around helps ensure you will be where they need you when they need you. When students complete their reading, they discuss the text in their groups by sharing notes, drawings, and having a conversation about the text. You then facilitate the whole-class discussion on the text (see Figure 18).

Benefits of Textbook Circles

Our students report that textbook circles help them as readers. They report that textbook circles help them do the following:

FIGURE 18
Textbook Circles Overview

Before Reading

Students do a text feature walk to predict. Students share text features from the text they are going to read and discuss how they feel this will relate to the text, connections they have, questions they have, clarification, background information they might know, etc.

During Reading

Students read and take notes on the text (using sticky notes or in a notebook), write questions they have, and draw pictures related to the reading. They may use stems from bookmarks to identify topics for discussion.

After Reading

Students begin discussing notes, questions, connections, etc. They may even pull in other resources to help them clarify and answer questions. The teacher pulls it together by facilitating a whole-class discussion on the content and themes, etc.

- **Be more accountable for their learning.** As Brittany put it, "It helps you think more...sharing with your peers makes you want to sound good when you talk."

- **Clarify learning.** Kaitlin says, "You can talk to people and they help you understand it...especially if you missed something, sometimes they go back to it in the text and then you get it."

- **Think.** Alana explains, "Someone in the group usually gives you something good to think about."

- **Communicate their knowledge.** As Andrea notes, "Sometimes people can jump into your conversation and help you out because they know something about it."

- **Build background knowledge.** Dorian comments, "You know some stuff and your peers know some stuff, and they sometimes have background knowledge that can help you."

- **Employ strategies.** Griffin says it best: "Sometimes textbooks are hard to understand because they have so much information, and when you can connect, question, predict, and visualize it helps you understand the text better."

Assessment: Pros, Cons, Suggestions

In our assessment-crazed culture it is tempting to try and take a grade on every activity we have kids perform. It's always important, though, to remember our primary goals for using literature circles: to have students read and enjoy a good book and then have a meaningful discussion about the text. If you are feeling the need to assess during this time, remember that the assessment should help you ultimately reach these goals.

We have found that when we assign grades for literature circle notes, students write eloquent and involved annotations. It is often difficult to get them to stop taking notes and discuss. These types of notes do not translate into high-quality discussions, however, unless the discussion is also being assessed. In fact, after students spend so much time writing down their thoughts, they mainly want their group members to listen as they share and are not too interested in what their classmates have to say.

Furthermore, you need to think about the motivation factor. Can you imagine having to write final-draft quality notes before you discussed something you have read with a colleague or spouse? What if you then had to assess your own performance in the discussion using a rubric? Would you be eager to do this? Would it be enjoyable?

We use informal formative assessment each time students engage in literature or textbook circles. We eavesdrop and coach as needed or plan minilessons based on what we hear during group work. We have many other opportunities to assess student learning. If you feel you must have a grade from a cycle of literature circles, consider asking students to write individual summaries of their books at the end.

With textbook circles, more formal assessment comes later when you have students do something with the information they have gained while reading. You can have them answer content-oriented questions, write a question-and-answer book about the topic, or even take a traditional test to assess learning. Just make sure your students understand that the textbook circle group members are there to help one another understand the content better so that they all can be more successful on the graded assignments.

Final Thoughts

Teaching students to engage in thoughtful, productive discussions is one of the most valuable investments of classroom time you can make. With these skills, students can help one another generate background knowledge, explore new texts, and consider the wide range of values and perspectives present in their class and the world.

In chapter 4 you will learn more about R^5 and how it promotes engagement, including some of the details and tools you need to make this structure work for you and your students.

Promoting Engagement in Reading Through R^5

> At first glance, it looks as if all is well during this Sustained Silent Reading (SSR) block. The class is still and quiet. Students sit calmly with open books, appearing to read intently. But take a closer look and you'll recognize a handful of disengaged readers doing the anything-but-reading shuffle. These students move from bookshelf to desk, from desk to restroom, back to bookshelf, switching books. Or they sit staring at and flipping pages of a book, maybe even reading words, but neglecting to make meaning of what they have read. Some of these readers like to share their progress with the teacher frequently, stating, "I'm on chapter 2 now," then later, "I'm almost to chapter 3." Add to these students those who are reading books well below their ability level, or those stuck reading the same genre, book after book, and you begin to get a clearer picture of what is actually occurring during this reading time.

Fake, Disengaged, and Mindless Reading

Does any of this sound familiar to you? Most teachers who provide independent reading time have witnessed students avoiding reading or pretending to read. In fact, it is one reason some teachers abandon the practice—it doesn't help those who need it the most. This is a genuine concern because there is a powerful link between time spent reading and reading achievement (Cunningham & Stanovich, 1997; Guthrie, Wigfield, Metsala, & Cox, 1999).

Many adults can relate to this phenomenon. At some point we have experienced our own disengaged reading, when our eyes passed over print but we didn't know what we had read. When this happens to us though, as expert readers, we do something about it. We might reread, stop and think, visualize, summarize what we have read, talk to an expert, find another text, or even abandon the text altogether. But many students neither have the tools to fix their reading when it breaks down, nor do they recognize when their reading has broken down. Here are some of the factors contributing to disengaged reading:

- A limited view of reading (i.e., just saying the words in the text and answering questions when they are finished)
- Lack of strategies to monitor comprehension
- No purpose for reading

- Difficulty choosing interesting books
- Difficulty choosing books at the right level
- Limited ability to self-assess and set goals for improving

Engaged readers read because they are interested in a topic, want to learn something, want to escape into a story, and many other reasons. We need to help our students build the skills required to comprehend a variety of texts. We also need to get students interested in reading other genres, including nonfiction, as well as new authors, series, and age-appropriate books. Our job (and it is not an easy one) is to find the right book for the right child, and then teach that child to fully engage every time he or she reads.

This chapter provides a rationale for independent reading and describes the structured independent reading block—Read, Relax, Reflect, Respond, and Rap (R⁵)—we developed to engage all readers, especially those who have the most trouble engaging with a text.

The Importance of Independent Reading

There is a significant amount of research supporting the practice of independent reading. Students who read more in school and for homework read better, have a stronger vocabulary, earn higher grades in school (Sweet, Guthrie, & Ng, 1998), and perform better on standardized tests (Anderson & Nagy, 1992; Donahue, Voelkl, Campbell, & Mazzeo, 1999; Gottfried, 1990; NAEP, 1988). The more children read, the more words they encounter, and the larger their speaking, listening, reading, and writing vocabulary grows (Anderson, 1996).

> I don't get to read a lot at home, and I just like the reading part [of R⁵]. I like to get into a really good book. —Griffin

Furthermore, volume matters. Researchers have found that the amount of time children spend reading is the best predictor of reading achievement (Anderson, Wilson, & Fielding, 1988; Guthrie et al., 1999) and is critical to developing a literate classroom culture (Davidson & Koppenhaver, 1993). ELL students, beyond the beginning reading level, benefit from wide reading in English (Pilgreen & Krashen, 1993). In-school free reading promotes reading comprehension (Krashen, 1988).

Access to appealing, interesting texts and time to read are critical if students are going to attain high levels of literacy (McQuillan, 1998). And, although research suggests that middle class families have more access to books (Feitelson & Goldstein, 1986), we find that many middle class students participate in numerous extracurricular activities, which limits their time to devote to reading; when given the opportunity, some don't actively engage in reading at all. We can't assume that students are reading outside of school, even though we ask them to do so.

Successful Independent Reading Programs

During the 1990s SSR (Sustained Silent Reading), DEAR (Drop Everything And Read), and USSR (Uninterrupted, Sustained Silent Reading) were commonly used as the independent reading block in many schools. During SSR, the teacher and students read materials of their own choosing for a specific amount of time. The rationale is that having students practice reading at their independent level develops fluency, increases vocabulary, enhances comprehension, and improves wide reading (Krashen, 1988; Pilgreen, 2000). While independent reading approaches such as SSR certainly have benefits, many teachers experience pitfalls during implementation. Students often read inappropriate books (too hard or too easy), and many students fake read during this time. The lack of response or feedback during SSR leaves some students without a purpose for reading. Furthermore, many students choose a new book each day, get stuck in genre or series ruts, and exhibit avoidance behaviors.

Reading workshop is another commonly used structure for independent reading in schools. Reading workshop is kicked off with a whole-class minilesson that lasts 5 to 15 minutes, followed by at least 30 minutes of students reading self-selected texts. Often students are asked to practice in independent reading what has been taught during the minilesson. While students read, the teacher records what the students are reading and then confers with students. Conferring can be done individually, in pairs, or in small groups. The theory behind reading workshop is that providing children with time to read, choice on what to read, and feedback will cause them to choose to read for pleasure outside of school. As in SSR, teachers can experience roadblocks with implementation. One problem is lack of stamina. Children do not always have the strategies and skills to read uninterrupted for 30 minutes; they need to develop this over time. In addition, keeping a minilesson to 5 to 15 minutes can be nearly impossible if the teacher is going to be explicit and direct. And, like SSR, book selection remains an issue. Even though book selection is monitored, kids still make inappropriate choices and get stuck reading the same genre or series constantly. Furthermore, all students may not receive feedback in the form of a conference or sharing on a daily basis.

So what has worked in the past? Successful independent reading programs have eight common elements (Pilgreen, 2000):

1. The environment is conducive to reading. The room is quiet and there are comfortable places to sit. The classroom is set up to invite reading.

2. Students have access to a variety of texts in the classroom.

3. The classroom library has appealing books. Self-selection is critical to the success of SSR, so the book collection should contain books students *want* to read.

4. Students have a distributed amount of time to read. Students are given time to read, and this is consistent and frequent. It may not be daily but it is scheduled on a regular basis.

5. Students receive encouragement from the teacher and peers. This could be time for one-on-one, small-group, or whole-class discussion about the books they have read. This can also include the teacher modeling reading while the students read.

6. The teacher has ongoing staff training, such as professional readings, workshops, or college course work.

7. The students are not held accountable. In other words, students do not receive a grade for reading and/or they are not required to meet a quota for reading during this time.

8. Students have engaging follow-up activities.

We kept these elements in mind as we built on what has worked in SSR and Reading Workshop to improve our own independent reading block (Clausen-Grace & Kelley, 2007). We added structured conferences so the teacher could better guide students as they applied metacognitive strategies (Pearson, 1985). We included time for students to reflect upon their own strategy use. We also provided time for students to share their strategy use with a partner and the whole class. These changes ensured not only that students were mentally engaged each day as they read, but also that they were practicing what was being taught in whole- and small-group lessons. It also removed some of the silence from our independent reading block. We dubbed our new independent reading block R^5, which stands for Read, Relax, Reflect, Respond, and Rap (see Figure 19). Nicki does R^5 three days a week, but it can be done daily.

FIGURE 19
Comparison of R^5, Reading Workshop, and SSR

R^5	Reading Workshop	SSR
Read and Relax: Students have a set purpose to read a book of their choice anywhere in classroom. Students practice strategy use. Teacher does a status-of-the-class and confers with students on strategy plans.	*Minilesson:* Teacher conducts a quick minilesson, which may set a purpose for reading—usually in a reading area. *Read:* Students read a book of their choice. Teacher reads, does a status-of-the-class and confers with students.	*Read:* Teacher reads. Students read a book of their choice.
Reflect and Respond: Students reflect and respond in their strategy log. Teacher circulates during this time.	*Record/Respond:* Students record their book titles in a reading log and then respond to the book they are reading.	*Record:* Students record their book titles in a reading record.
Rap (Share/Discuss): *Pairs:* Teacher continues to circulate. Students pair up and share something interesting from their book, actively listening to their partner share. *Whole class:* Teacher facilitates the pair-sharing and elicits the strategy being used. The process is repeated with a new pair.	*Sharing:* Teacher facilitates a whole-class share of reading.	*Sharing:* Students may or may not share what they have read.

How Does R⁵ Fit Into the Metacognitive Teaching Framework?

The goal of the Metacognitive Teaching Framework (MTF) is to develop students' strategies to the point where they can independently apply them with ease. We've already suggested that teaching comprehension strategies is not enough in itself to create a strategic reader. Furthermore, assessing independent strategy use can be difficult because it usually occurs in one's head and at a subconscious level.

As previously asserted, we believe metacognitive readers not only repair meaning when it breaks down but also glean a richer understanding from text by purposefully applying strategies while reading. So if metacognition is the key to thoughtful, active reading (Diehl, 2005), how do we assess it? The conferring and Rap portions of R⁵ afford the teacher a way to determine if students are applying strategies when reading texts, in the context of independent reading.

We are all familiar with the adage "practice makes perfect." Learning to ride a bike, play the piano, or speak a new language requires a lot of practice. In many cases, if we don't use a new skill we have learned, we lose it; if we practice a new skill without coaching, we may practice the same mistakes over and over again, cementing bad habits. Learning to be an effective independent reader isn't any different, and R⁵ provides the differentiated, supported practice our students need to help them become more metacognitive readers. In other words, all students get the correct amount of support for their particular reading needs, be it coaching, monitoring, or facilitating. During R⁵, you can coach students in the use of strategies, find out if they are really "getting it," and discover what you can do to help push students to think more deeply (Keene, 2002). R⁵ is intended to achieve the following:

- Increase reading proficiency through engaged reading
- Enhance students' metacognitive awareness by scaffolding and promoting the use of comprehension strategies (especially those being taught)
- Support wide reading
- Build student motivation to read
- Engage students in social interaction through discussion
- Improve active listening

The next sections discuss in greater detail each portion of R⁵. See Figure 20 for a snapshot overview of R⁵.

Read and Relax

I enjoy being able to just sit down and read with no interruptions. —Alana

The first observation visitors make when they come to see R⁵ is that the students are all engaged in reading. This is because the process is strategically crafted to promote successful independent reading and to help negate the obstacles we mentioned earlier.

FIGURE 20
R⁵ Overview

R⁵	What are the students doing?	What is the teacher doing?
Read and Relax 10–20 minutes	1. Reading self-selected texts (although they may be guided into another text by the teacher) 2. Employing strategies to promote comprehension 3. Sitting in an area of the classroom where they are comfortable	1. Taking the status-of-the-class to monitor book selections 2. Conducting intervention conferences as needed 3. Conferring with students individually on strategy plans
Reflect and Respond 3–5 minutes	1. Thinking about what they have just read 2. Recording thoughts in a response log 3. Noting metacognitive strategies used while reading	1. Walking around the room to monitor engagement
Rap 1 3–5 minutes	1. Sharing thoughts about their book with their assigned partner 2. Actively listening to their partner as they share their thoughts about the book they are reading	1. Walking around the room to monitor 2. Listening in on conversations to aid the whole-class rap
Rap 2 5–10 minutes	1. Sharing their partner's thoughts about the book they are reading 2. Identifying the strategies being shared by classmates	1. Facilitating the whole-class share 2. Calling on students to share their partner's thoughts 3. Calling on other students to identify the strategy being described

Finding the Right Book

Many fake readers just pick up a book and begin. Rarely do they read the title, look at the cover, open the book, and make a judgment, so a minilesson on how to choose a book is time well spent. Demonstrating how you select or reject a book can help those students who are "binge buyers" or those who have a "shop till you drop" mentality (Reutzel & Fawson, 2002). "Binge buyers" are the kids who are easily influenced by the cover and only choose those books displayed. The "shop till you drop" students spend so much time browsing that they never find the right book, and they are forced to select the nearest book for reading at the last minute. These students need to learn how to preview a book to decide whether it would be a good read or whether it should be left on the shelf. You may want to teach kids to read the front and back cover first to see if the topic interests them, then have them read the first page or two to see if the reading level and the writing style are a good fit.

> I usually decide if a book is right for me by reading the introduction or the first page or two and seeing if I actually understand it. —John

Read and Relax should be the time students read books that they can read. You do not want struggling students reading books that are too challenging during this time because this can lead to disengagement—exactly what you are trying to eliminate. Again, you will want to determine your students' independent and instructional reading levels, which will guide you as you monitor their reading (see chapter 2).

You can use the status-of-the-class (explained later in this chapter) to indicate who may be regularly choosing books that are too difficult. The biggest indicator is that the student jumps from book to book without finishing any. If you suspect students are doing this, you'll want to pause each time you notice a new book being read and ask them why they changed. If a child is frequently switching books, it is a good idea to confer with him or her as soon as you notice. Because you are aware of students' reading levels, you can determine if an intervention conference on book selection is necessary.

The five-finger test for selecting books can help readers who continually fail to get into appropriately leveled text (Routman, 2000). It is used to help students determine the level of support that may be needed to read the book independently, or whether they should select another text without teacher support. To demonstrate the five-finger test, ask students to read a page of text from the book they are thinking about selecting. As they read, they put up a finger for each word that is unknown to them. After reading the entire page, students should ask themselves, "What did I just read?" If they cannot remember, then they should select another text. If they can, they should refer to the chart according to the number of fingers they have held up. This will help determine whether the book is appropriate or if they should seek a new book. The Five-Finger Test for Selecting Books chart (see Appendix B, page 193) can become a class poster or just be a sheet inside their R⁵ folder.

If an intervention conference becomes necessary, you might have the students demonstrate the five-finger test right in front of you, with the book they are reading. While listening, you should note how many words they have difficulty with. That way, if they are not aware of their mistakes you can address the errors directly after the page is read. If students are unable to explain and understand what they have read, you might point out that most people read books that are a little lower than their instructional level when they are reading for pleasure. Take them to the bookshelf and show them a few titles that are on this level and might appeal to their interests. Some students just expect reading to be difficult and boring because it always has been for them. They don't see anything wrong with sitting down and struggling though a text. Helping them find an appealing book they are able to read is the best way to raise their level of expectation.

However, students who have the background knowledge and interest to read challenging books often can successfully comprehend. In addition, many students choose books because they have previously seen the movie. As Zach explains,

> I went to the theater with my friend. We saw *A Series of Unfortunate Events*, and they showed Book One, Two, and Three. It was so good. I saw the pictures and what it was really like. I just felt like I needed to read these books and see what happens in the series. As I read on, I kept reading. They're the best books I've ever read.

Having support for an accurate prediction, knowledge of vocabulary, and ready-made visualizations can provide enough scaffolding for kids who want to read a challenging book. The true indicators are whether the student is engaged when reading the book, can retell what he or she has read, and finishes the book.

Sometimes students are anxious to read a book that is far beyond their means. When this is the case, suggest they do so at a different time with some extra support. This can include having them pair up with a more proficient reader, obtaining the book on tape, or reading with a parent or sibling at home. We definitely do not want to discourage students from reading books they want to read—we just don't want them to struggle or fail in the process. And we don't want them to think that reading for pleasure should be a constant struggle to sound out words or read without attaching meaning, as often happens with difficult books.

Three Simple Rules

Three rules help students relax and settle into reading quickly and solidly. They make a dramatic difference for those students who typically spend time doing anything to avoid reading. Using these rules, students' choices are to sit and pretend to read or to sit and truly read. Only a few students make the former choice, and, as you will see, the structure of R[5] prevents them from hiding behind a book. The following three rules set the tone for R[5] and help to reduce off-task behaviors:

Rule #1. Students must have self-selected reading materials in their desks prior to the start of the R[5] period. If students forget or finish reading a book, we give them a new selection to read for the remainder of the time (although most students are prepared and have a new selection if they think they will finish reading their book that day). We are careful to ensure that this is not perceived as a punishment, and we try to choose something the student would be able to read and enjoy.

Rule #2. Students may not get up during Read and Relax. Restroom and water breaks are given before and after Read and Relax. Most students, when engaged in their reading, do not want to get up, but this rule provides a bit of extra discipline for fake readers who need to focus on reading.

Rule #3. Students may not talk unless they are in a teacher conference or it is time to Rap. If students talk instead of reading, they are reminded of the rules and asked to move back to their seats for the remainder of the read-and-relax time. Because they no longer can sit where they want, chatty students quickly begin to conform. Just as effective is peer pressure; many students will ask other students to be quiet as this is their time to enjoy a good book, and someone talking can be distracting.

Status-of-the-Class

You should use status-of-the-class each day to monitor student choices, provide encouragement, and support book choices (Atwell, 1990). The Status-of-the-Class Sheet includes students' names and cells for recording the date, title of each student's text, and the page they are on that day (see Figure 21 for a sample and Appendix B, page 194, for a reproducible). Circulating and recording the information on the status sheet takes less than five minutes—time well spent—and although there is never a minimum num-

FIGURE 21
Status-of-the-Class Sheet—Teacher Sample

Date	Student	Book/Page Number	Date	Book/Page Number	Date	Book/Page Number	Date	Book/Page Number
9/25	Brian C.	Sign of the Beaver p.8	10/9	Magic Finger p.38	10/12	Sign of the Beaver p.75	10/16	Disney Adventures p.33
	Hunter	Help! I'm Prisoner p.6		Ghosthunters p.4		Monster House p.14		Monster House p.23
	Taylor	Tigers at Twilight p.25		Runt p.27		Absent		Runt p.66
	Ashlyn	Mostly Ghostly p.15		Crossing Jordan p.8		Witch Catcher p.18		Witch Catcher p.24
	Victoria	B.S. Club #8 p.53		BS #12 p.107		B.S. Club #14 p.14		B.C. #15 p.12
	Brian H.	Shredderman #1 p.50		Flush p.6		Shredderman #2 p.12		Absent
	Lyndsey	H.P. #3 p.4		Colder than Ice p.18		Absent		Colder Than Ice p.64
	Josh	Blackwater Swamp p.57		Christmas/Camelot p.27		p.65		Frankenstein p.54
	Jessica	Absent		Frog Princess p.6		Absent		The Frog Princess p.25
	Aaron	Escaping the Giant Wave p.4		p.42		p.56		Escaping the Giant Wave p.62
	Prerna	Absent		Absent		Tales of a 4th Grade		Gifted
	Andrew	Absent		Absent		Runt p.69		Gifted
	Casey	Absent		Absent		Hidden Talents p.15		Gifted
	Chris	Secret of the Song p.74		Midnight on the Moon p.60		Hatchet p.15		Hatchet p.35
	T.J.	Circus Mystery p.94		Runt p.26		Capn Underpants p.66		Harry Potter and the Sorcerers Stone p.29
	Austin	Haunted Campers p.8		p.16		p.23		Haunted Campers p.27
	Katie	Girls to the Rescue p.40		Midnight Voices/Library p.5		p.52		The Midnight Library/Voices p.67
	Adam	Ice Magic p.124		Hoot p.32		p.271		Gifted
	McCall	B.S. Club #1 p.20		B.S. Club #1 p.132		Hi Fella p.46		Hi Fella p.104
	Ru	Shark Attack p.34		Oonawassee p.11		Colder than Ice p.47		Colder Than Ice p.53
	Autumn	Spiderwick #3 p.86		B.S. Club #4 p.18		p.73		B.C. #4 p.88
✓	Morgan	Tripping Over the Lunch Lady p.133	✓	Absent	✓	Tasso of Tarpon p.12	✓	N/A

Austin

Tasso of Tarpon Springs p.31

ber of pages required or a book quota, students quickly realize you are noticing what and how much they read.

Students choose their own reading material during this time, but some students may still need teacher assistance. The status-of-the-class offers you the opportunity to do on-the-spot intervention conferences with those students who are making poor book choices or having trouble finding a book that holds their interest. You can also tell who is reading their R[5] book outside of R[5]. The status-of-the-class is a quiet and subtle way to provide some accountability and support right when it is needed.

One-on-One Conferences

Graves (1983) puts it best: "When the teacher talks we learn...when the child talks, the child learns...and when the child talks, the teacher can help" (pp. 137–138). One-on-one conferences enhance the relationship between you and your students, gives you a better understanding of what each student is capable of doing, and what they need to do to move to independence. In addition, conferences can improve self-esteem and aid in the development of a literate community (Calkins, 1986). Each day after you take the status-of-the-class, you should conduct a one-on-one conference with one or two students.

At the beginning of the year, focus conferences on intervention. You will assess whether students are in an appropriately leveled and appealing book. You also should probe to see if students understand what they are reading. The focus in subsequent conferences shifts to strategy application.

During strategy conferences, on the other hand, ask students to describe how they have applied a strategy on that day with the book they are reading. If they have not used any strategies (or recognized their use), you can coach students toward effective, cognizant strategy use.

For each strategy taught, there is a self-assessment and goal-setting sheet, which students complete as the unit draws to a close. Once students have completed their first strategy unit and created a plan for continuing to improve, the plan is reviewed during the conference (see Figure 22). Again, you will coach the student in how to apply the plan.

While R^5 strategy conferences are still teacher-directed, more of your time should be spent listening than in intervention conferences. Listening is difficult but important

FIGURE 22
Student Discusses Strategies with Teacher During Conference

because, as Nichols (2006) states, "Listening to children talk gives us a window into their thinking. As we listen we gain an understanding of how actively they are constructing meaning, the level of complexity they are able to reach on their own and through purposeful talk with others, and the strategies they may be using to do so" (p. 34). Once you have completed the first strategy unit and students have written their first strategy plan, you can use more fully the R^5 Conference Form (see Figure 23 and Appendix B, page 195). The primary focus of the conference should be the students' plan. You want to know whether they are using strategies when reading and, furthermore, whether they are implementing the goal set for each specific strategy. Aim to meet with each student at least once during each strategy unit, approximately every six weeks. Of course, meet-

---

FIGURE 23
R^5 Conference Form—Student Sample

Student: _Megan L_   Date: _4/26/06_

Intervention (only if needed): ☐ Changing books   ☐ Stuck in genre/series   ☐ Books too difficult

1. Tell me a little about what you're reading. Title _Harry Potter and the Chamber of Secrets_   Genre _Fantasy_
   Excellent summary

2. Last time we met you were working on _Summarizing_ (goal). Have you done this today?

   If yes,

   ☑ Able to give a specific example of strategy use from your current book.

   ☐ Able to give a specific example of strategy use from any text. (go to #3)

   She demonstrated how she had asked questions which were later answered and this helped her to
   If no, _Summarize what she had read_

   ☐ Example was nonspecific or invented.

   ☐ Unable to give an example of strategy use.

   Can you give me an example of a strategy you have used today?

   ☐ Connecting ☐ Predicting   ☐ Questioning
   ☑ Visualizing ☐ Summarizing ☐ Other _____

   Described how she did this in HP.

   If needed, use probes on folded card to help students identify and/or better understand strategy use.

3. Let's look at your current self-assessment/goal-setting. Review plan:

   ☒ Plan is feasible. Have you been doing it? If yes, have student give example.

      If no, remind student to use plan, coach as needed.

   ☐ Plan is not feasible. Help student rewrite plan.

4. How can I help you become a better reader?

   "Give us more reading time, maybe change rap partners to mix it up, like a mix, pair, share."

5. Goal for next conference:

   She wants to notice her connections (our current unit).

---

ings will vary depending upon how often you do R[5], the number of students in your class, and your students' needs.

The Record of Conferences (see Appendix B, page 196) is one way to keep track of conferences. If you need to do a quick follow-up conference with a student this can easily be recorded on this sheet. Maintaining a binder that has the status-of-the-class, the Record of Conferences, completed conference forms, and blank conference forms can help with organization, too. Keeping completed conference forms in alphabetic and chronological order will help make the conferring time run more smoothly. You might even want to put each student's interest inventory with their forms for easy access.

Even though you have an agenda, this conference time should be conversational (Fountas & Pinnell, 2001). When calling on students to confer, ask them to bring the book they are reading, a writing instrument, and their reading folder. That way you will have access to all the materials you might need during the conference.

Types of Strategy Conferences

Overall conferences serve both formative and summative functions. They can inform future instruction and let you know if your instruction has been effective. You will not always know beforehand the type of strategy conference you are going to have; this usually emerges from listening and talking with the student. But because you instruct each student beyond R[5] you will have an idea of those students who may need some extra support. Strategy conferences are held with one student at a time and can take as little as 2–3 minutes or as long as 10 minutes. Conference time depends upon the book, the student, and the type of conference. Strategy conferences typically fall into three categories:

> I like conferring because that way you (the teacher) know what we're reading and you know, like, what strategies we are using and you can help us with our metacognitive strategy plan.
> —Kaitlin

1. Coaching—when the teacher provides the most support to assist readers
2. Monitoring—when the teacher reminds students to use their strategy plans
3. Facilitating—when the teacher nudges students to think more deeply and helps them to continue to develop as readers

Coaching conferences usually take longer than monitoring and facilitating conferences because they require careful listening and thoughtful remediation. When coaching students, you must listen carefully. As Kaufman (2000) points out, "A teacher who has listened well may discover that a student needs direct instruction in a specific skill or that the student simply needs to hear his or her own words back" (pp. 8–9). Sometimes the student sounds really good so you will want to probe a bit further if you have concerns.

Strategy Conference Segments

We suggest breaking strategy conferences into six segments, which align with the R[5] Conference Form.

Segment 1: Students tell the title, a summary of what they have read to date, and the genre of the book. The R⁵ Conference Form is used to note what they say but also to record any problems.

> Conferring helps me summarize because Mrs. Grace asks me what happened in the story. It also helps me realize the strategies I want to work on.
> —Alex

Segment 2: Review the students' goals from the last conference. This goal may be related to their last strategy plan, amount of time spent reading, new authors or genres read, or any other goal they set at the end of the previous conference. Very often the students have achieved this goal, providing an opportunity for them to get positive feedback.

Segment 3: Students share how they used any strategy during reading on this day. Again, this provides optimal opportunity for success. Students can almost always think of one strategy they have used, allowing you to celebrate their metacognition.

Segment 4: You and the students review the current strategy plan to ensure it is workable and to assess if it is being used. If the plan needs to be altered, you can work together to make it better.

Segment 5: Ask students how you can help them become better readers. This question is as much for you as it is for them. This transcript demonstrates the value of this query. After the transcript you'll read a description of how this influenced instruction:

Teacher: How can I help you become a better reader?

Reid: You could read more challenging books to us.

Teacher: How will that help you become a better reader?

Reid: Well, when you show us how you do something then maybe I can do that when I'm reading.

For the next read-aloud, Nicki chose an excerpt from the book *The Legend of Holly Claus* (Ryan, 2004). The students had been asking her to read it, and she had deemed it too challenging. She shared what Reid had asked her to do and read the first four chapters of the book, pausing occasionally to scaffold by questioning and sharing her thinking. The students enjoyed the text, and some of the more advanced readers continued to read the rest of the book.

Segment 6: Students set a goal for the next conference based on conversation during the current conference, which is not always the strategy goal on their current plan. Be sure to give students a little time to set a goal—to think more deeply before responding—and don't let them off the hook when they say, "I don't know." You might be surprised at how reflective their goals are. For instance, the goal for the next conference is often to find different books—such as a new series, new genre, or a more challenging book. We receive frequent requests for additional reading time, as well. Another com-

This **Vocabulary Bookmark** belongs to:	Good readers use METACOGNITION when they...
Barry	• make connections.
List at least three new or unusual words from your reading. Include the page number where you found the word when you write it on your bookmark.	• predict.
	• monitor their reading to make sure it makes sense.
astonishment page # 76	• use fix-ups to get unstuck.
Obligation page # 76	• visualize what they are reading about.
cautioned page # 76	• form and answer questions as they are reading.
immediately page # 76	• summarize.
_____ page #____	• reflect on (think about) what they are reading.
	I AM A GOOD READER!

mon response is asking for help with challenging vocabulary. When this is the goal, we give students a laminated vocabulary bookmark (see Figure 24 and Appendix B, page 197). While reading, students are to record unfamiliar words on the bookmark and bring it to you to discuss as necessary.

Reflect and Respond

After reading, students reflect and record their thoughts in an Independent Reading Log (see Figure 25 and Appendix B, page 198). The purpose of this reading log is to ensure students have engaged with their text, to monitor their use of various comprehension strategies, and to help them prepare for the Rap portion of R^5. After reading, students take three to five minutes to think and record the title of the book, its author, genre, and a strategy response about their book. Several response stems are listed on this log, including I'm wondering, I remember, I'm thinking that, I feel sorry for, Can you believe, When I read __ I was reminded of __, and WOW! These stems have been crafted to lead students to reflect on one or more of the strategies they used that day. The last column asks students to identify the strategy or strategies they recorded.

FIGURE 25
Independent Reading Log—Student Sample

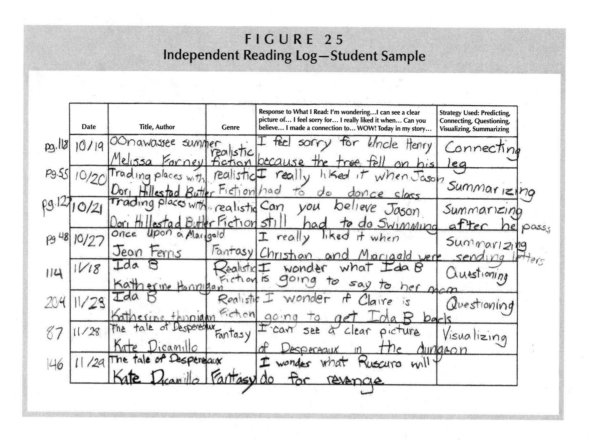

	Date	Title, Author	Genre	Response to What I Read: I'm wondering... I can see a clear picture of... I feel sorry for... I really liked it when... Can you believe... I made a connection to... WOW! Today in my story...	Strategy Used: Predicting, Connecting, Questioning, Visualizing, Summarizing
pg.118	10/19	OOnawassee summer Melissa Forney	realistic fiction	I feel sorry for Uncle Henry because the tree fell on his leg	Connecting
pg.55	10/20	Trading places with Dori Hillestad Butler	realistic Fiction	I really liked it when Jason had to do dance class	Summarizing
pg.12	10/21	Trading places with Dori Hillestad Butler	realistic Fiction	Can you believe Jason still had to do Swimming	Summarizing after he pass
pg.48	10/27	Once upon a Marigold Jean Ferris	Fantasy	I really liked it when Christian and Marigold were	Summarizing sending letters
114	11/18	Ida B Katherine Hannigan	Realistic Fiction	I wonder what Ida B is going to say to her mom	Questioning
204	11/23	Ida B Katherine Hannigan	Realistic Fiction	I wonder if Claire is going to get Ida B back	Questioning
87	11/28	The tale of Despereaux Kate Dicamillo	Fantasy	I can see a clear picture of Despereaux in the dungeon	Visualizing
146	11/29	The tale of Despereaux Kate Dicamillo	Fantasy	I wonder what Ruscuro will do for revenge	

Reflecting and responding is not intended as an evaluative tool for individual students, but it does provide some insight on each student's progress with strategy application. Most importantly, logging provides think time for students to mentally prepare for Rap, the next phase of R⁵, serving as a scaffold for conversations.

Rap

Rap enhances students' listening skills and auditory memory because it requires active listening; students cannot participate in the whole-class share (Rap Part 2) unless they know what their partner said during pair-share (Rap Part 1). Furthermore, Rap is critical to whittling away at fake readers—students have to engage while reading so they are prepared to share exactly how they applied a strategy to that text, on that day. This positive peer pressure encourages engagement because students do not want to be caught with nothing to say about their partner's book when the teacher calls on them.

The structure of Rap Parts 1 and 2 necessitates meaningful talk where student thinking is grounded in the text or understanding of the text. The conversations students have allow them to unpack their thinking. In other words, when they are conversing, they clarify ideas and are able to articulate their thoughts. Because each partner has time to share, they want to listen to one another and they value one another's thoughts. Often they begin to connect their ideas to one another's and to other books they have read. Rap helps cultivate a culture of readers. All students read and all students share; therefore, they feel as though they are part of a literacy community. This talk is integral to creating a literate community (Langer & Close, 2001; Marshall, 2002).

One bonus outcome from Rap is the generation of interest in other books. Students are sharing books and often reading the book through their partner's eyes. And many students choose their next book title based on these conversations. Some even form their own book club by reading the same text. When this occurs students can assist each other with monitoring understanding. Brittany noted, "I like to share at the end. And if you are reading the same book, they might really help because...if you don't understand something, then the person might understand and help you."

Rap Part 1: Pair-Share

After students log their responses, they share their reflections with partners. Conversations about books, or the rap pair-share portion of R^5, last three to five minutes. You should strategically pair students together during this time to improve the quality of the discussion and eliminate possible off-task behavior. For instance, pair students with people they would not choose on their own, but don't make the pairing so uncomfortable or incongruous that they choose not to participate at all. In other words, pair-share works best if students are not paired with their best friend or worst enemy. Changing partners every few months gives kids the opportunity to hear a new perspective and enlivens conversations. The following transcript captures the types of conversations students have during Rap Part 1:

> The most important (and interesting) part of R^5 for me is the part where we rap with our partners, because you get to hear what their story is all about and it sometimes makes you want to read the book also. —Gabbi

Andrew: I just finished *Runt* and now I'm reading *A Dog's Life* by Ann Martin and I can see a clear picture of the mother giving birth in a barn house. I see the squirrel and Bone, the dog, being born. Also, the writer described how dogs can see clearly out of their eyes after a few days, as their other senses become stronger...it was interesting.

Bryan: I'm reading *Drake & Josh: Blues Brothers* and Drake is going to be in a talent show. He is trying to beat Hewitt who is in the Choral Society. And Josh is a weatherman for the day, and he can't stop sweating and twitching.

Andrew: Oh, I saw that episode, that was funny.

Bryan: Yeah, I saw it too.

At first, most pair-sharing is summarizing because students are most comfortable with sharing about their books, and this is significant as we want our kids to be adept at summarizing. However, in order to get the most out of R^5, you may need to tease out other strategy use, either by facilitating the whole-class share during Rap Part 2 or by teaching a separate minilesson on how to vary strategy use. The depth of strategies shared increases as students progress through the first strategy unit.

Rap Part 2: Whole-Class Share

In the whole-class share, students are invited to share what their pair-share partner described. This can take anywhere between 5 to 15 minutes. At first you will need to call on students to report on their partner's reading, and then you will lead the class in identifying metacognitive strategies being shared. This format requires students to focus and engage during Rap Part I in their reading so they can meaningfully contribute in the whole-class rap. During the whole-class rap, you should call on volunteers as well as those who do not raise their hands so students know they must engage and listen during each session of R⁵. The following transcript demonstrates Rap Part 2 in action:

Teacher: We are going to go ahead and share. Let's see which pairs would like to share today? Barry?

Barry: [Reporting on his partner's book] Bobby is reading *Moby Dick* and he can see a clear picture of the sailor going whaling and he predicts that the sailors are trying to kill the whale.

Teacher: I heard two strategies there. Who can tell what strategies were shared? Patrick?

Patrick: He's using a...visualizing and predicting.

Teacher: What did he use to predict?

Patrick: Um...questioning?

Teacher: Was it questioning? [Looking to partner Barry, who shared] What did he use? Share his prediction again.

Barry: Bobby's prediction is that the sailors are going to kill, trying to kill the whale.

Teacher: Then what do you think he might be using? We do not know for sure, but what do you think he might be using?

Patrick: What I already know about the topic.

Teacher: We kind of know the story enough to know the whale gets killed.... Do you think he already knows about the story of Moby Dick? Bobby, is that what you used?

Bobby: Yes.

Teacher: How about your partner, Bobby?

Bobby: Barry is reading *The Secrets of the Droon: Journey to the Volcano Palace*, and he can see a clear picture of.... I think it was Eric and his friends in a trap and he predicts that Eric won't wake up.

Teacher: What strategies did you hear being shared?

Gabbi: Predicting.

Teacher: Predicting and what else?

Gabbi: Summarizing.

Teacher: Summarizing, and is there one more?

Gabbi: Visualizing.

Teacher: He did use visualizing. Good, can anyone tell what he used to predict?
[Discussion continues]

The cognitive flags posted in the classroom serve as a visual reminder during this time as kids turn to these flags when discussing the strategies being employed. You can facilitate the whole-class share by validating worthy responses (or validating those made by students who needed the most encouragement), as well as clarifying and amplifying student responses.

What Has R⁵ Meant to Our Fake Readers?

Many former disengaged readers say that R^5 was the key to helping them really enjoy what they are reading. As the year progresses the "reformed readers" clamor for more R^5 time. They report that R^5 and the strategy instruction is critical to fully engaging with their books. Many comment on how their mind used to wander off while they read, but when they use strategies they stick with the text. Notice the positive comments of the following reformed readers:

- When we are doing R^5 we do different strategies and maybe write them down. And when I do those strategies, I don't really think about wandering off, I just stick to the text.

- I know the strategies better. If I do the strategies, I'll focus on that text and the strategies and I won't wander off because I'll be visualizing...I don't want my visualizing to stop.

- I think that last year I didn't really know most of the strategies and how to use them as well. And now I know how to use those strategies so it makes it easier for me to, like, connect to the text.

Final Thoughts

Restructuring independent reading by implementing R^5 allows you to carefully and consistently monitor and guide the developing reading habits of students. It is another way in which we take the silence out of reading by engaging students in meaningful talk that requires them to think about text as they construct meaning and motivates students to read more. Introducing new authors, genres, and series to students increases wide reading. Scaffolding metacognitive awareness with self-assessment and goal-setting helps develop thoughtful literacy. Providing opportunities for students to share ideas and discuss text engages readers. For us, this strategic and thoughtful modification of independent reading has resulted in significant gains on formal assessments of wide reading, metacognitive awareness, and comprehension.

During R^5, students share book titles and describe pieces of their books three times a week (or more, if you choose to do R^5 daily), which entices many fake readers. R^5 creates a pervasive culture of avid readers. Students, even those who are reluctant readers, begin asking for specific titles to be added to the classroom library. They start coaxing their parents to purchase new titles (that they actually read, rather than just stacking) or to take them to the public library to get books. They request more R^5 time. The emphasis on metacognitive awareness benefits all—from fervent readers to the most reluctant.

Now that we have introduced the major learning structures involved in the MTF we will shift to the individual metacognitive strategy units to help you put the MTF into action.

PART III

Metacognitive Strategy Units

How do readers predict? Make connections? Question? Visualize? Summarize? Furthermore, how does each of these cognitive strategies aid comprehension? What techniques can you employ to explicitly teach each strategy? What role does self-assessment and goal-setting play in strategy acquisition? You'll find the answers here.

Each chapter in this section is devoted to teaching a different strategy: predicting, making connections, questioning, visualizing, and summarizing. We provide specific activities to scaffold strategy use. Think-alouds, direct instruction, guided-reading lessons, and independent learning activities are included to help you develop metacognitive learners.

CHAPTER 5

Predicting

A teacher previews a text with a small guided-reading group, encouraging them to make predictions. One child volunteers, "They're going to find a stray cat and they won't be able to find a name for him. So they'll try lots of different names and in the end they'll figure it out." It is an amazingly accurate prediction. Has this student already read the book? No, he is able to synthesize the small amount of information available on the front cover with what he knows about stray cats and genre to predict what will happen with precision. What skills and knowledge does this child pull together in order to predict so well?

What Does It Mean to Predict?

If we want our students to predict properly, rather than just guess at what a text will contain, we need to teach them how. We must show them the clues each text holds and teach them how to combine these clues with their own background knowledge to make reasonable predictions.

> If you read without predicting, it's just like you read without even thinking about what's going to happen. —John

Predicting helps us build internal tension or anticipate a satisfying ending. It helps us choose the right book to answer a question. It gives us a reason to read—we want to find out if we are right. Predictions serve as guideposts as we move through a text. We make a prediction then check in from time to time to see how it holds up.

When readers predict they must engage with the text. They use their prior knowledge and the text to set up expectations of what will happen or what information the text will contain. This might involve knowledge about vocabulary, a concept, text organization, the author, or other connections they may have to the text (Honig, Diamond, & Gutlohn, 2000). Accessing this background knowledge usually occurs substantially in the preview of the text and also during the reading of the text. This includes using text features and the text to make accurate and meaningful predictions. Students monitor their predictions as they read and adjust or confirm as needed in order to better understand the text.

The Importance of Predicting

Simply stated, good readers predict. When students predict they set a purpose for reading and anticipate what they will read (Lubliner, 2001). When students make and review their

> Without predicting you really wouldn't focus on the story that much because you wouldn't guess what's going to happen. —Chris

predictions they must interact with the text. Predictions help readers make connections between their prior knowledge and the new information being learned (Gillet & Temple, 1994). This schema serves as a basis for future learning, helping the reader create mental models (Gunning, 2003) and increasing the probability that they will remember what they have read (Recht & Leslie, 1988). Furthermore, when students predict as they read narrative text, they must pay attention to the sequence of events. When they support their predictions with textual evidence, critical thinking is enhanced, along with comprehension (Lubliner, 2001).

Because prediction and inferring are related concepts, it is helpful to look at what readers do when they infer. Tovani (2000) notes that when readers infer, they do the following:

- Ask a question and wonder about something in the text
- Consider textual evidence
- Think about what they know about the evidence in the text
- Use the clues in the text and their background knowledge about a topic and try to answer the original question

Problems With Teaching Predicting

Michael is referring to making meaningful predictions. We are familiar with predictions that have little or nothing to do with the text to be read. One problem students have

> When you're not really reading, you really can't predict because you have to be really thinking about it and really reading it to actually predict. —Michael

with predicting is that their predictions are often inaccurate, sometimes because of the text and at other times because of the reader. Some texts lend themselves to making predictions, while others are more obscure. Some of the textual factors contributing to difficulty in prediction include vague, clever, or misleading titles or chapter headings. Also, books without a teaser on the back or inside front cover make it harder for readers to predict with accuracy. For instance, mysteries are often intentionally misleading; but although mystery writers try to lead the reader astray with extraneous events or facts, effective readers weed through these to determine what to ignore as they confirm and revise predictions. And although readers may not always be able to predict a plot twist in these types of books, they can make assumptions about the way the piece is organized. They can tell that the mystery won't be solved in the first half of the book, for instance, because there wouldn't be a need for the rest of the text.

At other times the reader is the reason for problems with prediction. Students might make wild guesses about the text without using any background information or textual evidence. This is often apparent with nonfiction. Technical vocabulary and varying text structures make reading informational text more challenging, especially when students are required to demonstrate content learning. In addition, students underestimate the importance of text features, if they acknowledge them at all (Spencer, 2003). All of these issues can make it tricky for intermediate students to make meaningful predictions.

Perhaps the biggest issue with predicting is that many kids don't take the time to do it properly. They may take a cursory look at the cover as they choose the book, forming a general image of what it is about. They don't reflect on the title and cover art. They don't flip the book over to read the back to further solidify their prediction. As they read, they are often surprised or confused to see that the story is quite different than what they expected, at which point many kids usually abandon the book. Teaching children to predict thoroughly and accurately will enhance their reading experience from the first page to the last.

How and When We Predict

We've described prediction as something that is done not only before you read a text, but also during reading. Yet many commercial reading programs use prediction as a prereading skill only. To get the most out of predicting it needs to be something that you teach before, during, and after each reading session. Prior to reading, students look at items available to help them make predictions. These items could include the front and back cover, title, and artwork if they are just launching into a text or the illustrations, section headings, and text features if they are continuing with a text. While they read, students predict using what they have read and what has happened or been presented so far. They also pause to confirm or revise their current predictions. At the end of a reading session, we want kids to pause and reflect on whether their predictions were accurate and to confirm or revise their predictions based on what was read. Looking at what you think is going to happen and then reviewing and evaluating your predictions based on what actually occurred maximizes the effectiveness and worthiness of this strategy.

How We Predict and the Predicting Components

We approached the prediction components differently from our other units. While working with students we found that there were certain things we (and they) used that made our predictions accurate and meaningful. Creating the components this way eliminated many of the outlandish predictions we had experienced. Because students had to identify what component they used to make their prediction, they knew when they had made a weak or irrelevant prediction and quickly revised their thinking. As we researched, reflected, and worked with our students we revised our list of components to make the Predicting Tally Sheet mirror their thinking and verbiage. The following are the predicting components:

> I use prediction in the beginning and the middle of reading. I don't really use it at the end, mostly I do it in the beginning and middle. I guess what's going to happen next and then try to figure it out. —Markus

- I use the title and chapter headings to predict. I use the front and back cover to predict. I use pictures and captions to predict.
- I use questions that might be answered as I read to predict.

- I use what I already know about a topic (including vocabulary) to predict.
- I use what I know about an author, genre, or series to predict.
- I use what I know about text organization and text structure to predict.
- I use what has happened so far in the book to predict.
- I use meaningful connections to predict.
- I use what I know about a character to predict.

Predicting and the Metacognitive Teaching Framework

It makes sense to teach the prediction unit first because through it students become immersed in the language of the Metacognitive Teaching Framework (MTF). Before we launched this unit, we spent months looking at all the ways we and our students predict. We took our observations and broke them into discrete components that concretely describe the breadth of prediction strategies. These components are our way of breaking down the complex task of predicting into attainable goals. A reader who expertly engages a wide variety of the prediction components is operating on a higher level of understanding. We begin by introducing the components, and then we teach students how to use them.

It is important to note that we have developed components for each of the metacognitive strategies, and the prediction components described in this chapter lay the foundation for all the other strategies. The components also give you, the teacher, ready-made teaching topics for each of the strategies. Direct teaching of how to use the prediction components allows students to thoroughly understand and apply them in a variety of contexts. In addition, prediction is implemented first because most students usually come to us with at least the ability to make rudimentary predictions.

The purpose of this unit is to raise students' awareness of how they make meaningful predictions. Another goal is for students to be able to infer based on their predictions. Students need to be taught how to look at textual clues and their background to make informed predictions and draw accurate inferences. Because predicting and inferring are intertwined it makes sense to hit hard on this skill during this unit.

Because this is the first strategy unit in which students will be taught using all the stages of the MTF, it is important to not rush. In our experience, the amount of time spent teaching each strategy varies with each class. Some groups may acquire predicting more quickly than others and some students in your class may be good at predicting from the start. If this is the case, you would differentiate in small groups for those students who are having a difficult time with prediction. But all students will need direct instruction in the prediction components to establish a common language and set expectations. This occurs during think-aloud and follow-up lessons.

Explicit Instruction of Predicting

This will be the first time students will have experienced the MTF from the introduction of components through to self-assessment and goal-setting. Although they will be familiar with most of the teaching approaches you use—think-aloud, whole-group lessons, small-group lessons, literature circles, and R⁵—this will be the first unit in which the focus is a specific strategy using the methods you introduced during the first six weeks.

To launch prediction, it's helpful to choose a question-and-answer book because the structure of the text is predictable and there are usually visual supports. Prior to the think-aloud, read the text and note the prediction components you use while reading. Capture your thoughts on sticky notes and place them right in the book where you make your predictions. The sticky notes serve as a reminder during the think-aloud with students. The think-aloud may require two different sessions.

Explaining and Defining Components of Predicting

In the first think-aloud session, describe the predicting strategy in further detail. This is not the first time students will have heard the word *prediction*, but this may be the first time they are introduced to each component used when predicting. Ask students what it means to predict, thus establishing a common working definition. After constructing a definition for predicting with the class, call on individual students to read through each prediction component listed on the tally sheet. Model and give examples of each of the components, soliciting examples from students.

Then facilitate a whole-class discussion of each prediction component, providing students with meaningful examples of how to use the component. Elicit examples from students for those components they felt they might not understand. In the following transcript, you will notice that some components are discussed more than others. This will differ with the age and background knowledge of your students. The following transcript demonstrated Nicki explaining and defining prediction:

Teacher: How is a prediction different from a guess?

Lindsay: The difference between a guess and a prediction is with guessing you're just guessing what's going to happen and in prediction you're actually using background knowledge to think of what's going to happen and what might happen next.

Teacher: Excellent! So you're using background knowledge; it's not just right there. Do you want to add something to that, Lisa?

Lisa: A guess is when you don't even check on or look at something in the book. Predicting is when you look at the title and look at the pictures.

Teacher: What I hear you guys saying is that in a prediction you use something in the text and maybe your background knowledge to help you make that prediction. In a guess, you don't use anything, you just wildly guess. Is that right?

Class: Yes!

Teacher: So, let's look at the tally sheet. Once you predict you're going to think about what you used to make that prediction. The first heading says "To predict, I...." I want you to read this phrase at the front of each statement. What is the first thing that is on the tally sheet that you might use to predict?

Nicki proceeds through the list of components, defining, clarifying, and giving examples of what each component means.

Noticing and Applying Components of Predicting With a Text

In the second session, model your thinking out loud as you predict. Then ask students to identify from the list of components what you used to make your prediction. Each student should have a blank tally sheet, and you can keep a class tally chart on a full-size poster (see Appendix B, page 204, for a reproducible). The following transcript shows Nicki modeling and her students noticing and applying prediction components:

Teacher: Your job right now is going to be for you to listen. I'm going to do a think-aloud. By that I mean I'm going to read to you and share my thinking as I'm reading. I'm going to share my predictions, and you're going to help me identify which prediction component I'm using. Then, I'm going to get a lovely assistant to tally them for me. Do you have a question, Ru?

Ru: Why do we have to do the tally?

Teacher: We do this because it helps us become aware of how we predict. And once we're aware of what we do, then we try to get better at the other things we're not using. So in the end you become...SUPER PREDICTORS! And why is being a good predictor a good thing? How does it help you, Autumn?

Autumn: It helps you comprehend the books that you are reading and the other texts that you're reading, too.

Teacher: So this book is *Can It Rain Cats and Dogs? Questions and Answers About Weather*. I'm going to predict that this book will be about weather. What am I using to make that prediction, Lindsey?

Lindsey: Background knowledge and the book cover.

Teacher: Well, it's not background knowledge, but I am using the book cover. And what else?

Jessica: You read the questions and answers in the title.

Teacher: Right, the title. I used the title. Up top it says Scholastic Question and Answer series and so I think it is a nonfiction book, because I have read other Scholastic Question and Answer books and they are all nonfiction. What am I using to make that prediction, Casey?

Casey: What you already know about the genre or series.

Teacher: Good. [Addressing class] What else did I use? Where on the book is this?

Class:	[Students respond in unison] Front cover.
Teacher:	So, I also used the front cover. Alright! Here's my next prediction: I think it's going to have questions about weather followed by detailed answers about weather. Let me tell you why...because I have read other question-and-answer books, and they all had a kind of short question with a very detailed answer on the topic. So what am I using to make that prediction, Bryan?
Bryan:	What I know about the text structure.
Teacher:	Bryan, you're a genius! That's exactly right. Give him a round of applause. That was a tough one! Text structure. That is the way this book is organized. Question-and-answer books start with a question, then they have a big detailed answer. Do you want to add something? Is there another thing I use? There is. What is it?

After the think-aloud, ask students to go back to their seats and practice predicting as they read an article from a *Weekly Reader*, textbook, or another text to which all students have access. Have them predict, read, and tally their predictions.

Refining Strategy Use: Activities for Teaching Predicting

Now that the components of prediction have been introduced, it is time to practice so students absorb what they've learned. Activities are organized under the strategy components they teach, although many fit under multiple components. Not all activities listed under the component are described in that section, but we point out where you can find each activity for specifics.

> If there's a chapter and it is expository or a nonfiction thing, I always predict what that part is going to be about by using the subheadings or the chapter titles. —John

Your goal during these lessons is to assist students with recognizing their use of components through practice and discussion. As students work through the MTF they begin to assimilate the components and are better able to employ prediction. Several of the activities recommended were described in chapter 2, and most lessons are useful in other strategy units as well. Therefore, these activities will become familiar to students as you repeat them when teaching other metacognitive strategies.

I use the title and chapter headings to predict.
I use the front and back cover to predict.
I use pictures and captions to predict.

These three components have been grouped together because they all use text features that you want kids to pay attention to and use to make, confirm, and revise predictions. Ask students to forecast the main idea by looking at the title, front and back cover, chapter headings, and pictures and captions to help them. By doing this you will indicate that these text features are important aspects of the text and integral to comprehension. Students should know, too, that these early predictions might change as they read and that one goal they have is to confirm or revise their thinking as they read. Activities that assist with reinforcing these components include the following:

- Anticipation Guides (see below)
- Text Feature Walk (see chapter 2, page 40)
- Noticing Text Features (see below)
- Previewing, Predicting, and Learning From Text Features (see chapter 2, page 38)
- Text Feature Wall (see chapter 2, page 36)

Anticipation Guides

A common strategy used in classrooms is an anticipation guide, which helps students activate background information by having them agree or disagree to certain statements (Readence, Bean, & Baldwin, 1995). These statements are all related to what they are going to read and may include information from pictures and captions. Overall, this activity relates strongly to prediction and can support many of the other prediction components, especially "This prediction uses what I already know about a topic, including vocabulary." An anticipation guide helps students set a purpose for reading because they are more likely to read on to see if they were right or wrong. To facilitate this activity, you should ask them to agree or disagree before reading and then again after reading. An added step can include having students write a prediction summary based on these statements and their background knowledge. (Figure 26 shows a student sample of an Anticipation Guide for the Earth's atmosphere.) After reading, students write why they chose to agree or disagree, and they provide a page number or numbers where they found each answer.

Noticing Text Features

As we know, students usually do not take the time to preread the text features. Being aware of text features begins at a simplistic level when you ask students to pay attention to the front and back cover, the title and chapter headings, and pictures and captions. Teaching students how to navigate through text features is a vital before-reading skill. When students preview a text, they can make predictions on sticky notes, which they place in the text where they made their prediction. While reading, they try to confirm or revise their predictions. After reading, students discuss their prediction sticky notes and how their predictions relate to the main idea. Engagement is maximized when students take ownership of the process by working in pairs or small groups.

FIGURE 26

Anticipation Guide and Prediction Summary for the Earth's Atmosphere—Student Sample

Earth's Atmosphere
Anticipation Guide

Student Name _Elsita_   Date _4/3/06_

Directions: Read each statement. Check off whether you agree or disagree with the statement in the Before Reading columns. While reading think about each statement, were you right or wrong? After reading the section, reread each statement. Check off whether you agree or disagree in the After Reading columns. Explain why you agree or disagree in the space provided below each statement. Write the page number where you found evidence to support your statement.

Before Reading   After Reading

Agree	Disagree	Statement	Agree	Disagree	Page #(s)
	X	1. The atmosphere begins about 30 miles above the surface of the earth. _because it has different layers and the layers are far apart._		X	D7
X		2. The trophosphere is the top layer of our atmosphere. _because the thermosphere is._		X	D8
X		3. The atmosphere has five layers. _because their is the Thermosphere, mesosphere, stratosphere, Troposphere_		X	D8
X		4. The atmosphere has a solid crust at the very outer edge. Rockets must break through this crust to reach outer space. _because it is soft blanket of air._		X	D6
	X	5. Airplanes fly in the stratosphere. _because they do not get in a lot of bad weather_	X		D8
	X	6. Almost all weather occurs in the mesosphere. _because it happens in the troposphere_		X	D8

I predict that the text is going to talk about the atmosphere and how air pressure is inside the atmosphere. I think the trophosphere is under the atmosphere. The stratosphere is under the trophosphere and where airplanes fly. The mesosphere is under the stratosphere and thermosphere is under the mesosphere

I use questions that might be answered as I read to predict.

Have students focus on asking questions they expect to have answered while reading the text. This means they must use clues left by the author via text features and text and their own background knowledge to develop meaningful questions. This type of questioning is designed to facilitate student engagement with the text and to get students to anticipate their reading. Activities that can be used to teach this component are as follows:

- Sticky Note Questions (see below)
- Preview, Read, Question (see below)

Sticky Note Questions

This simple activity builds on the earlier lesson, Noticing Text Features. Have students read the text features and relate them to the main idea. Before they read and throughout their reading, have students write on sticky notes questions they think will be answered by the text. These questions should have a direct relationship to the text and what students know about the topic. Have them place the sticky notes in the text where the question arose. Students read on to answer their questions and to get the big idea. When finished reading, students can discuss the text in pairs, small groups, or as a whole group. A teacher-led discussion on the value of their questions can help them with writing thoughtful questions that lead to predictions.

Preview, Read, Question

For this lesson, students use the Preview, Read, Question Think Sheet (see Figure 27 for a student sample and Appendix B, page 199, for a reproducible). The students begin by previewing the text. In the first column of the think sheet, they write down two or three questions they expect to have answered as they read. In the second column students list what they previewed in the text that caused them to think those questions would be answered. They include the page number(s) as textual evidence.

Before students read they should share their questions in pairs or a small group, so if they realize their initial questions are not thoughtful they can revise or rewrite them. Again, these conversations are all about getting the kids to anticipate what they are going to read and to generate an interest in the text. While reading, students determine whether their questions are answered, and they fill in the answers in the last column of the Think Sheet. Students can discuss the text read in a small group, focusing on whether their questions were answered.

I use what I already know about a topic (including vocabulary) to predict.

Many students have a wealth of knowledge they can tap for anticipating what they are going to read. Those students who don't step into your room with enriched home back-

FIGURE 27
Preview, Read, Question Think Sheet—Student Sample

Before Reading: Preview the text, read the text features. Write 2–3 questions you expect to have answered as you read.	During Reading: What in your preview caused you to write the questions? Cite any relevant page numbers.	After Reading: What was the answer to your question?
How do they hunt?	1213 Pictures	Harris hawks hunt in teams. The great horn owl eats eats chickens. The American kestrel eats grasshoppers mice lizards
How far can they see?	7 lable digram	sharp eyes that can see far away and under water.
How do they take care of there young?	14,15,16,17 Title Heading	some hawks nest in bushes and osprey build with seaweed nests. they hunted for the young and tear the meat into little pieces so the young wont chook.

grounds at least have prior exposure to lessons or texts about many topics from school. You want kids to use their background knowledge to make informed predictions—especially helpful in content area studies. You want kids to think about what they know about a topic before they jump into reading about it.

Start by having students identify boldface or italic words. Students do not always pay attention to them, even if you have already taught this skill, but it's important to reinforce that the author chose to identify those words for a reason. Helping students develop the routine of noticing boldface or italic words and connecting them to the big idea in the text will aid comprehension. For example, the author might define the bolded and italicized words or provide an example within these features, or these words might appear in the glossary with a definition.

Techniques that teach passage-critical words front-load learning by getting students interested, activating prior knowledge, and setting a purpose for the reading. Robb (2003) specifically recommends limiting direct vocabulary instruction in grades 3 through 5 to three to four new words and grades 6 through 8 to four to five new words per reading. So although you may share more than four or five content-critical words before reading, expect that some are already known to students and help them begin to formulate an idea of what the text will be about. Activities you may find useful to help students access background and vocabulary knowledge include the following:

- Word Splash (see chapter 9, page 164)
- The Power of Words (see below)
- Knowledge Rating Scale (see chapter 9, page 165)
- Text Feature Walk (see chapter 2, page 40)
- Word Alert! (see this chapter, page 91)
- Concept-Definition Sort (see chapter 9, page 162)

The Power of Words

Having students preview a text is an excellent way for them to access background knowledge and anticipate what they are going to read about. Using the Power of Words Think Sheet (see Appendix B, page 200) scaffolds this process. Students begin by skimming the text and reading the text features. As they preview, they write what they think they are going to learn based on important vocabulary and what they know about the topic. In the left-hand column students identify words they think will be important to the understanding of the text. While reading, the student puts check marks next to words in the left-hand column that were important and in the right-hand column writes new words that they feel are essential.

After reading, students discuss the key words and how they related to the reading (see Figure 28 for a student sample). This can be done in pairs, small groups, or in a

FIGURE 28
The Power of Words—Student Sample

Name Kaitlin   Title Life in the Grand Canyon

1. What do you think this book will be about?

Different animals that live by the Grand canyon and how they live.

2. What important words would you expect to see in this text?

Important words I identified before reading... (while reading check mark any words you have written that have been important to the text)	Important words I added after reading...
Grand Canyon shelter Animals sun snakes plants life food river	Valley river bank rock habitat forest deserts

whole group. A follow-up lesson could include having students write a summary using some of the important words they identified. This think sheet facilitates students in making associations among words and helps them to connect the new to the known.

Word Alert!

Using a Word Alert! Think Sheet (see Appendix B, page 201) helps students activate prior knowledge and self-assess their knowledge of words that they will be reading (Graves & Graves, 2003). We created the Word Alert! Think Sheet by adapting various student self-evaluation tools already in existence (see, for instance, Blachowicz & Fisher, 2006). Before having students read the text you should preselect words to include on the Word Alert! Think Sheet. Again, the words should be important to the text and words you think students may see again. Put the words on the Word Alert! Think Sheet, leaving space for students to add words, and photocopy the sheet so all students have a copy in front of them.

Before reading, students complete the first three columns by noting with a "Y" (yes) or an "N" (no) whether they know the word. If the word is known, students move to the next column and write how they know the word and what they think it means. If students do not know the word, they move to the third column and make a check mark and highlight the word so they can focus on that word when reading. Students look for confirmation of their definition or the actual definition in the text and note a page number in the fourth column, so they can refer back to the page if needed. After reading, the students discuss the preselected words and any new words added in relationship to the text's content. (You can leave blank cells at the bottom so students can add their own words, or students can write new words on the back. Figure 29 shows a student sample, and Appendix B, page 201, contains a reproducible.) An extension activity would be to have students write a summary statement using the words from the Word Alert! Think Sheet.

I use what I know about an author, genre, or series to predict.

In the primary grades we use predictable, illustrated texts with rhyme, rhythm, and repetition to scaffold success with reading. Even if students have not yet completely learned how to "break the code," the repetitive nature and supports offered through illustrations allow them to feel successful. Familiarity with an author, series, or a genre is the support older readers can use to help them better anticipate their reading.

For example, when reading the A Series of Unfortunate Events books, readers can use the author's unique writing style to anticipate what they are going to read. For example, the author addresses the reader directly, as exemplified in the following excerpt: "So I must tell you that if you have opened this book in the hope of finding out that the children lived happily ever after, you might as well shut it and read something else" (Snicket, 2000, p. 3). Another predictable aspect is explaining vocabulary right in the text so that

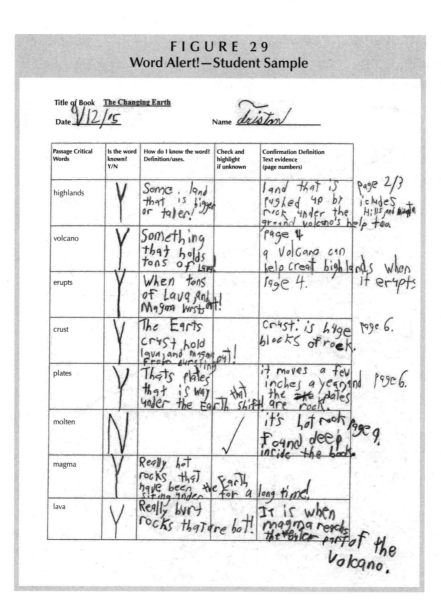

FIGURE 29
Word Alert!—Student Sample

Title of Book **The Changing Earth**

Date 9/12/15   Name Triston

Passage Critical Words	Is the word known? Y/N	How do I know the word? Definition/uses.	Check and highlight if unknown	Confirmation Definition Text evidence (page numbers)
highlands	Y	Some. land that is bigger or taler!		land that is pushed up by rock under the ground volcano's help too. page 2/3 icludes Hills and Mnta
volcano	Y	Something that holds tons of lava		page 4 a volcano can help creat bighlands when it erupts
erupts	Y	When tons of lava and Magma birst out!		page 4.
crust	Y	The Earts crust hold lava, and magma From bursting out!		crust. is huge blocks of rock. page 6.
plates	Y	Thats plates that is way under the Earth shift	that	it moves a few inches a year and the plates are rock. page 6.
molten	N		✓	it's hot rock found deep inside the book. page 9.
magma	Y	Really hot rocks that have been siting under the Earth for a long time!		
lava	Y	Really burt rocks that are hot!		It is when magma reachs the outer part of the Volcano.

the reader understands the word's meaning and how it relates to the story of the Baudelaires:

> "Children, children," Mr. Poe said sternly. "Not so many questions."
> Uncle Monty smiled at the orphans. "That's quite all right," he said. "Questions show an inquisitive mind. The word inquisitive means—
> "We know what it means," Klaus said. "Full of questions." (Snicket, 2000, p. 13)

When students are familiar with an author's style, the characters in the series, or the genre, their predictions are much stronger. To help students in this area you can use

- Story Maps (see page 93)
- Read, Relax, Reflect, Respond, and Rap (R⁵; see chapter 4 for more detail)

Story Maps

Story maps are commonly used to help students identify the key elements of a narrative text in order to aid summarization and the students' ability to retell the story. Students list the title, characters, setting, problem, solution, and main events in the text within the appropriate boxes. Figure 30 shows an example of what a story map might look like, and you'll find a reproducible Story Map Think Sheet in Appendix B, page 202.

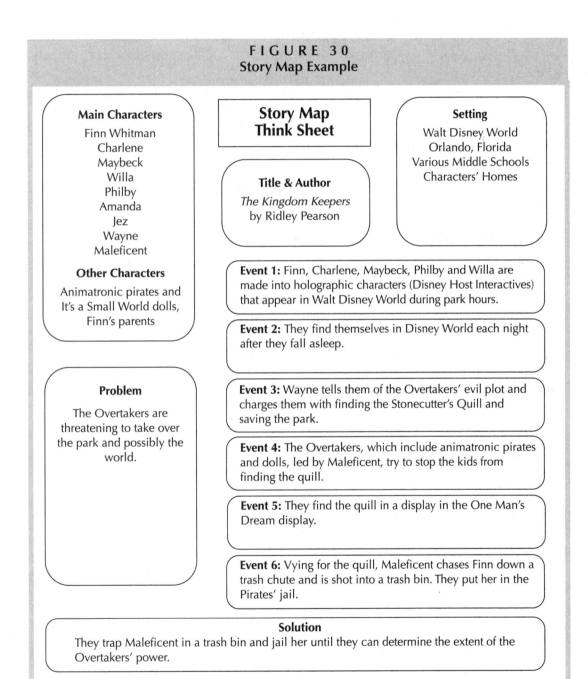

FIGURE 30
Story Map Example

Story Map Think Sheet

Main Characters
Finn Whitman
Charlene
Maybeck
Willa
Philby
Amanda
Jez
Wayne
Maleficent

Other Characters
Animatronic pirates and It's a Small World dolls, Finn's parents

Title & Author
The Kingdom Keepers by Ridley Pearson

Setting
Walt Disney World
Orlando, Florida
Various Middle Schools
Characters' Homes

Event 1: Finn, Charlene, Maybeck, Philby and Willa are made into holographic characters (Disney Host Interactives) that appear in Walt Disney World during park hours.

Event 2: They find themselves in Disney World each night after they fall asleep.

Event 3: Wayne tells them of the Overtakers' evil plot and charges them with finding the Stonecutter's Quill and saving the park.

Event 4: The Overtakers, which include animatronic pirates and dolls, led by Maleficent, try to stop the kids from finding the quill.

Event 5: They find the quill in a display in the One Man's Dream display.

Event 6: Vying for the quill, Maleficent chases Finn down a trash chute and is shot into a trash bin. They put her in the Pirates' jail.

Problem
The Overtakers are threatening to take over the park and possibly the world.

Solution
They trap Maleficent in a trash bin and jail her until they can determine the extent of the Overtakers' power.

I use what I know about the text organization and text structure to predict.

We've all witnessed it: An intermediate-grade student appears to read on grade level but is unable to grasp the content area concepts he or she reads in textbooks. Or, when given a research assignment, a student reports with frustration that the resources provided don't contain the information sought—even when they do.

My brother is in high school and he let me read his Harcourt textbook, and I noticed that when they have a bolded word they explained it in the text. And then when we just read our Harcourt text on Early Americans, they did the same thing. —Jessica

Researchers often lament the so-called fourth-grade slump in reading achievement (Chall, Jacobs, & Baldwin, 1990). Teachers will tell you a big part of the problem is that once students hit fourth grade, they are expected to know how to read a wide variety informational materials (Yopp & Yopp, 2000), but many times the bulk of students' primary reading instruction has been focused on reading narrative stories (Duke, 2004). Because of this, students attack every text as if it should be read from beginning to end, like a narrative story.

Traditional instruction in text structure awareness has been focused on identifying and teaching common text patterns such as cause–effect, comparison–contrast, problem–solution, description, and sequence (Robb, 2003) in conjunction with recognizing signal words and using graphic organizers (Irvin, 1998), which support comprehension. And although this practice is worthy, many texts use multiple text patterns that often confuse readers; rarely is a text purely one structure. Therefore, we have broadened the teaching focus to include text organization. Knowing how a text is organized helps students access content and makes them more likely to commit the information to memory (Simpson & Nist, 2000). Tierney and Readence (2005) suggest that readers who have knowledge about a text's organization have more of an advantage in recall and comprehension over students who are not aware of text structure. The activities in this component are offered to engage students in analyzing text structure and organization. Furthermore, this is extended into writing when students experiment with the various writing forms about they are learning which:

- Distinguishing Between Narrative and Expository Text (see chapter 2, page 34)
- Story Maps (see this chapter, page 93)
- Expository Text Investigation (see below)
- Question-and-Answer Book Writing (see chapter 9, page 170)

Expository Text Investigation (ETI)

ETI is designed to help students purposefully read and write a variety of expository genres, each with a unique and discernible difference in organization. ETI sensitizes students to aspects that make a text considerate or inconsiderate (Armbruster, 1988), all in an effort to maximize students' learning. Often expository text can be challenging for students because the vocabulary includes multisyllabic words and content-specific words that students may not have the background knowledge to comprehend. In addition, the text features designed to support them can also present a challenge. ETI is an inquiry process that helps students identify and investigate the characteristics of a specified expository text genre. More importantly, it gives students a procedure they can use to evaluate new texts as they encounter them and provides a model for writing in various expositions.

You want students to approach each text with a purpose and a plan for obtaining the information they want and need to know (Purcell-Gates, Duke, Hall, & Tower, 2002). For example, you want a student who is working on a report on the International Space Station to know to look in the textbook's index or a nonfiction trade book and then go to the correct pages. Once there, you want the student to read the section headings and text features to get his or her bearings and know where to focus when reading. The student wouldn't just start at the beginning and read everything in a futile attempt to find information.

Another goal for this activity is to help kids write using a variety of expository text types. This will be further discussed in the activity of question-and-answer books. This is also described in chapter 6 on questioning with a description of alphabet books.

Prior to the investigation, make sure students can distinguish between narrative and expository texts. (See the detailed lesson in chapter 2 on how to accomplish this.) In addition, time spent using story maps will ease the transition to reading expository text. At the start of an ETI, you should define the purpose of analyzing text. *The Literacy Dictionary* defines text analysis as "the structural characteristics of text...as they relate to comprehensibility" (Harris & Hodges, 1995, p. 255). One possible way to explain this to students is "the way a text is organized and put together in order to help us learn." The Expository Text Investigation Think Sheet (see Figure 31 for a student sample and Appendix B, page 203, for a reproducible) is a graphic organizer that offers scaffolding, along with peer support. As students discover how a text is organized they begin to use this knowledge to anticipate and better understand what they read. In addition, they can use this knowledge to produce writing in the text form being investigated.

After establishing a purpose for the investigation, put students with partners (mixed ability works well) and give each pair a few book types you want them to explore, such as question-and-answer books. (See Figure 32 for a list of suggested types of expository texts for ETIs.)

Give each pair a Text Investigation Sheet and explain the directions. You will probably need to explain that a characteristic is something unique about a text; for example, a question-and-answer book has questions followed by answers throughout.

Give students time to look through and discuss the features of the texts they have been given to explore. Monitor by listening to conversations to make sure students are discussing the texts' organization and not the content. After students have identified several characteristics, bring pairs together for a whole-group share. Record on chart paper to refer to later. Discuss how you would go about reading this type of text and for what purpose. Talk about the author's purpose in writing this style of book, and why the author might have chosen this particular style for the content or audience.

ETIs can be done in about 45 minutes. They are usually done using a pair-share structure but could also be done in a small group for those who need more support. Many different expository genres can be used, and we recommend repeating this activity throughout the year so students can compare types of books.

FIGURE 31
Expository Text Investigation of a Q-and-A Book—Student Sample

Researcher(s) _____Victoria_____

Title	Genre or Structure	Characteristics of this Book (What do we notice about how it is written?)
S is for Sunshine	ABC Book Expository	1. The letter that that the page is talking about is bolded. 2. The page says what the letter is for. 3. The pages are on topic. 4. The title says a letter, and what it is for. 5. The book has Question and answers
A is for Abigail	ABC Book Exspository	1. On each page it tells something about the topic. 2. Each page has tons of text features 3. The book has a page for all 26 letters. 4. The picture shows what the text is talking about. 5. The index in the back has the same information as in the text.
The Sea is Salty	Q & A book Exspository	1. The First Question relates to the next one. 2. It gives more text features than text. 3. It has realy good text features.
Scholastic Children's Dictionary	Dictionary Nonfiction	1. All words are in alphabetical order. 2. It gives a word than a definition(s). 3. In the upper left hand and right hand corners, these are guide words. 4. It gives a text feature for every few definitions.

FIGURE 32
Suggested Types of Expository Texts for ETI

- Question-and-answer books
- Alphabet books
- Encyclopedias
- Picture dictionaries
- Textbooks

- Newspapers
- Magazines
- Advertisements
- Brochures
- Invitations
- Menus

I use what has happened so far in the book to predict.

Having students use what has happened so far in the story to make predictions requires using textual evidence. It also reminds students that predicting doesn't just happen before they read but is an ongoing process. We need to readjust predictions as we continue to read. In other words, as the plot develops so should our predictions. The following is a list of activities you could use to help students understand this component:

> I predict when something exciting is going to happen and then after every chapter I predict what the next chapter is going to be like.
> —Scott

- Story Maps (see this chapter, page 93)
- Cut-Up Story (see below)

Cut-Up Story

Janet Allen shared this strategy during a workshop using the short story "A Mouthful" (Jennings, 1998). We have adapted this activity and tied it in with our prediction components. First, break the story into meaningful chunks. We have broken this particular story into 12 parts. We assign numbers to each part, 1–12, then have the person with number 1 read first:

> Parents are embarrassing. Take my Dad. Every time a friend comes to stay the night, he does something that makes my face go red.... He loves to play practical jokes. This behavior first started the night Anna came to sleep over. Unknown to me, Dad sneaks into my room and puts Doona, our cat, on the spare bed. Doona loves sleeping on beds. What cat doesn't? Next Dad unwraps a little package that he has bought at the magic shop. Do you know what is in it? Can you believe this? (Jennings, 1998, p. 37)

After someone has read aloud the first part, the students make a prediction about what is going to happen next, and then they identify which component(s) they used to make their prediction. From this excerpt, most students predict that the dad is going to have plastic cat poo from the magic shop that scares Anna and makes her want to go home. Students definitely rely on what has happened so far in the book, but they also use other components such as "what I know about a character" and even "what I know about the topic" of items that are sold at a magic shop.

The activity continues with the person with number 2 reading his or her part, and we move through the story, stopping to predict and identify what components students are using to make their predictions. This activity can be done with other texts, too, but we stuck with this story because it has been effective and the students really enjoy the humor and plot twists.

I use meaningful connections to predict.

You want your students to make meaningful connections to what they are reading and to use these connections to make good, strong predictions. First of all, you really want students to focus on the word *meaningful*. For the purposes of this component, a *meaningful connection* is one that will help readers predict something in the text. For example, if students are reading a story about a family who is on a sailboat during a storm and they had a similar experience or had seen a movie about a similar event, they might predict that the boat will be tossed in the waves, the dishes will fall out of the cabinets, and that the kids will be locked below while the parents navigate the boat. This prediction is based on something they have seen or experienced, making it feasible. It is also based on the text, making it related and meaningful.

One simple way to elicit these kinds of meaningful connections from students is to give them some generic questions to use as they read. You might write on the board, "Has anything like this ever happened to me? Have I ever read a story or seen a movie where something like this happened? What was the outcome? What might happen in the text?" Another activity to support this component is making a Two-Column Chart.

Two-Column Chart

This activity has been adapted from the two-column notes created by Santa, Havens, and Valdes (2004). For the two-column chart have students make two columns with the following headings: My Connections and My Predictions Based on My Connections. Model for them how to make a meaningful connection and then a related prediction. As they read and fill in their charts, ask students to draw a line under each connection–prediction pair. Make sure to circulate and probe to help those who have trouble getting started. After they have a few connection–prediction pairs, have them share with a partner.

I use what I know about a character to predict.

Just as knowing the author, series, or genre helps us to predict, so does knowing a character. As we become familiar with characters' traits and attributes, we are better able to determine what they might do next or anticipate their reaction to events as they unfold. We especially get to know characters if they are in a series, such as Violet in the A Series of Unfortunate Events books. We know Violet is the oldest of three siblings and we know that when she ties her long hair up in a ribbon she is getting ready to clear her head and think of an invention. We know that her inventions are usually made from everyday objects, but they always help her and her family get out of tricky situations. We do not have to read several books with the same character to know a character well, however. Even in a short story, such as "Mouthful" (Jennings, 1998), we can ascertain that Dad is a prankster and predict what he will do based on this. The following activity assists teaching this component:

- Story Maps (see this chapter, page 93)

Self-Assessment and Goal-Setting

After a few data-gathering sessions, usually after a few weeks of being immersed in prediction, you can clean off the large class tally sheet and use it to collect class data on strategy use. Read through each component and have students look at their own tally sheets to assess which components they have been using over the course of the unit. Tally the number of students who have been using a component regularly and write the number directly on the tally chart next to each component.

The following transcript describes how Nicki used class data to model self-assessment and goal-setting. After showing students how, she has them mimic her process and develop their own plans relevant to their individual data and needs:

Teacher: Today, we are going to wind up our prediction unit. You need to have your tally sheet and the self-assessment and goal-setting sheet for prediction on your desk. [She waits until students have needed materials] How many of you remember when I asked you during an R^5 conference, "What can I do to help you become a better reader?" [Hands go up] Well, when I ask you that question I want you to set a goal. What is your thought when I ask you that question about what I can do to help? [Pause] Some of you are not sure how to answer that question. Today, I want each of you to make a plan, or set a goal, for prediction. But first, I will show you how.

Take a look at your prediction tally sheet. Think about those things you have been doing really well. [Pause] Count the number of tallies you have for each component and write the number on each row. [Pause] Now, I am going to go through each component and I am going to mark our class data on the class tally chart. Let's start with the first component. This prediction uses title/chapter headings. If you marked four or more tallies in that area raise your hand. [Thirteen hands go up and she records on the class tally chart] How about front and back cover? [Seven] Pictures and captions? [Nine] Questions that might be answered as I read? [Seven] What I already know about a topic, including vocabulary? [Seven] What I know about an author, genre, or series? [Six] What I know about text organization and structure? [Five] What has happened so far in the book? [Twenty] Meaningful connections? [Four] And, what I know about a character? [Nineteen] Wow! Take a look at our class data. Tell me what we are doing really well as a class?

Joshua: What has happened so far in the book.

Bryan: What I know about a character.

Teacher: Do you think we need to set a goal for these, if we are doing them well?

Class: [In unison] No.

Teacher: What would be something we might want to work on to get better at predicting?

Ashlyn: What I know about text structure.

Austin: Meaningful predictions.

Teacher: Are we doing a good job with using what we know about an author, series, or genre?

Class: [In unison] No!

[Nicki turns on the overhead and puts up a copy of the Predicting—Self-Assessment and Goal-Setting Sheet (see Appendix B, page 205, for a reproducible)]

Teacher: If we were going to write a plan based on our class data, I would check off Uses Titles, Uses Pictures, What I Know About Character, and What Has Happened So Far, because we are already doing a good job with these. [She checks them off her form] Then I would highlight components to improve, and those are the ones that are not checked off—Use the Front and Back Cover; Create Questions to Help Me Predict; Use What I Know About a Topic or Vocabulary; Use What I Know About Author, Genre, or Series to Predict; Use What I Know About Text Organization; and Make Meaningful Connections to Predict. Then I'll choose one goal that I would like to work on improving. I'm going to write a plan to improve on this goal so that I can get better at predicting. [Pause]

I have already made a sample of a plan to show you how you are going to write your own plan. Your responsibility is to listen well as I share my plan so you can write your plan based on your data and needs. This will be your own plan to use while you read and when you confer with me on your reading. We are doing this to help you become a better predictor.

Okay, look up here at the overhead screen. I chose to work on using what I know about the author, genre, or series to predict. Does everyone understand why I chose this? [Pause] That's right, I used our tally chart to figure out where we needed to improve. For step 1 of my plan, I wrote, "Choose a book by the same author or from the same series as another book I've read." Why do you think I put that down first?

Jessica: Because if you are going to use what you know about the author or series you have to read more than one book by that person.

Teacher: Yes, I need to use what I know about the author's style. If I read a new book by Peg Kehret, the fact that I have read many of her books and know how she writes helps me anticipate what I am going to read. And when I read the Magic Tree House series I know that Jack and Annie, the main characters, always travel through time. This can help me predict. [She continues reading steps number 2 and 3 from her form] Ru, because I know you are going to ask, I'll go ahead and tell you that yes, I am going to make myself predict this way. I need to practice predicting, even if I have to force myself, to get better at it. And, then finally, step number 4, I am going to read and confirm my predictions. I think this will be the last line of everyone's plan because the goal is to predict and confirm or reject your prediction.

Now, I used our class data to write a plan. You are going to use your own data on your personal tally sheet to write your plan.

Austin: Are we going to do this for visualizing?

Teacher: What a good question. Yes, we are going to do this for every strategy unit. Now, someone tell me what you are going to do? [She calls on students to repeat her directions and she emphasizes that the plan is to help them become a better predictor] Does anyone not understand what they are supposed to do? [Pause]

At this point, Nicki walks around the classroom, working with students individually on their plans. (See Figure 33 for a student sample tally sheet, and also Appendix B, page 204, and Figure 34 for a plan based on that tally sheet. See also Appendix B, page 205, for a reproducible Self-Assessment and Goal-Setting Sheet.) Students read independently while they wait for her to circulate to their desks. Sometimes she notices a trend and can stop and discuss it with the whole group. Instead, you may want to meet with students in small groups according to the component they have identified as one they want to work on. In this case, you would have students do independent work and call students to meet with you according to the component they selected, such as using the title and chapter headings to predict. These students would bring their goal-sheet and a pencil when meeting with you. This may be the first time students have been asked to make a plan for improvement based on their needs and, therefore, the small-group or one-on-one attention can greatly reduce frustration you may experience when initiating goal-setting. It can also strengthen the quality of their plans.

A good follow-up to the self-assessment and goal-setting lesson is to have students use their plans with a text and attempt to do each step of their plan as they read. An example would be stopping to predict based on a text feature and then writing down the prediction. This way, students can work out any kinks in their plans and get immediate practice while predicting is fresh in their minds. Be sure to gather the plans and read through them so you can help those who may need to make revisions. It also helps to meet with students in small groups and have them practice using their plans under your watchful eye. Again, have students share how they used their plans to help them predict.

FIGURE 33
Predicting Tally Sheet—Student Sample

To predict, I...	Tally
use title and chapter headings.	卅卄 | 卅卄 卅卄
use the front and back cover.	卅卄 ||
use pictures and captions.	卅卄 | ||
use questions that might be answered as I read.	卅卄 |
use what I already know about the topic, including vocabulary.	卅卄 卅卄 卅卄 卅卄卄 |||
use what I know about the author, genre, or series.	| |||
use what I know about text organization and text structure.	卅卄 ||||
use what has happened so far in the book.	|卅卄 卅卄| 卅卄 ||||
use meaningful connections.	||
use what I know about a character.	卅卄 ||||

Final Thoughts

Students who have spent time and energy learning how to effectively use prediction as they read can seem almost psychic in their abilities to foretell what they will read. They are better at selecting books that meet their expectations, and they find the reading more satisfying.

We want kids to fully engage with books. During this thorough introduction to the MTF and the components of the prediction strategy, students get the idea that reading is an interactive process. They learn that you can't make a meaningful prediction if you are fake reading. We are not going to let them fake read. Whether they are listening to a read-aloud, sharing the

> If you don't predict while you're reading, there's really not much point of reading the book except, like, if your teacher or your mother and father tell you to. Like, if you don't really predict and you're reading, you're really just fake reading and you're just trying to get through the book. —Markus

FIGURE 34
Thinking About My Reading: Predicting—Student Sample

Name _____   Date ___11-9-06___

Directions: (1) Put a check mark by the things you do well as a reader when making predictions.
        (2) Highlight the things you think you need to work on to become a better reader.

- ☑ I use the title and chapter headings to predict.
- ☑ I use the front and back cover to predict.
- ☑ I use pictures and captions to predict.
- ☐ I use questions that might be answered as I read to predict.
- ☑ I use what I know about topic (including vocabulary) to predict.
- ☐ I use what I know about an author, genre, or series to predict.
- ☑ I use what I know about the text organization and text structure to predict.
- ☑ I use what has happened so far in the book to predict.
- ☑ I use meaningful connections to predict.
- ☐ I use what I know about a character to predict.

Choose one highlighted item to improve upon:

Make meaningful connections while I read to

predict.

Create a plan to improve upon this skill.

1. _I would like to choose a reilistfiction more._
2. _I would read the book very careful._
3. _I will stop and ask me if this ever happen to me?_
4. _Do I know anyone like this? If yes write a predict_
    about the character. 5. read to see if my
    prediction comes true.

reading in a small, guided group, doing literature circles, or in R⁵, students have to interact with, respond to, and learn from text. And their thinking is going to be made public. They also learn that all readers can improve and the teacher will be there to guide each of them all the way through to setting and working toward meaningful reading goals.

The next four chapters are on the other strategy units. It is not necessary to present them in a particular order, as you will differentiate their use based in your students' needs. These chapters share the structure provided by the MTF but provide research and activities specific to the strategy being discussed.

CHAPTER 6

Making Connections

A teacher sits reading in a rocking chair; students perched comfortably around her feet are entranced by the story she reads. She pauses strategically to ask if anyone has a connection to the text. A forest of hands springs up, and all begin to wave urgently. They all have connections and they all want to share. It is the only time during the read-aloud that she asks this question. She has opened the floodgates, and the rest of the story is punctuated by eager hands signaling frantically for a chance to share a connection.

What Does It Mean to Make Connections?

Connections are the way we make sense of our information-saturated, fast-paced world. They help us find our place and learn about the people and places around us. Our connections help us define who we are. We see ourselves in the things we experience or read about, and these connections can help us better understand something new. Cognitive scientists tell us that we must connect new knowledge to something we already know to acquire the new information. These neural connections occur at a physical level and are vital to assimilating knowledge. Although the connections we make while reading begin at this neurological level, they also tap into the part of us that makes us uniquely human—our emotions, imagination, and compassion. Our connections help us infer almost intuitively as we read.

When readers make connections they take the one-dimensional world of text and flesh it out by making the text come to life. Readers who connect well are able to place themselves in a story or situation. They can visualize because they have a ready-made picture of a similar place or event. They use their prior experiences to help them predict and form questions as they read. Connections provide the background knowledge we need to glean a richer understanding of text. Good readers combine connections with what is presented in a text to help us grow—personally, professionally, or spiritually.

The Importance of Connecting

The National Reading Panel (National Institute of Child Health and Human Development, 2000) concluded that "text comprehension is enhanced when readers actively relate ideas represented in print to their own knowledge and experiences and construct mental representations in memory" (p. 14). Connecting is one way students do this. Tovani (2000) offers several reasons why students should connect:

- To relate to the characters
- To visualize
- To avoid boredom
- To pay attention
- To listen to others
- To read actively
- To remember what they read
- To ask questions

These are all skills that good readers use. When students are actively engaged with the text their motivation improves along with their cognition (Guthrie & Wigfield, 2000). Students comprehend better when they make connections among their personal lives (including experiences), texts they are reading, and the world (Keene & Zimmermann, 1997). These have come to be known as text-to-self, text-to-text, and text-to-world connections.

Problems With Teaching Connecting

Teaching about connections is a double-edged sword. On the upside, it is the perfect gateway to metacognitive awareness. Kids seem to be able to recognize some connections quickly. Educators who teach this skill should be ready to field comments from excited students about their connections throughout the day. It is an excellent way to help students feel successful about their ability to think metacognitively.

On the downside, students too easily become focused on the type of connection—text-to-self, text-to-text, or text-to-world—and not on how that connection helps them better comprehend. They can muse over all kinds of connections for considerable amounts of time, trying to decide if they are more of text-to-self or text-to-world. They can get into heated discussions about the classification of a particular connection. Unfortunately, if students don't move past this identification phase, their initial success can stall. The important part of making connections is not necessarily what readers are connecting to in their own experiences; it is that strong connections can help them understand the text better.

Focusing on what they connect to in the text and how that connection helps them better comprehend will help eliminate the biggest problem students have with connecting: making irrelevant connections. For instance, there may be a student who is compelled to tell you that she has been to New York and her book mentions New York, even though the text is not set in New York and knowing about New York does not assist the reader in better understanding the story. You can use the Making Meaningful Connections Think Sheet (see Appendix B, page 206) with students to help eliminate this issue.

How We Connect and the Connecting Components

When we make connections, whether deliberately or subconsciously, we do so to better understand the text we are reading. As we worked with both narrative text and expository text we found that when our connections were most effective they related to something specific in the text, such as the characters, plot, and setting, or our connections helped us to employ another strategy, such as visualization and prediction. Upon practice and reflection we identified these and others as our making connections components and included them in the Making Connections Tally Sheet (see Appendix B, page 207):

- I connect to the characters.
- I connect to the plot.
- I connect to the setting or place.
- I connect to visualize, taste, smell, feel, or hear the text.
- I connect to predict or infer what will happen in the text.
- I connect to what I know about a topic or word.
- I connect to help me feel emotions related to the text.
- I connect to what I know about the text organization and text structure.

Making Connections and the Metacognitive Teaching Framework

Although many commercial programs include teaching the strategy of making connections, the focus is typically on helping students distinguish among text-to-self, text-to-text, and text-to-world connections; we only use this as a stepping-off point. Early in the year, as we teach students how to discuss text in literature circles and textbook circles, we lay the groundwork for this unit by teaching them what connections are and the different ways readers connect. During the school year they will continually practice making, noticing, and discussing connections during literature and textbook circles, as well as during Read, Relax, Reflect, Respond, and Rap (R⁵).

As soon as we begin our formal unit on connecting, we shift the focus away from the type of connection and onto the text itself. We ask kids, "What in the text are you connecting to?" and, more importantly, "How does that connection help you understand the text?" In this way, students don't worry so much about where their connection originated. Instead, they focus on how the connection helps them deepen comprehension—how it helps them predict, visualize, question, summarize, and infer.

Explicit Instruction of Making Connections

As with any think-aloud, text selection is very important. In this case, you want to use a text that captures students' interest, one they can relate to. We've successfully used *The Talking Earth* (George, 1987) because the book is set in the Everglades, an area we spend time studying and where some students have visited, so students have related background knowledge. The students also research and write survival stories set in Florida, which is what *The Talking Earth* is.

Another way to ensure success is by reading a related picture book prior to the start of the think-aloud lesson. In this case, we had read several picture and nonfiction books set in the Everglades region. We also had viewed a slide show of photographs from the Everglades, narrated by a student's father who had spent time camping there. These pieces of background knowledge helped guarantee that each of the kids could successfully connect to the story.

Explaining and Defining Components of Making Connections

To begin the first think-aloud session, ask students to silently read through each of the connecting components on the tally sheet. Then facilitate a whole-class discussion of each connecting component, providing students with meaningful examples of how to use the component and eliciting examples from students for those components you feel they may not understand. Some components will need to be discussed more than others. This may differ according to the age and background knowledge of your students.

Noticing and Applying Components of Making Connections With a Text

Next, explain to students that you will be doing a think-aloud to model how you connect as you read. They need to pay attention and notice how you connect and what you are connecting to. Tell them that at first you will be modeling, but when they are ready, they can help you identify the connecting components you are using.

Students should have access to their own tally sheets and the large, laminated class tally chart should be displayed so all students can see it. Assign a student to tally the strategies you model as the class identifies them. Begin reading, pausing every so often to demonstrate how you connect. At first you will identify the component(s) you are modeling, but as soon as the students begin volunteering you should allow them to do so. Try to model all of the components at least once. There will definitely be some overlap here—one connection might require a tally in two or more components. It's important that you acknowledge this for students because intermediate-level learners and above will be developmentally able to understand this dichotomy. The following transcript demonstrates steps of the think-aloud in action:

Teacher: I have prepared a think-aloud to model the connection components. The title of this book is *The Talking Earth* by Jean Craighead George. This is a story about a Native American girl who lives in the Everglades. Her tribal chief is sending her away for a couple of days on a retreat because she doesn't believe in some of the tribal beliefs, such as that animals talk to you. He thinks she is too modern. In the beginning she is having a conversation with the tribal chief. He asks her to bring him a lightning bolt, and she almost

	understands, but not quite. This has happened to me—when I have a thought and I think I've figured out something and then I get distracted and it is gone.... How am I connecting?
Elsita:	I connect to the character.
Victoria:	I connect to help me feel the emotions in the text.
Teacher:	Exactly. [Reads from the text] I can see the airboat in the Everglades because I have ridden on one in the Everglades.
Reid:	I connect to visualize, taste, or hear?
Teacher:	Yes! What else?
Lisa:	To help me feel my emotions?
Teacher:	Did I mention any emotions?
Joey:	I connect to what I know about a topic or word.
Teacher:	Yes, good. [Reads from the text] I can picture what she is wearing because I have seen pictures of Seminole Indians dressed in their formal wear and I see the colors of red, black....
Lisa:	I connect to visualize.
Teacher:	Yes. [Reads from the text] I am connecting to the word *frantically*. I know from other things I have read that animals act frantically when they are worried or scared.
Alex:	I connect to what I know about topic or word.
Teacher:	Right. I am also thinking there might be a fire because that is something animals fear sometimes.
Ciara:	I connect to predict or infer.
Hayden:	I connect to what I know about topic or word.
Patrick:	I connect to the plot.
Teacher:	Yes, I am thinking about what is going to happen in the story and how it will be developed. [Reads from the text] I can smell the forest burning I remember when we had fires last summer and the air was smoky.
Alex:	I connect to the smell.
Patrick:	To the setting.
Teacher:	Yes.

Refining Strategy Use: Activities for Teaching Connecting

Now that you have introduced the components of connecting, it is time to help students recognize, practice, and assimilate them into their reading toolbox. As with the predicting unit, we've organized some lessons under the specific strategy components they help to teach. With making connections, however, there are several important activities that cover all the components or other aspects. These can be done before you teach lessons on each of the specific components or after, depending on your

students' familiarity with the concept of connecting. One simple way to do this is to follow up your think-aloud with an R⁵ session dedicated to connecting. Although we think it is important to let students read and relax during R⁵, it doesn't hurt to guide their thinking a few times a year when initially using a new strategy. The following short transcript demonstrates how you might launch an R⁵ session dedicated to connecting:

Teacher: As you are reading today I want you to make connections and write down a few of them [on sticky notes]. You do not have to write all of your connections on sticky notes but you do need to tally them all.

Ru: Do we have to connect?

Teacher: Well, why do you think I'm telling you the strategy to use and write about during R⁵?

Ru: To practice what we just learned about.

Teacher: Exactly. Are there times when we might make more than one tally for a strategy? [Students nod] You are going to be very metacognitive during R⁵ today. I want you to really be aware of your use of connections. I expect you to have at least four to five tallies during this time. R⁵ will last a little bit longer because after the reading we will all share the connections you have put on sticky notes.

After students read, relax, reflect, and respond, they rap in pairs. During Rap Part 1 they are asked to share connections with their partners. The following transcript illustrates Rap Part 2, the whole-class share, in which students share their connections with the class:

Joey: Nicholas is reading *Raven's Gate*, and Matt took a trail and it led him back to where he began, and in *Gregor the Overlander* the character went down a tunnel and came back.

Teacher: How did that connection help him understand the story?

Hayden: He connected to the plot, and maybe the setting.

Teacher: Great.

Nicholas: Joey is reading *A Week in the Woods* and it is an adventure. His connection is that Mark has a big screen TV and he has one.

Teacher: How did it help him understand the text better?

Joey: It made me understand how he feels.

Teacher: Really?

Joey: Maybe the emotions?

Teacher: Was this about how he felt or about having a TV?

Joey:	[Smiles and shrugs]
Alex:	Tristan is reading *Gregor the Overlander*, and it is fantasy. He could connect because when Gregor woke up he didn't want to get up, and when he wakes up he does not want to get up.
Emily:	I make a connection to help me visualize.
Nicholas:	To a character.
Teacher:	Good.

The Connections Continuum activity that follows can be used to teach any or all of the making connections components.

Connections Continuum

Early on in the unit, it is a good idea to have students evaluate the relevancy of various connections. A Connections Continuum can help them do this. For this lesson, you need to carefully choose a book that your students will be able to connect to. We used an Eyewitness Reader book entitled *Bermuda Triangle* (Donkin, 2000). This book includes a series of narratives about mysterious happenings in the Bermuda Triangle. Students find the stories irresistible, and many can relate them to television shows or books they have read previously on this topic. Also, because of our proximity to the ocean, many students have boating experience. To provide some additional background, Nicki previously read a picture book about the *Mary Celeste*, a ship that was found floating in the Bermuda Triangle. We used a different story about the *Mary Celeste* from the *Bermuda Triangle* book for a think-aloud lesson.

Once you select the text, plan a think-aloud in which you will share 8–10 connections. The Connections Continuum in Figure 35 shows the connections we used during this think-aloud. Be sure to prepare some connections that are shallow and some that will deeply enhance comprehension. Type up the connections you will share and format the paper so that each connection is no wider than 4 inches. Copy enough sets of connections so that your students can work in pairs using a complete set. Read the story and share your connections. Afterward, give each pair of students a set of the connections to order from the most meaningful to the least meaningful. Once students are done, lead a discussion to determine what made some connections more meaningful than others. You can list these ideas and post them in the classroom during the unit to help students remember how to connect meaningfully.

I connect to the characters.

If the characters in the book are doing something that you've done before, it's easier to understand and it can help you understand the book better. —Kaitlin

Our past experiences, be they in person, through a text, or through some other media, strongly influence how we connect to characters. For instance, if we are reading about a character that is similar to ourselves, we might predict the character's actions based on what we would do in the same situation, or we might picture the character as resembling ourselves. If we are reading

FIGURE 35
Connections Continuum Sample

There used to be a band called "The Drifters." I think they played dance music. p. 9

I've been to England. They serve wonderful fish and chips there. The weather is different than in Florida. p. 9

I read another story about the *Mary Celeste*. It said that there was still food on the table and the bedsheets were rumpled.
p. 11

I would have done the same thing as Captain Gould. You'd never catch me staying on that ship. p. 15

This reminds me of a scary movie I saw called "Ghost Ship." When the sailors got on the abandoned ship, it was <u>eerie</u>. p. 10

I agree with Morgan. I wouldn't want to command a ghost ship either. p. 12

My uncle told me a very scary survival story about him riding on a boat through the Bermuda Triangle. p. 14

about a character who reminds us of someone else, we will base our internal pictures and predictions on attributes of that person.

You can start the conversation about connections to characters during read-aloud. The simple question "Does this character remind you of anyone you know or have read about before?" may get the ball rolling. An activity that supports connecting to characters is as follows:

- Story Maps (see chapter 5, page 93)

I connect to the plot.

Before you can help students notice and make connections to the plot of a story, you must be sure they know what *plot* is. Explain that plot is how the author structures the action of a story (Harris & Hodges, 1995). The plot of a story includes the events that unfold the problem and that lead to a solution in the story. We connect to the plot of a story when something like it has happened to us before. For example, when Reid connected the dog running away and getting hurt in *Brian's Hunt* (Paulsen, 2003) to his own dog running away and getting hurt, he was using his own experiences to help him understand what happened in the book.

Also, when we read series books we can connect to patterns in the plot from one story to the next. For instance, as children read the Magic Tree House books, they make connections between how the story they are reading is launched and how the other stories in the series are launched because they all start in a similar way: Jack and Annie go to the tree house, open up a book, and point, then they are swirled around and transferred to another place and time. These plot connections are important for all our readers, especially the reluctant ones. Students can rely on their past reading experiences to help them easily understand the new story and to free them up to focus on other aspects of the text that may be more problematic for them. It makes for a smoother, more fluent read—a missing commodity for some readers. These are a couple of activities you can use to help students connect to the plot:

- Expository Text Investigation (see chapter 5, page 94)
- Story Maps (see chapter 5, page 93)

I connect to the setting or place.

As we read in a small group one day, Elsita connected right away to several places in the nonfiction book we were reading, *A Guide to Rocks and Minerals* (Fuerst, 2005). She had been to two places pictured in the text, Bryce Canyon National Park and the Grand Canyon, during family vacations, and suddenly a topic that hadn't appealed to her at all became quite fascinating. These connections helped her visualize the places certain rocks and minerals are formed, as well as what the formations look like in their natural settings. Even more importantly, it piqued her interest in a subject she hadn't considered to be interesting before. Story maps (see chapter 5, page 93) can help students connect to a setting or place.

I connect to visualize, taste, smell, feel, or hear the text.

Because they live in central Florida most of our students have been to Walt Disney World a number of times, so it is not surprising that they make many connections during a read-aloud from *Kingdom Keepers: Disney After Dark* (Pearson, 2005). As the characters in the story hop on the "It's a Small World" ride or look up at the fire station on Main Street, our kids have a clear picture of what these places look like. Most of them can hear the tinny sound track for "It's a Small World" playing through their minds as the characters progress through the ride.

> I think connecting helps you to visualize because you connect, and if you can connect to a book, you can get a better picture of what's going on. —Sarah

These kinds of connections help put readers at the center of the action, giving them a fuller, richer understanding of the text.

Most of these connections are text-to-self, relying on personal experiences to help us more deeply immerse ourselves in the story. *Oonawassee Summer* (Forney, 2000) brings forth memories of favorite foods during a beachside picnic—potato salad, hot dogs, sliced tomatoes, sweet tea, and homemade chocolate cake. And while being able to taste these foods in their minds doesn't further students' understanding of the plot, it does help them enjoy the story as they vicariously feast at the beach. One activity that would help students connect this way is Common Senses (see chapter 8, page 149).

I connect to predict or infer what will happen in the text.

Our background knowledge helps us predict and infer what will happen in a narrative or what information might be included in an expository text. For example, when reading *Escaping the Giant Wave* (Kehret, 2003), our students connected what they had learned about tsunamis through news reports, student periodicals, and family discussions about the devastating tsunami in 2005 to help them predict that the characters who were on the beach naïvely awaiting the waves would be swept away.

Students might also connect one work by an author to another by the same author to predict characterizations or plot points. Students who read *Hoot* (Hiaasen, 2002), for instance, might predict that the bad guys in Hiaasen's other young adolescent book, *Flush* (2005), will meet their just rewards because that is what happened to the antagonists in *Hoot*. The following activities can help:

- Anticipation Guides (see chapter 5, page 86)
- Text Feature Walk (see chapter 2, page 40)

I connect to what I know about a topic or word.

Background knowledge of vocabulary and concepts are an integral part of comprehension. It is extremely difficult for young readers to construct knowledge from something they are reading if the topic and important vocabulary are completely foreign. As teachers, we carefully select the texts we use, videos we show, websites we visit, and topics we bring up for discussion, to help build some background before we teach a new concept. These bits of knowledge serve as crampons for new learning.

For instance, as we took a text feature walk through the book *Hurricanes* (Simon, 2003) one student commented on the boldfaced word **diameter**. She used this word, which she had learned in math class, and a diagram of a hurricane to understand that hurricanes are measured by their diameter because they are round.

Some of the activities you can use to help students activate background knowledge include the following:

- Word Alert! (see chapter 5, page 91)
- Text Feature Walk (see chapter 2, page 40)

> For me the easiest books to connect to are those that have topics that I like or that I know a whole lot about, because if the topic was about space then I probably wouldn't connect too much. But if it was about the ocean I would connect so much and I could really make a great discussion for that. —Sarah

I connect to help me feel emotions related to the text.

We all have different reasons for reading at various times, but most people who read for pleasure occasionally choose texts because they want to feel an emotion related to the text. Whether it is the heart-racing excitement of a good suspense thriller or a tear-jerker, we delight in experiencing someone else's feelings. Although we don't provide activities specific to this component, it is important to select texts that might cause students to emote. Pointing out how you personally connect to feel emotions as you read and encouraging students to do the same is powerful.

I connect to what I know about the text organization and text structure.

This is something to really hit hard in the beginning of the year and during the prediction unit. As students begin to read and recognize common text patterns such as beginning, middle, and end, or as they recognize that headings in expository text precede important information, they connect the organizational patterns of one book to another. These connections help them make a plan for reading. Students might remember being able to use the index to go directly to the desired information when reading a nonfiction trade book, so they might try the same strategy on a new nonfiction trade book. As students are exposed to and recognize more text structures, they begin to use this component more. The following activities can help:

- Expository Text Investigation (ETI) (see chapter 5, page 94)
- Distinguishing Between Narrative and Expository Text (see chapter 2, page 34)

Self-Assessment and Goal-Setting

As students become comfortable connecting and have an understanding of the various components, remind them to record their strategy use on their Making Connections Tally Sheet during R[5] and other lessons. You will know when students are ready to self-assess and set goals based on your teacher observations during whole- and small-group lessons related to connecting. As in the prediction unit, use class data to model this process. After showing students how to write a plan, they can use the same process to set goals and develop plans relevant to their data and needs.

The first step is to wipe off the class tally chart for making connections. Have students take out their personal tally sheets on which they have recorded the components they have used to make connections. Have them add up the number of tallies they have in each row (see Figure 36 and Appendix B, page 207) and have them write down the total in each row. Read out loud each component listed on the class tally chart and have students raise their hands to share whether this is something they have been doing on a regular basis. Note the total number of hands raised on the large class tally chart.

Next, model on the overhead how to write a plan for making connections based on the class data. Think aloud as you work through writing your plan. Ask the students to

FIGURE 36
Making Connections Tally Sheet—Student Sample

I make connections...	Tally	
to the characters.	|||	3
to the plot.			1
to the setting.	||	2
to visualize, taste, smell, feel, or hear the text.	⊤HL |||	8
to predict or infer what will happen in the text.	HL ||||	9
to what I know about a topic or word.	HU HL ||	12
to help me feel emotions related to the text.	|||	3
to what I know about the text organization and text structure.		0

look at the large class tally chart and have them determine which components the class is doing well enough to be checked off the plan form. Then have students tell you which components should be highlighted for further practice because the class has not done them as often as other components. Select one of the highlighted components for the class plan. We prepare a plan ahead of time because we have an idea which component is troubling students or which component may be most helpful to students as readers.

After you have completed modeling how to write the plan, pass out the Thinking About My Reading: Making Connections—Self-Assessment and Goal-Setting Sheet (see Figure 37 for a sample student plan and Appendix B, page 208) to each student to complete. You can discuss their plans with students in either of two ways. You could have students work on this independently and call up groups to work with you based on the component they have chosen to improve upon. Or you could have students work inde-

---

FIGURE 37
Thinking About My Reading: Making Connections—Student Sample

Name _____   Date _____

Directions: (1) Put a check mark by the things you do well as a reader when making connections.
       (2) Highlight the things you think you need to work on to become a better reader.

   ☑ I make connections to the characters.
   ☐ I make connections to the plot.
   ☑ I make connections to the setting or place.
   ☑ I make connections to visualize, taste, smell, feel, or hear the text.
   ☑ I make connections to predict or infer what will happen in the text.
   ☑ I make connections to what I know about a topic or word.
   ☑ I make connections to help me feel emotions related to the text.
   ☐ I make connections to what I know about the text organization and text structure.

Choose one highlighted item to improve upon:

Make connections to what happens in the story.

Create a plan to improve upon this skill.
1. _Read something which I think I can relate to._
2. _When something important happens ask myself_
3. _whether that has ever happened to me before?_
4. _Then think about when that happened and how it relates to what I'm reading._

116

pendently to write their plan and you could circulate around the room and talk to students individually. The approach you use depends on your students' needs and your teaching style.

Once students have workable plans, it is important for you to remind them to use their plans during R⁵ and other reading times. From this point until the next strategy plan is written, R⁵ conferences should focus on students' application of their plans. Because connecting is such a natural process for most learners, the biggest concern at this point is to make sure students continue to make meaningful connections that help them comprehend the text more deeply.

Final Thoughts

Connections are personal; who we are shapes the connections we make. Kaitlin finds it hard to connect to fantasy, but other kids read fantasy and form strong connections. Connections draw us into the text and help us own it. Students can easily call forth surface-level connections. It is up to us to help them sift through and find the connections that help bring a text to life for them. If we don't, our students will never fully immerse themselves in a text. In the next chapter we explore how students question the text and, more specifically, how to help them ask meaningful questions that help them deepen their understanding of a text.

> If there's something like fantasy, it might be harder to connect to it, but if there's something that's realistic fiction, it's things that can actually happen in your life. So it could be easier to do it for realistic fiction. —Kaitlin

CHAPTER 7

Questioning

"Why is the earth round? How do we pay for the space program? What would we do if we found life on another planet? Why don't we fly off into space?" Questions soar out of students' mouths as quickly as the teacher can type them. Combining the questioning unit with a unit on space has pushed this K–W–L session into hyperspeed. The questions are so big, so important, so numerous, the teacher knows her students will continue trying to answer them long after this unit is over.

What Does It Mean to Question?

Children are born curious. They look at the world around them and ask why, how? Unfortunately, what is second nature to our toddlers and primary-grade students often dissipates as they move into the intermediate grades. Although many of our students become relatively proficient at answering teacher-generated questions, they forget the most important questions—their own.

> I think questioning helps you go deep into the text and, like, understand it better because you're asking your questions that you want to know about the text.
> —Kaitlin

The questions students ask before, during, and after reading satisfy their curiosity and illuminate the text. Questioning helps us understand the world around us as well as the texts we read. We might ask questions to clarify, connect, conduct research, or summarize. Questions help us anticipate and focus our reading. If our questions are going to be substantive, however, we usually need some background in the topic to be explored. Harvey and Goudvis (2000) suggest that if we read without questions we might as well abandon the book. Asking questions sets a purpose for reading and allows us to interact with the text. In short, questioning gives us a real reason to read.

The Importance of Questioning

The National Reading Panel (NRP) identified question answering and question generating as two strategies for teaching comprehension that have a solid scientific basis (National Institute of Child Health and Human Development [NICHD], 2000). The NRP differentiated between question answering—the time when students answer questions from the teacher and then receive immediate feedback—and question generating, when the reader asks questions about the story. According to the NRP, question answering and question generating give students a purpose for reading, encourage comprehension monitoring, and assist students in connecting newly learned material to known concepts

(NICHD, 2000). When students question what they are reading, they interact with the text, motivate themselves to read, clarify information, and infer beyond the literal meaning of the text (Tovani, 2000). Tovani emphasizes this point, stating, "Readers who ask questions when they read assume responsibility for their learning and improve their comprehension" (p. 86).

We decided to focus on asking questions because our students already experience a lot of question answering. Our schools are good at this; in fact, students often think that the sole purpose of reading is to answer teacher and text questions. Most have learned to do it well or have developed coping strategies. They are especially adept at "right there," or literal questions, those that require factual recall of information in the text. They have a bit more difficulty with inferential questions and are often dumbfounded when asked to write their own response or interpretation. With these questions they often think there is a trick and there must be a definite right answer. This unit centers on teaching students to ask and answer their own meaningful questions about a text.

Problems With Teaching Questioning

When we began trying to figure out all the reasons or ways students use questioning, we quickly realized there was a lot more to it then just having kids create questions. Student questioning is only as effective as the questions asked. Our students initially created questions that were irrelevant to the text— the question was unconnected to the reading, off topic, and lacking depth—students already knew the answer, or the question was on the surface level.

It took us a while to help students understand our goal. We wanted to help them uncover their true questions—the ones their brains asked without permission, the questions that caused them to select a text and keep reading.

> You're usually more interested in the questions that you have created than the ones the book asks. When I have a question and I'm looking for the answer in the book, I really focus on that question, and it helps me because I just keep looking for the answer until I find it. —Alana

Perhaps part of the problem is that our early schooling focuses on answering other people's questions, which causes kids to choke back their own. Why ask a different question than the one you get credit for answering? We had to reconnect our students with the inner wonder they were born with.

How We Question and the Questioning Components

Good readers ask questions before, during, and after reading. During literature circles training and the prediction unit it's important to introduce students to questioning. Early in the school year have students skim the text (especially text features) they are going to read and write questions on sticky notes. This is important because we expect kids to explain why they ask each question from the very start, and we address any unrelated or unimportant questions early. Have students focus on answering these questions and verifying or confirming their learning both during and after reading. To help students succeed with asking questions you need to model your own questioning. We initially identified several reasons why we ask questions. As we worked with students, we revised this into a list of components that became the questioning tally sheet (see Appendix B, page 209, for a reproducible Questioning Tally Sheet). The following are the questioning components:

- I ask questions to clarify something in the text or a text feature.
- I ask questions to help me understand vocabulary.
- I ask questions to help me find specific information in the text.
- I ask questions to help me connect to the ideas or characters in the text.
- I ask questions to put myself in the text by using my senses (visualizing, tasting, smelling, and feeling).
- I ask questions to understand choices the author made when writing the text.
- I ask questions to help me understand the text organization and text structure.
- I ask questions to summarize what I have read.
- I ask questions to help me extend my learning beyond the text.
- I ask questions to help me understand a character or an object.
- I ask questions to help me predict.

Questioning and the Metacognitive Teaching Framework

Because so much of school is focused on answering questions, it is important to familiarize students with the self-generating learning strategy of asking good questions, then reading to answer them. Students will have begun to explore asking questions during the prediction unit, while in small- and whole-group instruction; during teacher read-aloud; during Read, Relax, Reflect, Respond, and Rap (R⁵); and in literature circles. The relationship between questioning and the other strategies continues to be important in this unit.

Explicit Instruction of Questioning

Thinking aloud is one of the best ways to model and teach questioning. By this point, using think-aloud to introduce a new strategy and its components is a familiar structure for students, but questioning is very complex, so students may need this lesson broken into smaller segments. The first step is to go over the components on the Questioning Tally Sheet, and the second step is to model the expert's questioning using the components.

To launch questioning, choose an informational text that relates to your social studies and science curriculum. Nicki used a book about the Donner Party's journey during Westward Expansion, which was highly motivating to students because of its description of survival in the harsh climate of the U.S. Sierra Nevadas. As with other units, it is important to read the text to yourself before sharing with students, jotting your thinking on sticky notes and specifically honing in on questioning.

During the first session, model and give examples of each questioning component. In the next session you will model your thinking as you apply each of the components to help you question the text. Nicki used think-aloud to demonstrate her use of the questioning components as she read *The Donner Party* (Werther, 2002). For both sessions, students should have a blank tally sheet and a class tally sheet on a full-size poster should be displayed at the front of the room.

Explaining and Defining Components of Questioning

To begin the first think-aloud session, ask students to silently read through each of the questioning components on the tally sheet. Then facilitate a whole-class discussion of each questioning component, providing students with meaningful examples of how to use the component and eliciting examples from students for those components they feel they understand.

Noticing and Applying Components of Questioning With a Text

Now begin reading the text aloud, pausing where you have placed sticky notes to demonstrate your use of the questioning components on the tally sheet. Continue the think-aloud and ask students to begin to identify their component use. One student should serve as the tally recorder during this phase of the lesson. Call on students to identify the component or components you use when thinking aloud.

Refining Strategy Use: Activities for Teaching Questioning

Two commonly used strategies for both question answering and generating are Question Answer Relationship (QAR) developed by Taffy Raphael (1982) and Thick and Thin Questioning (Harvey & Goudvis, 2000). QAR questions can be any of four types: right there, think and search, author and me, and on my own. In other words, students determine if the answer is directly in the text, in different parts of the text, requires their own thinking along with the authors, or includes only their ideas. You can model how identifying key words can help students determine the question type being asked by the teacher or in the text. By recognizing the type of question being asked, students are better able to find the answer. You can also teach students how to write questions that represent each type. This question generating helps students develop question asking skills.

Learning about thick and thin questions helps students think more deeply about the questions they ask as they read. You can use Thick and Thin Questioning with either narrative or expository text. Distinguish the difference between thick questions, which deal with large concepts and the big picture, and thin questions, which deal with specific content or ideas. Thick questions are usually open-ended and require complex answers. Thin questions require short, definite responses. Clue words to thick questions include *why* or *what if*, while clue words for thin questions usually include *how far*, *when*, or *what*.

The NRP (NICHD, 2000) suggested the following as effective procedures to teach students to generate questions:

- Ask students to generate questions during reading and include information across different parts of the text.
- Ask students to evaluate their questions and determine whether they are answered from the text or are inferential.
- Provide students with feedback on the quality of their questions asked and encourage and assist them in answering the questions generated.

We had both used QAR and Thick and Thin Questioning with students but still felt our students could benefit from more direct instruction in questioning, such as those activities presented in this chapter.

Now that students are familiar with the components of questioning, you will need to support them as they ask their own questions. In addition, you will need to continue to model asking questions to help students understand the various components better. Activities are organized under each strategy component and often fit under more than one. Many activities have been introduced earlier in chapter 2 and chapter 5.

The first activity, Categorizing Questions, helps students become aware of many different questioning components. It is good to use this activity early in the questioning unit so that it may serve as a springboard for clearing confusions about components.

Categorizing Questions

In this activity, pairs of students are given a shared text, possibly an excerpt from something related to content. They are also given a set of questions that can come from the text, but it might be most helpful if you have developed these questions to assist students in identifying the component the question represents. The questions are numbered and each question is cut into a strip (one question per strip). Students read the text and then use their Questioning Tally Sheet to help them determine which components each question represents. For example, the question "What is a Nebula?" is asked to help understand vocabulary and find specific information in the text. Students can write the question's number on their tally sheets to reference later during the discussion (see Figure 38 and Appendix B, page 209).

The focus should be on the discussions students have about the possible question categories, and you should walk around the classroom to help clarify components for kids. During the wrap-up, lead a whole-class discussion about the questions and components.

Questioning Tally Sheet—Student Sample

I ask questions...	Tally
to clarify something in the text or a text feature.	1, 9
to help me understand vocabulary.	
to help me find specific information in the text.	5, 2
to help me connect to the ideas or characters in the text.	
to put myself in the text by using my senses (visualizing, tasting, smelling, and feeling).	3
to understand choices the author made when writing the text.	4
to help me understand the text organization and text structure.	
to summarize what I have read.	8
to help me extend my learning beyond the text.	7, 6, 10
to help me understand a character or an object.	
to help me predict.	1

I ask questions to help me clarify something in the text or a text feature.

Many students (especially those who struggle to make sense of text) come to us with the idea that a text is something to get through. Failure to comprehend what they read while getting through the text is only an issue if someone else discovers their mistake. It's critical to teach students that if a text is important enough to read, it is important enough to understand, and questioning is one way to understand a text more completely. You will lay the groundwork for this component during the first six weeks when you teach students what it means to clarify and as you consistently affirm that reading is always done for meaning.

This component reminds readers that questions can be used to help us repair meaning as we read. Good readers don't gloss over mistakes by quickly reading ahead. They stop a moment and ask, "Did I read that word right?" or "Did the text really say what I just read?" Good readers also take the time to read the text features, figure out what they mean, and determine how they relate to the text as a whole. While reading *The Guinness Book of World Records* one might ask, "Did that man really get a Frisbee stuck in his lower lip, or did I read the caption too quickly?" The following activities can help students focus questioning to clarify text and text features:

- Using Text Features to Question (see below)
- Preview, Read, Question (see chapter 5, page 88)
- Questioning My Textbook (see this chapter, page 126)

Using Text Features to Question

During the first six weeks of school we hope students make reading text features a pre-reading habit through the Text Feature Walk activity. This is reinforced during textbook circles and most textbook reading. But we have learned that we need to remind students in each new unit to pay attention to the text features. Using Text Features to Question Think Sheet is a simple t-chart activity that can be done in a whole or small group. You should model how you read a text feature and then how you might write a question related to it. For example, after reading a table of contents with a guided-reading group, the teacher asked, "Why is it called the Big Bang?" The first column would list the text feature and the second column would list the questions. After identifying a section of text to read, students work in pairs and read the text features in that section. They complete the Using Text Features to Question Think Sheet for that section of text (see Figure 39 for a student sample and Appendix B, page 210, for a reproducible form). Then they read the text to find the answers to their questions.

After reading, lead a discussion about whether questions were answered and whether the question(s) have helped students understand the text. Questions remain unanswered usually for one of two reasons: (1) the question may have been poorly constructed, or (2) the question wasn't answered yet in the text. The student sample shown in Figure 39 shows how the student wrote the answer to questions after reading.

I ask questions to help me understand vocabulary.

As students stretch into more advanced texts, they occasionally come across words that are completely unfamiliar. A strong reader will pause briefly to ask, "What does this word mean?" They might read the text around the word to see if it is defined in context. They might look for clues in the text features. If they cannot make sense of it quickly, they might note the word on a slip of paper to investigate later.

Of course, part of what makes some readers proficient is their ability to prioritize which new words to pursue and which to let go. They might notice that a new word is a proper

FIGURE 39
Using Text Features to Question Think Sheet—Student Sample

Text Feature Read	Question I have...
1. Title	1. When was michell Anderson born! 1959 born.
2. P.C.	2. Why did he stand with those people instead of other astronauts!
3. P.B.	3. because those wore his crew people
4. P.G	4. I'm wondering what that thing is on top of the shuttle Mir
5.	5. Why did he set up savent experementions in space; science research mission.
6.	6.
7.	7.
8.	8.
9.	9.
10.	10.

noun and just read on with the understanding that each time they see the word it names the same character or place. They might decide that the word is critical to understanding the passage they are reading and look it up or ask someone what it means right away.

You need to help students understand the differences between passage-critical words and others. You can teach them to recognize proper nouns for what they are and to make good decisions about which words to invest time in. Much of this is done one-on-one in the reading conference. You can also directly teach minilessons on these skills:

- The Power of Words (see chapter 5, page 90)
- Word Alert! (see chapter 5, page 91)

I ask questions to find specific information in the text.

As they progress through school and life, students have a greater need to access information in texts. You must enable them to find what they want to know in an efficient and satisfying manner. There is nothing more frustrating for a child to be full of great questions and to flounder around in the wrong texts or the wrong section of text while trying to answer them. If you are going to reunite students with their inner curiosity, then you had better teach them how to satisfy it.

Questions that address this component are pretty straightforward. They could include "How many planets are there?" or "Who were the first Europeans to settle in our state?" They might also relate to the plot of a story as in "Who lit the fire?" or "Where is this story taking place?" The following activity, Questioning My Textbook, can be helpful when teaching how to seek specific information in the textbook.

Questioning My Textbook

Questioning My Textbook helps students hone their questioning skills and ask important questions that are likely to be answered in a section of the textbook (see Figure 40 for a student sample and Appendix B, page 211, for a reproducible form). Students learn to use the section headings and text features to guide them as they formulate questions. This activity also emphasizes the importance of answering or trying to answer the questions that are asked. As Gabbi, one of our students, explained, "To find a question that has been answered, you have to read it (the text) over and over and the more you read it, the better you understand." Finally, Questioning My Textbook gets students to begin summarizing by asking them after reading to write questions that *were* answered in the textbook.

Before reading a designated section of text, students preview and read the text features. Next, they write two questions that are not already posed in the text features, which they expect to have answered as they read. They read the text, then answer their questions if they can. After reading, students write two new questions that were answered by the text. Remind students that you are looking for important questions, not minor details. They are to write the answers to these questions as well. When students have completed the activity, have them share and discuss with the class. This whole-class share is a valuable way to ensure comprehension. Says Alex, "There was a whole bunch of information in there, and I didn't get it all. When other people shared their questions and answers, I picked up on it."

I ask questions to help me connect to the ideas or characters in the text.

If we can connect to a character or important idea in what we read, then our comprehension is greatly enhanced. When we ask "Has anything like this ever happened to me?" or "Have I ever read a book or seen a movie with a similar idea?" we are striving to connect. Sometimes self-questioning is the quickest way to help us connect as we read. You can help students hone this skill during reading conferences or in a whole-group minilesson by sharing some generic questions they can ask themselves to help connect. The Character Quilt activity (see chapter 8, page 142) can be helpful, too.

FIGURE 40
Questioning My Textbook—Student Sample

Name _____

Directions: Preview and read the text features for this section of text. Write two questions, not found in the book, that you expect to have answered as you read. During or after reading, write the answers to your two questions.

Question 1: How did pepole get the Characters and objects for the constillations?

Answer: Pepole saw them as outlines pℊ of objects, mythological characters or animls.

Question 2: Do any constillations look the same as another?

Answer: Not in text.

_____

After reading, write two new questions (not in the textbook or above) that were also answered by the text. Write the answers to these questions as well.

Question 1: Where is Polaris located?

Answer: almost directly above the North Pole

Question 2: Wich 2 constillations told Pepole that it was safe to plant?

Answer: Leo & Virgo

I ask questions to put myself in the text by using my senses.

Our questions can help put us right into the text as we read. For instance, asking "What does Turkish Delight taste like?" plants us in Edmund's shoes in C.S. Lewis's (1950) *The Lion, The Witch and the Wardrobe*. Asking yourself what it looks like to see a tsunami headed straight for you helps you understand the fear experienced by survivors. If students have trouble automatically visualizing, tasting, smelling, or feeling something in the text, remind them that pausing to ask themselves what something looks, tastes, smells, or feels like is a great way to make this happen. Taking the time to ask these questions can greatly enhance one's reading experience.

I ask questions to understand choices the author made when writing the text.

Students need to know that texts don't just spring forth from printing presses, book club boxes, or library shelves. Someone had to conceptualize and write the text. Someone else thought about and produced the visual supports. All of this means that if a character does something surprising, or the first six chapters only have one sentence each, or if the ending is not the way you expected, it was not by accident. The author made choices and, right or wrong, whether or not you agree with those choices, those choices shaped the text.

How does this component help readers? It helps them become better connoisseurs of texts. And it helps them have faith that if something doesn't seem quite right, it should make more sense as they read on. With good nonfiction, it means each text feature was chosen for the specific way it supports the main idea. When a child asks "Why did they include a picture of the International Space Station?" he is really asking "How does this relate to the main idea?"

I ask questions to help me understand the text organization and text structure.

In a recent literature circle, our students were trying to figure out the beginning of *Granny Torrelli Makes Soup* (Creech, 2003). They had a lot of questions for the author, most stemming from their lack of satisfaction with the way the book began, but they also wondered if the story was starting in the beginning or the middle. They were trying to figure out how the text was organized. This questioning component also comes into play as students determine the best way to approach an expository text. Should they start at the beginning and read to the end, or would it make more sense to jump in on the section in which they are interested?

This component can come naturally for students if you frequently ask questions to determine text structure or organizational patterns as the occasions arise in class. For example, if you are preparing to read a narrative text aloud, you might read the title and then ask if this book will start at the beginning, progress to the middle, and conclude at the end. If you are sharing an excerpt from an expository text, you might model asking yourself out loud if this book has an index that you can use to go directly to the information sought. Another activity that provides opportunity for students to use this component is Expository Text Investigations (see chapter 5, page 94).

I ask questions to summarize what I have read.

If students want to remember what they read, they should stop every so often and ask "What was that section about?" or "What happened in this part of the story?" These questions ensure that the reader both understands and remembers what has been read. They also require students to slow down and process the information. As with all components, you should model these summarizing questions in your think-aloud. Questioning My Textbook (see page 126) is an activity that can help reinforce this component as well.

I ask questions to extend my learning beyond the text.

We hope our students become lifelong learners, and what they learn with us is just a start—that we will awaken a need in them to find out more. Maybe we will inspire a career or a satisfying hobby.

This component validates those questions students have because they have read a text. It signals their current reading as a jumping-off point, not an end. Sometimes a reader has a question early in a text that never gets answered. Sometimes the question is formed as the reader thinks about what was read: "If _____ is true, then is _____ true as well?" Encourage kids to ask these questions, then to find the answers to the most compelling questions on their own.

> Usually when a book asks the question, it's like—they're asking it for review. So it's going to be in the text. But if you ask the question, sometimes you're not going to answer it in the text. So you might have to look somewhere else. —Kaitlin

I ask questions to help me understand a character or an object.

Good readers strive to fully understand the characters or objects they are reading about. For example, students might question the motivation of a character "Why did she run away if she wants to make friends?" Or, they might try to figure out how a crystal is able to cast light in a fantasy story. In a book about weather, students might ask "How does a barometer work?" The important thing to stress about this component is the fact that students should be trying to better understand the characters or objects about which they read.

> You learn more about the text if you can find the answer to the question you have, because, like, if you're asking who is this—why is this character important—and then you find the answer, you understand the text better. —Alana

I ask questions to help me predict.

As students begin R^5 most of their Rap questions will fall into this component category. They will ask questions such as "Will the girls ever be friends?" or "I wonder who stole the book?" These questions are important because they help propel our readers forward and make their purpose for reading clear— to find out "who dunnit"! As soon as these questions emerge in Rap, you should follow the identification of the strategy (questioning) with the question "And what other strategy does this question help you do?" (predicting). Students will be proficient at this component before you even begin your questioning unit. A specific activity to reinforce this component is Preview, Read, Question (see chapter 5, page 88).

> Questioning helps me with all the strategies because when I ask questions, I want to figure it out. And so on. —Andrea

Self-Assessment and Goal-Setting

Students record their strategy use on the Questioning Tally Sheet during whole- and small-group lessons (see Figure 41 for a student sample). We use just about any reading material to teach questioning, especially science or social studies textbooks and

FIGURE 41
Questioning Tally Sheet—Student Sample

I ask questions...	Tally
to clarify something in the text or a text feature.	卌
to help me understand vocabulary.	卌 卌 卌 Ⅰ
to help me find specific information in the text.	卌 Ⅱ 卌 卌 Ⅱ
to help me connect to the ideas or characters in the text.	卌
to put myself in the text by using my senses (visualizing, tasting, smelling, and feeling).	卌 Ⅱ
to understand choices the author made when writing the text.	卌 卌
to help me understand the text organization and text structure.	Ⅱ
to summarize what I have read.	卌 卌
to help me extend my learning beyond the text.	卌 Ⅱ Ⅱ
to help me understand a character or an object.	卌
to help me predict.	Ⅱ

other nonfiction materials. During this unit, you should designate several whole- and small-group sessions for students to read and tally their questions. At the end of each lesson, set aside time for students to share the components they have used.

After a few data gathering sessions, use the class tally chart to collect class data on strategy use. As you have done in previous strategy units, read each component aloud and have students look at their own tally sheets to assess which components they have been using over the course of the unit. Tally the number of students who have been using each component regularly and show students how to look at the data to figure out what they need to improve upon. Then develop a sample plan based on whole-class needs. After modeling, ask students to use the same process and create their own plans based on their own data and needs. (See Figure 42 for a sample student plan for questioning and Appendix B, page 212, for a reproducible.)

Immediately after the self-assessment and goal-setting lesson have students use their plans with a short section of text you have preselected. This way, students can work

---

FIGURE 42
Thinking About My Reading: Questioning—Student Sample

Name _____   Date __1/23/06__

Directions: (1) Put a check mark by the things you do well as a reader when questioning.
           (2) Highlight the things you think you need to work on to become a better reader.

☑ I ask questions to help me clarify something in the text or a text feature.
☑ I ask questions to help me understand vocabulary.
☑ I ask questions to find specific information in the text.
☑ I ask questions to help me connect to the ideas or characters in the text.
☑ I ask questions to put myself in the text by using my senses (visualizing, tasting, smelling, and feeling).
☑ I ask questions to understand choices the author made when writing the text.
☑ I ask questions to help me understand the text organization and text structure.
☑ I ask questions to summarize what I have read.
☑ I ask questions to extend my learning beyond the text.
☑ I ask questions to help me understand a character or an object.
☐ I ask questions to help me predict.

Choose one highlighted item to improve upon:

I ask questions to help me predict.

_____

Create a plan to improve upon this skill.

1. Read Text.

2. I will ask questions that can help me predict anywhere in the text.

3. Think about a prediction and ask it in question form.

4. Write questions on post it notes.

5. Try to answer questions.

out any problems in their plan and get instantaneous practice, and you can use this time to circulate and proofread plans to identify students who need help revising. Give students time to read and remind them to use their plans to assist them with understanding the text. Once students are done reading, have them share how they used their plans in a whole-class share.

Collect students' plans and determine who may need to make further revisions. It helps to meet with students in small groups and have them practice using their plans with your guidance. During regular R⁵ sessions remind students to focus on using their plans and confer with students to continue supporting growth with questioning. You will also want to provide specific opportunities for other practice. For instance, have students read a content area text using their questioning plans. After students have finished, ask them to share with the class how they used their plans and how they worked.

Final Thoughts

This book is the result of our questioning. We wanted to know if metacognition mattered and we wondered why some students did not engage in reading while others would not be torn away from their reading. We probed and questioned ourselves as readers and anyone who would make their thinking visible to us. The components for each strategy were developed from inquiry. This unit was difficult to develop because there isn't a lot of research on how students question as they read, and students are not used to focusing on their own questions. It was also the most rewarding unit to develop because, through it, we awakened our students' innate inquisitiveness. When we combined the teaching of questioning with a unit on outer space, students' questions took them further than we ever imagined possible.

Chapter 8 details how to help readers visualize as they read and how to help students make the text come into clearer focus through the technique of visualizing.

Visualizing

A student walks into class on Monday with a slight scowl on her face. She says she's mad because she finally got to see the movie version of her favorite book and they got it all wrong. It didn't look anything like she had pictured it. She proceeds to give the class a blow-by-blow description of everything the filmmakers got wrong.

What Does It Mean to Visualize?

The child in the vignette is one, like many, who visualizes as she reads. We live in a visual world, after all. Students are bombarded with graphic images through video games, television, movies, and the Internet. In fact, visualization is a cognitive strategy we often use without realizing it. Have you ever used drawings to help you figure out a math problem? Or a diagram to help you understand a scientific process, like the water cycle? Have you found that perfect outfit and imagined yourself wearing it before you even put in on? Or when asked to give directions, do you picture yourself driving them and picture the major landmarks in your mind?

Visualization is important in our lives and is one skill that many readers can relate to quickly. Visualizing is especially important and helpful for athletes, actors, and musicians. This mental rehearsal helps them perform better by enhancing and improving their execution. Certainly teachers visualize each year as they plan how they will set up their classrooms. We picture where students will be working and the flow of traffic around desks; we visualize students gathering on the floor and working at activity tables. We create a mental image of what we want the bulletin boards and other display areas in our classrooms to look like, then we work hard to make the room match our mental image.

> Whenever I'm reading good descriptions, they kind of just come naturally. For some reason I can just picture it. We had a discussion the other day about visualizing, and it comes when you're sleeping. I can have a clear picture when I'm sleeping, and sometimes it's from books that I've read during the day and sometimes it's not. —Brittany

The Importance of Visualizing

Harvey and Goudvis (2000) suggest that the images readers create through visualizing are deeply personal and make the reading experience more pleasurable and engaging, like movies in the mind. Furthermore, visualizing can help readers better understand the text by calling on all their senses—conjuring smells, tastes, sounds, textures, or images that bring the text alive and make reading a much more enjoyable and satisfying endeavor. Those of us who have been lost in a book know what it feels like to ignore our surroundings and be transported into the story. Sometimes it is so real that we forget who and where we are.

Tovani (2000) wrote, "If they can see it, they often understand it" (p. 53). This is simple, but true. Good readers form mental images as they read (Armbruster, Lehr, & Osborn, 2003) by using their background experiences and the author's words to form images. At other times readers rely on textual supports such as illustrations and photographs to help them picture the text. The pictures in our mind personally connect us to the text or what we are learning, and they often leave lasting impressions (Keene & Zimmermann, 1997). Readers who visualize while reading have better recall (Pressley, 1977) and perform better on standardized tests (Jerry & Lutkus, 2003). Students who visualize expository passages can determine if information is not complete, and therefore they are able to clarify, even if visual aids are not at their disposal (Gambrell & Bales, 1986). People who read without visualizing are simply gliding across the surface of a text, missing out on the rewarding experience of being immersed completely in another world or the complete cognitive engagement that comes from using all their mental resources to fully understand what they read.

Problems With Teaching Visualizing

The biggest concern with visualizing is that some students feel they can't do it. It doesn't come naturally to them, and they've never been shown how to pause and create mental images. These kids tend to be concrete, linear thinkers and many times prefer nonfiction or realistic fiction. They are often fake readers, too. Because they don't take the time to make sense of the text and may not even realize that this is what they should do, visualizing is out of the question. Furthermore, these students are often working so hard to decode the words that they are unable to make connections between words and images (Hibbing & Rankin-Erickson, 2003). At other times they may lack the background knowledge and vocabulary to assist them in visualizing the text. Although some visualization clearly enhances comprehension of the main idea or theme in a text more than others, we feel that every time readers pause to put themselves in a text, it enriches the experience and helps it stick in their memory.

To help students make visualizations that help them to better understand the text, you can use a two-column Making Meaningful Visualizations Think Sheet, such as the one used in the connecting unit (see Appendix B, page 213, for a reproducible).

How We Visualize and the Visualizing Components

You read the description to help you see it better in your mind and have a better visualization. —T.J.

Visualizing occurs before, during, and after reading. When we visualize we use our prior knowledge and text clues. If the text is less detailed and lacks picture or text feature support, the readers are left to create their own image. When expert readers visualize they do the following:

- Make the words in the text into pictures, sounds, scents, and feelings
- Make connections among the ideas in the text, the world, and their own experiences
- Place themselves in the text and become involved with the text
- Improve comprehension
- Enjoy reading
- Remember what was read

We began with a list of how readers visualize based on research and our own reading experiences. As we worked with students, we revised this into a list of visualizing components that made up our Visualizing Tally Sheet (see Appendix B, page 214, for a reproducible) and became the basis for our lessons on visualizing. The following statements are the visualizing components:

- I visualize to help me predict.
- I visualize to help me clarify something in the text.
- I visualize the characters, person, or creatures.
- I visualize the events.
- I visualize the setting or place.
- I visualize using my senses (smelling, tasting, hearing, or feeling).
- I visualize using a physical reaction (hot, cold, thirsty, upset stomach, etc.).
- I visualize using an emotional reaction (happy, sad, excited, lonely, etc.).
- I visualize using illustrations or text features in the text.
- I visualize to help me remember.

Visualizing and the Metacognitive Teaching Framework

This unit focuses on helping students use visualization to experience, remember, and understand what they are reading. In it we teach those who have never seen text through their mind's eye to focus in and create mental images. For those who are proficient with mental imagery, we provide experiences that expand and broaden their visualizations. Using the MTF to teach visualizing strategies allows students to have a richer experience with the text and deepens their comprehension.

The relationship among all of the metacognitive strategies is important, but it is integral with visualizing, as the act of imagery intersects with all of the metacognitive units, especially connecting and summarizing.

Explicit Instruction of Visualizing

At this point, using think-aloud to introduce a new strategy and its components should be a familiar procedure for our students. They should expect to learn what the components mean, and they should begin identifying examples of strategy use, both yours and their own. Although we differentiate between defining components and demonstrating component use as two discreet sessions, you may be able to introduce visualizing during one class sitting. The first step is to go over the components on the tally sheet and the second step is to model your visualizations using each component.

To launch visualizing, choose an excerpt from a previous read-aloud; Nicki chose *The Kingdom Keepers: Disney After Dark* (Pearson, 2005) because her students had thoroughly enjoyed this book during read-aloud and had previously discussed some of their visualizations and connections. Nicki also felt that because this text was familiar and set in Walt Disney World, where most of the students had visited, it would be easier for the students to identify the application of the visualizing components. As with other units, you should read the text to yourself before sharing with students and strategically choose a section of text that conjures images for you; jot these on sticky notes so you can concentrate on teaching during the think-aloud. Focus the first part of the lesson on defining each component and the second part on application of the components with an excerpt from the read-aloud. Each student should have a blank tally sheet, and the large class tally chart should be positioned so that all students can see it.

Explaining and Defining Components of Visualizing

Before launching this think-aloud, ask students to silently read through each of the visualizing components on the tally sheet. Lead a whole-class discussion of each visualizing component by providing students with meaningful examples of how to use the component and eliciting some examples from students for further explanation of each component. In the transcript that follows, you will notice that Nicki discussed some components more than others. The amount of time you spend on each component will differ depending upon the age and background knowledge of your students.

Noticing and Applying Components of Visualizing With a Text

Now, read aloud your preselected excerpt, pausing and sharing your visualizations as you read. Ask students to identify which component or components you use each time you pause to visualize. One student should serve as the class recorder, placing a tally mark on the large, laminated tally sheet posted in front of the class every time students identify component use or you explain your component use. The following transcript demonstrates how quickly students began to notice and identify Nicki's component use and share their own during her visualizing think-aloud:

Teacher: So I decided for our think-aloud I would use a book we are very familiar with, *The Kingdom Keepers*. Can you guess which part I am deciding to start us at?

Victoria: The scene you shared with us for your book talk...when they're at the teepee?

Teacher: No.

Aaron: When they're going down the sled of the trash?

Teacher: Yep, that's exactly the one I picked. The trash chute. Prepare to be grossed out. Alright, here we go. [Reads aloud from page 317] "Seeing this, Finn jumped down the trash chute. From high overhead he heard Amanda's gleeful voice echo as he fell. 'I'll never forget what you did!'

As he was sucked down the foul-smelling tube, Finn tucked the roll of plans away under his belt. He took a deep breath and gagged. He thought he might throw up."

Teacher: I can already smell the rancid, sickly-sweet rotted garbage. It's making my stomach turn. What kind of visualization was I using there? Adam?

Adam: You were using your sense of smelling.

Teacher: Yes, I was using my senses. Let's start right there.

Austin: A physical reaction.

Teacher: I did have a physical reaction. I'm still having a physical reaction. Autumn?

Autumn: The events.

Teacher: Well, I haven't pictured the events yet, because I am just smelling it. But we'll get there. [Continues reading aloud from page 317] "The tube reeked of rotting trash. Gooey bits and sticky globs of rancid food and soggy litter stuck to him like leeches, licked his face and slopped into his hair and clothing. Again, he felt himself gag." I can see the metal tube and I can see trash all around. It's mostly dark, and Finn is just kind of tumbling through. What kind of visualization is that? Victoria?

Victoria: The events.

Teacher: Well, a little bit of the events, but more so something else, Ru?

Ru: Character, person, creatures?

Teacher: Did I talk a lot about what he looked like?

Ru: The setting.

Teacher: The setting. I'm picturing where he is. Very good. [Continues reading aloud from page 317] "In the distance, far down the tube, echoing through the metal, Finn heard hoots and hollers—Maybeck and Philby. The suction spit trash into his face." Now I don't understand how suction can spit trash into your face if you're going in the same direction, so I'm going to pause for a minute and picture this. Let's see, so there's a fan and he's heading toward it, and maybe he's being pulled faster than the trash. [Uses her hands to show how Finn could be moving in the same direction as the trash, but faster so the trash hits him] So here's the trash being pulled, and as he's being pulled faster than the trash it sticks to his face. And the fan is out ahead. I drew a little picture to help me. [Shows students her sticky note, where she's sketched a fan] This is the fan, and he's moving quicker than the trash. What strategy was I using there? Take a look.

Austin:	Helping me to remember.
Teacher:	I wasn't trying to remember there. Autumn?
Autumn:	To help you clarify something in the text.
Teacher:	Right! To help me clarify. I had to stop, because I didn't know what that meant. Good job, lovely assistant. [Continues reading aloud from pages 317–318] "He slammed into some kind of mesh gate, an intersection of converging trash-evacuation tubes. On the other side, black garbage bags and trash raced past. Then the gate opened and it was his turn. He tumbled down and rolled into the next tube, picked up speed, and headed off again, upside down and backward." So, I can just see Finn tumbling through the trash tube upside down and backward. What am I using, Josh?
Josh:	An event.
Teacher:	I am visualizing an event. Good. Anything else?
Austin:	The character, person, or creatures.
Teacher:	The character.
Teacher:	Yes. You are already good at this and you're going to get even better.

Refining Strategy Use:
Activities for Teaching Visualizing

Once students are familiar with the visualizing components, they will quickly begin to use them and share their component use. Because visualizing is deeply personal, students seem to pick up on it more swiftly than some of the other cognitive strategies. Right after you launch the visualizing unit, students should engage in Read, Relax, Reflect, Respond, and Rap (R^5).

Although many students catch on to this skill quickly, there are some for whom visualizing is a real challenge. All students will need continued support and modeling to help them better understand each component and see how visualizing helps them make sense of text. The following activities do just that. After the first three, which work for a number of components, activities are organized under strategy components and may fall under one or more component.

Visualizing During Shared Reading

This activity helps students become more aware of their visualizations. While students read a section of text that you have selected, have them draw pictures on sticky notes to capture their mental images. You will want to carefully select the section of text, either from a trade book or textbook, to make sure students will be able to visualize, and students should read the same selection of text in order to promote discussion.

After reading, ask students to share their sticky notes in pairs or small groups. Have students focus on how these images contribute to the reading experience and, more importantly, how their drawings assist them with understanding.

Sharing Visualizations in Think-Pair-Share

Another simple activity is to give students prompts to help evoke images while reading. This can be done effectively in a formal shared-reading lesson or judiciously during a read-aloud (however, we don't like to interrupt a read-aloud session too often for strategy work). The following questions can encourage and assist readers as they visualize text:

- After reading this section of text, what pictures come to mind?
- What images did you see as you read? Why do you think you saw these images?
- How did the author help you picture the ideas in the text?
- Did you use your senses: smell, hear, taste, and feel? How?
- Highlight five words or phrases from the text that help you get a picture in your head.

After reading a section of text out loud, in either a shared reading format or sparingly during read-aloud, pause and ask students one of the questions above. Have them talk with their elbow partner about the prompt, and then call on a few pairs of students to share.

Visualization Continuum

The Visualization Continuum is a modification of the Connections Continuum (see chapter 6, page 110), and it addresses a number of components. Although the Connections Continuum helps students see how valuable connections are, depending on what text elements they help readers understand, the Visualization Continuum helps readers understand that the clarity of the visualization is what counts. Students begin to notice how well their visualizations help them bring the text to life.

For this think-aloud, select an excerpt from a trade book that lends itself to visualizing. (We've used a short story from *Dog to Rescue: Seventeen True Tales of Dog Heroism* [Sanderson, 1993] with success.) As done with other think-alouds, before reading aloud to students, write on sticky notes seven or eight examples of how you visualized the text. In this case, be sure to vary the depth of your visualizations as well as model several of the visualizing components. Give students a copy of the text you are reading, so they can follow along and refer back to it as you read and share your visualizations out loud.

After your think-aloud, have students work in pairs to read through the set of visualization examples you shared as you read the story. As they read them, have students determine which components the visualizations exemplify and record the visualization number on a blank tally sheet in the appropriate component boxes. Once this is done, have them order the visualizations from least effective to most effective, in terms of bringing the text to life.

Once pairs have discussed and placed the visualizations in order, encourage them to look at the tally sheet and continuum to determine what factors contribute to meaningful, stronger visualizations. Lead a whole-class discussion on what makes visualization meaningful. Make sure that students understand you are asking them to tell which visualizations were more powerful, not which descriptions were written better. We hope your students will be able to see that it is not necessarily what you visualize but how deeply you visualize, and that the more ways you visualize something, the more real it becomes. Below are some responses Nicki's students gave to the prompt "What makes a visualization meaningful?" after completing the visualization continuum activity:

- What makes a visualization meaningful is how clear you can see it. (Adam)
- What makes some [visualizations] better is that you are looking at everything from the character's point of view and they are physical feelings and emotional feelings. (Casey and Brian)
- A meaningful visualization has details you can see in your mind. You can see a clear picture. (Prerna)
- Some texts have descriptive words so powerful that you are able to feel how the author wanted the character to feel in that event. (Ashlyn and Jessica)

I visualize to help me predict.

When we are completely immersed in a story, when we can see the action unfold in our mind's eye, when we are so familiar with a character that we can anticipate its next move, we are likely to picture what we think will happen next. This type of visualization helps us predict well. Once this occurs automatically as students read, then they are truly tapping into the power of visualization.

> If you visualize your prediction... then you try to find out which way it's more likely to happen. —Griffin

- Previewing, Predicting, and Learning From Text Features (see chapter 2, page 38)
- Text Feature Walk (see chapter 2, page 40)
- Anticipation Guide Extension (see chapter 5, page 86, for original Anticipation Guide description)

Anticipation Guide Extension

After students complete an anticipation guide (see chapter 5, page 86), direct them to write a prediction paragraph about what they think they are going to learn. Then have them draw a picture showing something that they will predict will be in the text. In the student sample shown in Figure 43, Gabbi added a labeled diagram to her paragraph so that she could picture what the layers of the atmosphere were going to look like. She used visualization to help her predict what she would learn.

I visualize to help me clarify something in the text.

When we visualize to help us clarify a character, event, or setting, we stop and reread, hoping the fuzzy picture becomes clearer. Our images become flexible, and we are able

FIGURE 43
Anticipation Guide Extension for Visualizing—Student Sample

Earth's Atmosphere
Anticipation Guide

Student Name _Gabbi_   Date _4/3/06_

Directions: Read each statement. Check off whether you agree or disagree with the statement in the Before Reading columns. While reading think about each statement, were you right or wrong? After reading the section, reread each statement. Check off whether you agree or disagree in the After Reading columns. Explain why you agree or disagree in the space provided below each statement. Write the page number where you found evidence to support your statement.

Before Reading   After Reading

Agree	Disagree	Statement	Agree	Disagree	Page #(s)
	✓	1. The atmosphere begins about 30 miles above the surface of the earth. _This statement could be true because we live in the troposphere._	✓		_D8_
✓		2. The trophosphere is the top layer of our atmosphere. _The troposphere is the bottom layer of our atmosphere._		✓	_D8_
	✓	3. The atmosphere has five layers. _The atmospher has four layers: the troposphere, stratosphere, mesosphere, and thermosphere._		✓	_D8_
	✓	4. The atmosphere has a solid crust at the very outer edge. Rockets must break through this crust to reach outer space. _The atmosphere does not have a solid crust._		✓	_D8_
✓		5. Airplanes fly in the stratosphere. _Airplanes fly in the stratosphere when they have to fly a long way or to avoid bad weather._	✓		_D8_
	✓	6. Almost all weather occurs in the mesosphere. _All weather occurs in the troposphere._		✓	_D8_

I predict that this section of our Science text will be about all the layers of Earth's <u>atmosphere.</u> I predict that there are 4 layers of the atmosphere; the troposphere, stratosphere, mosophere, and thermosphere. The thermosphere controls the weather, the stratosphere controls the clouds, the troposphere e controls air pressure on Earth and the mesosphere controls the oxygen. Also I think it will talk about how thunder and lightning forms.

Vocab.
atmosper
air pressure
trophospere
stratospheri
mesosphere
thermospher

to adapt them as we continue to read. This technique is especially helpful with nonfiction and can be closely tied to using text features to visualize. An example might be if you were reading about the earth's size relative to the sun, and the text gave a scale example such as a mustard seed to a beach ball, which seemed different from what you thought you knew. You would visualize the items in the text example to help you clarify your understanding. An activity that can help teach this component is a Guided Reading Lesson during direct small-group instruction.

Guided-Reading Lesson

Use a section of text that may be difficult to understand, reading aloud one idea at a time and encouraging students to form mental images. Remind students that sometimes we need to take the time to picture what is being read to fully understand. Have students describe what they see in their mind's eye. If they misinterpret the text, go back and reread for them.

Visualizing can be a powerful ally in content areas, as kids strive to understand new ideas or read about things they have never seen. A cross-curricular example of this activity could occur during solving word problems in a math lesson. You could work with a small group and encourage students to visualize as you read each idea the problem presents. Again, have them describe what they see and reread if they misunderstand.

I visualize the characters, person, or creatures.

Fantasy authors visualize characters or creatures well. Because many of the characters and creatures in fantasy books are not in our regular schema, authors of fantasy must use vivid descriptions to allow the reader to imagine them. Authors may include illustrations to help, but many times readers are left only the author's words and their own imaginations to picture what the characters and creatures look like. While writers in other genres may have an easier job of it, the more familiar fantasy authors can make readers feel with the characters or creatures in the text, the more the story is enjoyed and understood.

- Character Quilt (see below)
- Using a Picture Book With a Strong Character (see page 143)

Character Quilt

What is great about this activity is how adaptable it is to some of the other visualizing components. You just tweak it to meet your students' needs.

Students will need to write words for the following categories, related to the main character in the book they are reading or one that you have shared with the whole class: what the character looks like, feels (emotions), tastes, smells, and hears. You can use other categories, such as says, acts, and touches, but you need only four categories for this activity—one category for each corner of the quilt square. Students can then write describing words about the character on the inside of each corner according to the category labeled. For example, for "feels," you might say that Brian in the book *Hatchet* (Paulsen, 1987) is scared, hopeless, angry, frustrated, and alone.

Students fold in the corners of a piece of drawing paper so that they meet at the center, creating four triangles on the outside and a box in the center. Students then open up the corners and draw the character in the center using their written descriptions from each category. This sketching helps students create a more vivid image of the character. The picture becomes the center of the quilt. Along the edges, on the inside of the corners of each flap, students write their descriptions according to the categories they were given. On the outside of the flaps (corners) students write the title of the book and the character's name. This can become a bulletin board display.

Using a Picture Book With a Strong Character

This activity helps readers as they visualize a character. Often, struggling readers will overrely on the illustrations in a text to help understand the story. Although this is a decent strategy to use, students may not be aware that the author's words can help them formulate their own mental pictures. By choosing strategic places in a think-aloud text to pause and have kids share their mental images, you can guide them in the process.

Choose a picture book that has a strong character. Traditional fairy tales and folk tales are good examples, as are their adaptations. Biographies are also a good choice for this activity. Once you have chosen a text, such as *The Rough-Faced Girl* (Martin & Shannon, 1992), a version of Cinderella, read the text to yourself to identify places where you want the students to make mental pictures without the aid of illustrations. For example, while reading *The Rough-Faced Girl*, we selected specific pages where we paused and had students share with their elbow partners what they would draw to support the text, specifically to portray the main character. After reading the entire text without revealing the illustration of the girl's face, we had students draw a picture of what the Rough-Faced Girl looked like before and after she bathed in the lake (see Figure 44).

I visualize the events.

Brittany needed to clarify what was happening in the text so she pictured the event and then could understand what happened. If readers slow down and take the time to watch important events unfold in their minds, they will have a much richer reading experience as well as deeper comprehension. The following activities can help:

- Visual Timeline (see page 144)
- Draw to Remember Events (see page 144)
- Scene It! (see page 145)

> In *Among the Hidden* it said that he tried to open the sliding glass door and he put a hole in the screen, and that didn't really make sense. But then I understood it because he, like, punched his hand through the screen, and I saw him punching his hand through the screen and trying to unlock the door. —Brittany

FIGURE 44
Student Illustration of Rough-Faced Girl

Visual Timeline

During read-aloud, after you have read an exciting sequence of events, give students a thick strip of paper (wide adding machine tape works well here). Have them list the events on the strip of paper chronologically according to when they occurred. They need to leave space after each event listed on the timeline where they can illustrate the event, as well. Encourage students to picture fully what they want to illustrate before they begin to draw on the timeline. You may want students to talk with an elbow partner about their visualizations to make their ideas more vivid.

Draw to Remember Events

This activity encourages students to use visualization to remember events, and it can be modified to focus on specific story elements as well. This activity can be done with a short read-aloud, or kept over time as you read aloud a chapter book.

Give students drawing paper and have them fold it in half lengthwise. Instruct them to make three to four vertical cuts on the front flap from the edge to the center fold. While you are reading or just after you read, ask students to sketch on each section of the page an image from the story that shows a major event. Students then open up each section and write a brief summary of what is happening in the picture on the above flap. The pictures they draw serve as reminders while they write their summaries (see Figure 45 for a student sample). Once students are able to do this activity independently, you can have them do the drawing in class and then write the summary for meaningful homework.

Scene It!

This activity has multiple benefits, but it is most helpful for visualizing the events in the text and visualizing to remember what has happened previously. This activity can be done while students are reading, but is best done as a follow-up activity after reading. Students can work in pairs or teams if the text or book is one that they all have read. They need to identify the 6–10 most important events from the story and sketch these on drawing paper like a movie reel. After they complete their illustrations, they should go back and write a sentence or two that describes what happened in each scene.

I visualize the setting or place.

Being transported to another place or time is the motivating factor for many readers. And, whether or not escapism is our goal when reading, being fully engaged in a text means that we can see where events are taking place or picture a place the author is describing. Imagine reading the Harry Potter series without ever picturing Hogwarts Academy of Witchcraft and Wizadry or reading a nonfiction book on Niagara Falls without pausing to visualize the awe-inspiring spectacle! Being able to place ourselves virtually in a text reaps a richer understanding of what we read. The following activities can help reinforce this component:

- Setting Quilt (see below)
- Draw to Remember Setting (see below)

Setting Quilt

By shifting the focus of the Character Quilt (see page 142) to setting, you have created another useful activity. Before creating the sample in Figure 46, the student had read *Hatchet* (Paulsen, 1987). The category headings she brainstormed included feel and climate, see, hear, smell. In the center she drew a picture of Brian at the lake, which supported him throughout his survival ordeal. By using her senses she was better able to visualize an important setting from this book.

Draw to Remember Setting

This variation of Draw to Remember Events (see page 144) focuses on setting and helps students pause and use text clues and their own mental imagery to fully imagine where a story occurs. In the example shown in Figure 47, Nicki had read the story *Roxaboxen*

FIGURE 45
Draw to Remember Events—Student Sample

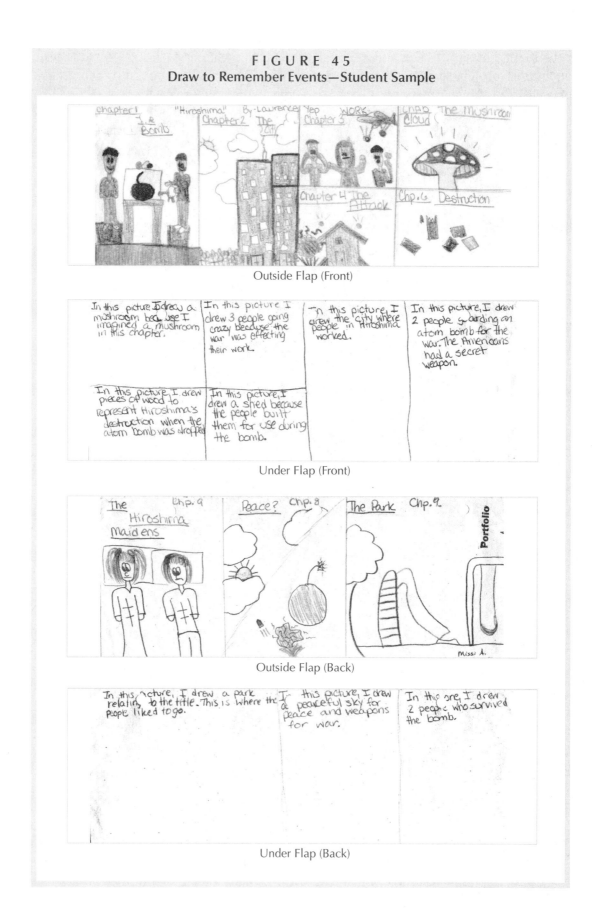

Outside Flap (Front)

Under Flap (Front)

Outside Flap (Back)

Under Flap (Back)

FIGURE 46
Setting Quilt—Student Sample

(McLerran, 1991). She paused three times in the story, after strong descriptions of the setting, to have students draw the town of Roxaboxen from different perspectives. In the first picture, they are looking at the town from across the road. In the next they are actually in the town, and in the final drawing they are looking up close at one of the houses in Roxaboxen. After each drawing, students wrote a description of what they visualized.

After reading the entire story, students were given a choice of whether they would get to see the book's illustrations. Before revealing the illustrations, however, Nicki reminded students that the focus of the activity wasn't to see who matched the actual illustrations best, but to create strong mental images of the setting.

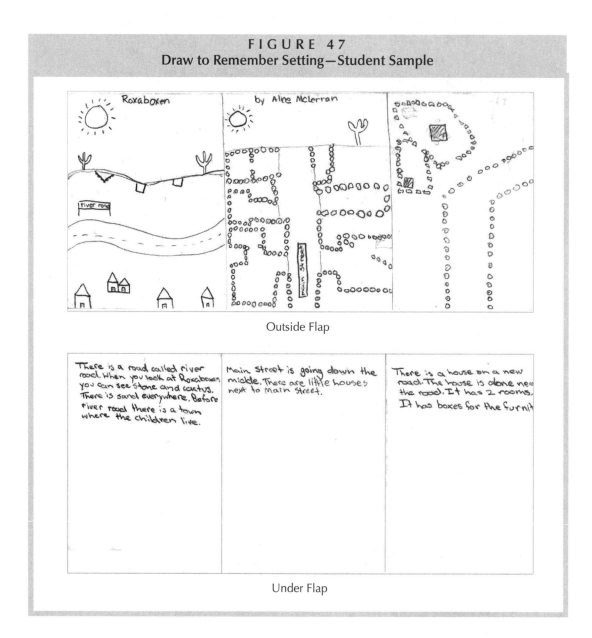

FIGURE 47
Draw to Remember Setting—Student Sample

Outside Flap

Under Flap

I visualize using my senses.

Sensory images that emerge as we read can be connected to our own memories or created from scratch, relying heavily on the author's words and our own imaginations. These impressions can be powerful and go far to help us become fully submerged in a text. For instance, one might remember for years the feeling of sinking one's hands and face into the silky, sun-warmed fur of Aslan's mane in *The Lion, The Witch and the Wardrobe* (Lewis, 1950). This mental experience helps the reader connect physically and emotionally with the character and creates a lasting impression.

> Visualizing is when you sort of relate to the text, when you picture it or feel it or you smell it and stuff like that. —Eric

- Common Senses (see below)
- Character Quilt (see this chapter, page 142)
- Setting Quilt (see this chapter, page 145)

Common Senses

This simple activity helps students slow down and practice using their senses as they read or listen to a story. First, choose a few sensory-laden excerpts to read aloud. These should be both fiction and nonfiction, as we want kids to know visualizing is used in all genres. You might choose descriptions that call on one particular sense, such as tasting, each day. Read each excerpt expressively and slowly enough that students can form images, then lead a think-pair-share. (Students should have about 30 seconds to fully experience their image, then a minute or two to share with an elbow partner.) Then ask a few students to share with the whole group.

A good follow-up activity is to give students their own selection of sensory-heavy excerpts to read and interpret, which helps them begin to use their senses as they read independently. Students really enjoy doing this—expect them to want a snack afterward on the day you explore the sense of taste!

I visualize using a physical reaction.

Few of us can read of Stanley Yelnat's ditch-digging experiences in *Holes* (Sachar, 1998) without working up a thirst. It's also hard to not feel a sense of urgency and tension when looking at photographs of volcanologists walking among the cooling lava near the peak of an active volcano. These physical reactions are not always pleasant, but they always indicate a submersion into the text. When, as Eric says to the right, you experience the world through the character's senses, you have truly escaped into the text.

> Visualizing sort of goes with connecting, because when you visualize a character and the character is hot, it makes you feel hot. So you sort of connect to the character by what they are experiencing. —Eric

- Setting Quilt (see this chapter, page 145)
- Character Quilt (see this chapter, page 142)

I visualize using an emotional reaction.

Our emotions are strongly tied to our memories and, therefore, intertwined with our connections. When readers are so engrossed in a text that they empathize with the characters or feel emotions tied to an event, they have reached a deeper, more personal level of comprehension. These vicarious feelings can run the gamut from the exhilaration of winning the Super Bowl to the heartfelt sorrow of losing a friend, but they always help readers more fully submerge in the text. The following activities can help you teach this component:

- Setting Quilt (see this chapter, page 145)
- Character Quilt (see this chapter, page 142)

I visualize using illustrations or text features in the text.

Illustrations and other text features, such as diagrams or maps, help readers visualize something that may be hard to comprehend otherwise. In a science text, for example, the concept of the water cycle is made clear by a simple diagram. Students can call on this diagram to imagine the cycle occurring as they watch rain fall or see clouds forming in the sky. In fantasy books, illustrators sometimes provide maps of the imaginary world to help readers get their bearings and visualize the different settings with greater ease.

Visualizing sometimes helps me picture different types of stars and planets like a picture of a Black Hole or planet. If I didn't know what the planets looked like, I'd be totally clueless of what's going on and what they're talking about, unless there was a picture to help me. —Eric

The best way to help students use this component is to use illustrations or diagrams from the texts you are reading in class. You might work with students one small group at a time and teach them how to look at a diagram and visualize exactly what it means. In the water cycle example, you could question students about times they have seen evidence of each stage of the cycle and allow them to pause and remember what it looks like. Remind them to think about the diagram the next time it rains or is foggy. You can refer back to the small-group work you did when talking about this component in other visualization lessons.

I visualize to help me remember.

Those strong mental images we create in tandem with authors remain burned in our memories forever. Remind students that they can use these impressions as a framework for remembering the text. On a more personal level, mental images help us remember what was important to us as we read, reminding us not only about what happened or what we learned but also about what moved us. Visualizing helps us draw conclusions, interpret the text, and recall significant events.

Visualizing can help you summarize because if you read a book and you start to visualize it, then you can tell what you saw in the book. You can play it like a movie [in your mind] and then you can remember. —Allie

- Draw to Remember Summaries (see page 151)
- Scene It! (see this chapter, page 145)
- Sketch to Stretch (see page 152)

Draw to Remember Summaries

Draw to Remember Summaries focuses on helping students remember longer, more complex texts. Each day as students read, ask them to record a drawing on the top of the flap (as they have done in other Draw to Remember activities) and write a short description of the most important idea or event in the text underneath each drawing. For homework or as an independent activity, students can write a formal paragraph on the inside of the flap summarizing what has been read thus far. When they have finished reading, they will have a visual and written record of the entire text. More importantly, these images will be cemented in memory because students took the time to flesh them out with a drawing, a description, and a summary (see Figure 48 student sample from *Hiroshima* [Yep, 1995]).

FIGURE 48
Draw to Remember Summaries—Student Sample

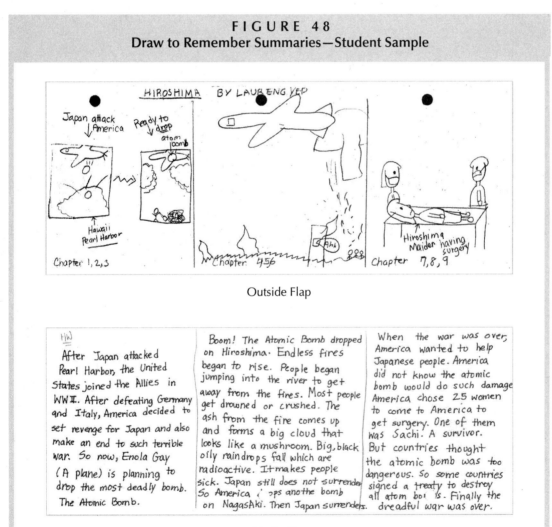

Outside Flap

Under Flap

Sketch to Stretch

This activity (Short, Harste, & Burke, 1996) is helpful to build listening comprehension as well as improving visualizing and summarizing. While you read or after you read a selection aloud, ask students to draw an image from the story that helps them remember what you have read. Students continue to add details as they listen to the story. Once students complete their sketches, they share them in pairs, discussing what they drew and why they drew that image. Then students come together as a whole group and share.

Self-Assessment and Goal-Setting

In addition to modeling your own visualization strategy use, designate several whole- and small-group sessions for students to read and tally when they visualize (see Figure 49 for a student sample). During most lessons, time is set aside for students to share the

FIGURE 49
Visualizing Tally Sheet—Student Sample

I visualize...	Tally
to help me predict.	II
to help me clarify something in the text.	IIII
the characters, person, or creatures.	IIII IIII
the events.	III
the setting or place.	IIII I
using my senses (smelling, tasting, hearing, or feeling).	IIII III
using a physical reaction (hot, cold, thirsty, upset stomach, etc.).	I
using an emotional reaction (happy, sad, excited, lonely, etc.).	II
using illustrations or text features in the text.	I
to help me remember.	IIII I

visualizing components they have used with the text being read. Text selection for visualizing is extremely important. In general, the more descriptive the text, the easier it is to visualize.

After collecting data over a few weeks, clean off the large laminated class tally chart that the class has been using to document strategy use for visualizing. As you read each component, ask students to look at their personal tally sheets and raise their hands if they have been using a component regularly. Count the hands and note the number on the chart next to the component. You can use this data to model how to choose a meaningful goal and how to make a plan to support growth in it. (See Figure 50 for a student sample and Appendix B, page 215, for a reproducible.)

After the self-assessment and goal-setting lesson it is helpful to have students practice using their plans with a short section of text or when reading independently. This

FIGURE 50
Thinking About My Reading: Visualizing—Student Sample

Name _____   Date _____

Directions: (1) Put a check mark by the things you do well as a reader when visualizing.
　　　　　 (2) Highlight the things you think you need to work on to become a better reader.

- ☐ I visualize to help me predict.
- ☐ I visualize to help me clarify something in the text.
- ☑ I visualize the characters, person, or creatures.
- ☑ I visualize the events.
- ☑ I visualize the setting or place.
- ☑ I visualize using my senses (smelling, tasting, hearing, or feeling).
- ☐ I visualize using a physical reaction (hot, cold, thirsty, upset stomach, etc.).
- ☐ I visualize using an emotional reaction (happy, sad, excited, lonely, etc.).
- ☑ I visualize using illustrations or text features in the text.
- ☑ I visualize to help me remember.

Choose one highlighted item to improve upon:

　I visualize to help me clarify something in the text.

Create a plan to improve upon this skill.
1. When I read and I get confused stop and reread.
2. A I reread use the author's words to picture what is happening.
3. Slow down my reading to see it.
4. Ask myself, does this make sense now.
　 If not, try again.

helps students work out any kinks in their plans and get on-the-spot practice and feedback. Help students find the types of texts they need and give them time to read and use their plans. Use this time to continue circulating the room and proofreading plans to identify students who need immediate help rewriting. Once students are done reading, ask them to share how they used their plans in a whole-class share.

Collect the plans and determine who may need to make further revisions. As we have recommended in previous units, you may next want to meet with students in small groups and have them practice using their plans with your guidance. During R^5 remind students to focus on using their plans and confer with them to continue supporting their use of visualizing. You may want to provide other opportunities for them to practice using their plans.

Final Thoughts

Visualizing as we read is one of life's great pleasures. It transports us to another time and place or even into another being. It is what brings us back to reading when we stray into other pastimes. What can be a better vacation from reality than escaping into the movies in your mind? In addition to motivating us to read, visualizing plays another important role: If we do it well, it helps us to more fully comprehend text. We visualize what is important to us and remember what we visualize. If we want our students to get the most out of what they read, then we must teach them how to do this, and to do this well.

In the next chapter, you'll learn how the MTF can assist you in effectively teaching summarizing to your students. Once again, activities to support students with their summarizing are described, as well as suggestions for explicit teaching.

CHAPTER 9

Summarizing

Three students are hard at work summarizing the cover story from a popular periodical. One is busy rephrasing the entire first section, sentence by sentence. Another lists every detail from the story in an almost random fashion. A third student summarizes each section of the text but fails to tie it all together with the main idea. These are just a few of the ineffective techniques we see intermediate learners use as they attempt the complex task of summarizing.

What Does It Mean to Summarize?

If we want students to do a better job summarizing, we must teach them that the process begins *before* they start reading. From predicting the main idea to pausing to remember as they read, to going back and eliminating unimportant details, students need to learn that a good summary isn't just written after reading. It is the culmination of reading and fully understanding a text. The quality of the summary is dependent upon the depth of a student's comprehension and his or her ability to communicate that understanding.

We have previously described summarization as the ability to glean the essence of the text and report on only the most essential parts (Keene & Zimmermann, 1997). Wormeli (2005) describes summarizing as restating the essence of the text in a new manner using as few words as possible. This can be done orally or in writing; artistically or dramatically; and individually, in pairs, or in small groups. Summarizing is different from retelling, in which students are expected to provide an in-depth account of the story—including most facts, events, and details—as they occurred in the text. Summarizing, conversely, is a succinct statement of the text's major points. One goal of this unit is for students to be able to understand the difference between a summary and a retelling. When teaching this strategy, we approach summarizing from its briefest form (such as a one-sentence summary) to a more in-depth synopsis that requires the main idea and supporting details. To summarize effectively, readers must understand what has been read and also what type of summary they are being asked to create.

The Importance of Summarizing

The National Reading Panel (NRP) identified summarization as one of seven types of instruction that has a solid scientific basis for improving comprehension in nonimpaired readers (National Institute of Child Health and Human Development, 2000). Marzano,

Pickering, and Pollock (2001) identify summarization as one of the top nine effective teaching strategies in the history of education. Summarization improves students' comprehension and their long-term memory (Wolfe, 2001). Yet according to Wormeli (2005) it is an underutilized teaching technique.

Teaching students to summarize can be challenging. First, students often have a hard time summarizing because they may not understand the text well enough, or they may not be adept at sifting through and assigning priority to the most significant and important ideas. Second, it takes a lot of time to teach children to summarize because it is a complex task that requires strong comprehension and higher-level thinking. Also, in order to teach summarizing, students have to have completed a reading. Third, teachers often find it less than exciting to teach students how to summarize because, frankly, who wants to rehash the text when you could move onto something new?

Problems With Student Summaries

If you were to generate a list of the difficulties your students have as they summarize, you would probably identify the following:

- They do not include what is important.
- They do not know what is important.
- They include too much information, retelling rather than summarizing.
- They do not include enough information.
- They copy the text, not knowing how to use "their own words."
- They leave out the main idea or supporting details.

The root of many of these issues is that students often don't take the time to fully comprehend what they have read before launching into writing. You can't effectively summarize what you don't understand.

How We Summarize and the Summarizing Components

Think about when you read and summarize something. The process you use and the degree to which you summarize depend upon the genre and your purpose for reading. After reading for pleasure, you might simply describe the book to someone you think would enjoy it. Or, if you read the newspaper in the morning, you might share something you read with a spouse, coworkers, or students. Usually this involves summarizing the text, but it is not an intentional process because you are merely eager to pass along some new information.

Summarizing in school is different from what we described above. Students are required to write summaries to help them learn and to demonstrate learning. It is important to teach children to summarize a variety of texts for a variety of purposes and to offer different strategies to aid them. The genre being read and the purpose for summarizing influence both the approach and the outcome.

For example, expert summarizers of nonfiction might look at the title and sub-headings and think about what they are going to read. Or, they might read the text features to orient themselves to the text. While reading, they identify the main idea, often found in the topic sentence, and look for supporting details, perhaps by using a highlighter or sticky notes to remember the information later. After reading, they think about what they read to determine what will go in their summary. If they need to clarify, strong summarizers reread the text. When writing, they delete unnecessary or redundant information, reword the remaining information, and include only the most important ideas and vocabulary.

In another example, when processing narrative text, a good summarizer might use the title, chapter headings, or front and back cover to predict what will happen in the story. Understanding narrative text structure, the reader expects each chapter to build upon the next as the author crafts the problem and solution. When they are finished reading, good summarizers might share the gist of the story with a peer, parent, or teacher. Sometimes students are required to do a formal summary in the form of a book report. Typically, these summaries are given in narrative form.

Summarizing is not an easy task because the reader is required to complete multiple steps to have a successful product. It takes a lot of cognitive effort. Marzano and colleagues (2001) explain the cognitive complexity behind summarizing:

1. To effectively summarize, students must delete information, substitute information, and keep some information.
2. For students to effectively delete, substitute, and keep information, they must analyze the information at a deep level.
3. For aid in summarizing, students must be aware of the structure of text.

Wormeli (2005) writes, "The big secrets of how to summarize are not secrets at all. Students must be tenacious, must learn multiple methods of summarizing, must practice, and must be inclined to revise their thinking as perspective and information warrant" (p. 8). In other words, summarizing requires the reader to cognitively engage with the text many times on various levels and is often text dependent. As we researched and reflected on summarizing, we identified several components. As we worked with our students, we revised our list of components to create the Summarizing Tally Sheet (see Appendix B, page 216). The following statements are the summarizing components.

To help me summarize:

• I read the text features and predict the main idea.
• I reflect on my prediction and either confirm or revise it.
• I read the text features and think how they relate to the main idea.
• I notice bold and italic words and think how they relate to the main idea.
• I read subheadings and titles and think how they relate to the main idea.

- I identify a section of text that I can read and remember.
- I stop at the end of a section of text to connect, visualize, or remember what I've read.
- I answer questions I have asked.
- I reread to verify important ideas.
- I reread to clarify meaning.
- I reread to choose supporting details and facts.
- I eliminate unimportant details.

Summarizing and the Metacognitive Teaching Framework

Summarizing is not a new skill for intermediate and older students. It will have been introduced and reinforced many times before they enter our classroom, and they will surely have done some form of summarizing in our classroom before we begin the formal unit. In fact, the structure of Read, Relax, Reflect, Respond, and Rap (R[5]) leads students to orally summarize their reading each time they engage in the Reflect, Respond, and Rap portions. Also, when students confer with the teacher they are asked to give a quick summary of the story they are reading, and the other strategy units include summarizing as a component. For example, students may ask and then answer questions to help them summarize what they have read. Although most students are able to define the goals of summarizing, they still need lots of support to achieve those goals.

We begin teaching summarizing with the very first metacognitive unit, prediction. As we stated earlier, the first step in summarizing is to fully understand what is being read. Students must predict the main idea before they begin reading, then confirm or revise that prediction as they read. Strategies such as questioning, connecting, and visualizing lead to the depth of understanding a student must reach before being able to capture the essence of the text. The direct and explicit strategies presented in this chapter will help all students use effective summarizing strategies from the moment they pick up a piece of text and begin predicting, to the moment they put down their pencils after writing a summary.

Explicit Instruction of Summarizing

By this time our students have experienced the Metacognitive Teaching Framework (MTF) and they are familiar with the think-aloud structure of introducing a new strategy and its components; thus we are able to present more content during one lesson.

To launch the summarizing unit, choose a text. Nicki chose a children's newspaper article tied to the social studies curriculum. Prior to the lesson with students, read the text and mark with sticky notes the places in the text where you want to share in your think-aloud particular components of summarizing.

It may be helpful to break your modeling of the summarizing components into two separate sessions. In the first session, model and give examples of each of the summarizing components. In the second session, model your thinking as you apply each component to help you summarize a text. Again, use the method of think-aloud to demonstrate your use of the summarizing components as you process a text. Each student will have a blank summarizing tally sheet, and there should be a class tally sheet on a full-size poster at the front of the room. It's also helpful for students to have their own copy of the text to follow as you read and explain your thinking during the second . session.

Explaining and Defining Components of Summarizing

Before launching this think-aloud, ask students to silently read through each of the summarizing components on the tally sheet. Then facilitate a whole-class discussion of each component, providing students with meaningful examples of how to use each component and eliciting examples from students for those components you feel they may not understand. In the transcript from Nicki's classroom that follows, you will notice that some components are discussed more than others. This will differ with the age and background knowledge of your students.

Noticing and Applying Components of Summarizing With a Text

Read the text aloud and pause at predetermined points to demonstrate the use of components and mark them on the class tally chart. One student should serve as the tally recorder during this phase of the lesson. Call on students to identify the component or components you use, and ask the student volunteer to mark the class chart accordingly. In the transcript that follows, you can see how Nicki gets the students to recognize her component use.

Teacher:	[Reading the text] "This week, British Florida; Florida goes to England." I don't think that means Florida is going to England. I think it means that England is going to take over Florida. What am I using?
Hayden:	To help me summarize I read the text features and predict the main idea.
Teacher:	Right. [Reading the newspaper deck, the bit of text below the headline] "Well, who's going to colonize Florida this week? Last week, the French and Spanish competed for that privilege. Each of those countries had a chance to be in charge of our great state for awhile. This week, the eyes of merry old England are turned to the Florida beaches!" I am going to confirm that Florida is going to be taken over by England. What am I using?
Ciara:	To help me summarize I reflect on my prediction and either confirm it or revise it.
Teacher:	Yes. Now, the title, "The British Are Coming!" I think The British are trying to take over Florida. What am I using?
Elsita:	To help me summarize I read the title or subheading and think about how they will relate to the main idea.

Teacher:	[Reading the photo caption] "The British wanted their backyard to include all of the New World." What am I using?
Lisa:	Read subheadings to summarize?
Teacher:	Is this a subheading? What is it?
Lisa:	A text feature.
Teacher:	What else am I using?
Reid:	Confirming your prediction?
Teacher:	Exactly. When I read the bolded word **persecution**, I think this is why the British came to America. What am I using?
Barry:	Noticing bolded vocabulary.
Teacher:	Yes. [Reading the text] "The French came to Florida to escape religious persecution." Oh. It's not just going to tell me that the British are coming but it might also tell me why. What am I using?
Lisa:	To reflect and revise prediction.
Teacher:	Yes! "The Spanish came to kick out the French." I need to stop here and picture this, the French came, then the Spanish. What am I using?
Gabbi:	Stop at the end to visualize.
Teacher:	What else?
Gabbi:	Identify a section of text I can read and remember?
Teacher:	Exactly. "Next came the English. What on Earth did England possibly want with Florida?" Aha! I'm right. What am I using?
Hayden:	Confirming a prediction.

Refining Strategy Use: Activities for Teaching Summarizing

We remember best what we experience first in a lesson and what we do last (Sousa, 2004). This is especially true with teaching summarizing. You need to introduce summarizing thoroughly, revealing to students what they are going to learn, then conclude by revisiting what they've learned through further reflection and recap.

Although it is not realistic to formally summarize every reading, it is important during this unit to focus many student readings on this strategy, especially during content area reading and guided reading lessons. Students should mark personal component use on their individual tally sheets while reading, which helps them identify which components they use frequently and which areas they would like to strengthen. In addition, providing real-world situations in which summarizing is important—such as reading newspaper articles, interpreting memos, restating video and board game directions, and making sense of technical manuals—will go far to make learning more meaningful.

Now that you have introduced the components of summarizing, it is time to roll up your sleeves and help students recognize and practice the components and assimilate them into their repertoire of reading tools. We've begun the activities below with the Summarizing Rubric, because you will want to introduce this early in the unit and refer to it often. Then we've organized the activities under the strategy components they help teach, and many fit in more than one place. Several activities have been described in previous chapters, while others are specific to this unit. Some of the activities that are in earlier chapters only require the emphasis to be shifted to the specific summarizing component being taught.

Summarizing Rubric

The summarizing rubric can be used throughout the unit as the evaluation tool for students' summaries (see Figure 51 and Appendix B, page 217, for a reproducible form). After you have launched the summarization unit you will want to introduce this rubric to students. It's helpful to begin by going over the three categories: Completeness, Correctness, and Quality of Writing. Next, review with students the Advanced level column and discuss the expectations for each category. Finally, ask students to evaluate a summary they have previously written or to write a new summary, making sure they exhibit the qualities described in the rubric. As students become more familiar with this evaluative tool, they should use it to help them write, revise, and assess their own summaries.

FIGURE 51
Summarizing Rubric

Name: _____

CATEGORY	Intervention (D)	Instructional (C)	Independent (B)	Advanced (A)
Completeness	Included 1 or 2 facts, may include extra unimportant information	Partial summary with some important ideas, a few facts, may include extra unimportant information	Adequate summary with many important ideas, some details, facts, and important vocabulary	Adept summary with most important ideas, details, facts, and important vocabulary
Correctness	Main idea is not expressed; it may include incorrect information	Main idea is partially expressed; it may include misinterpretation	Main idea is expressed; all facts included are correct	Main idea is clearly expressed; all facts included are correct
Quality of Writing	Written in own language or in copied text	Generally written in own language, may be presented as a list of disconnected ideas	Written in own language, generally flows from one idea to another	Written in own language, flows smoothly from one idea to another

I read the text features and predict the main idea.

We have students begin by predicting the main idea even before reading the text. They learn to look at the title, front and back covers, and graphic features of a text before they read to help forecast the main idea. This way, students are able to look at each new piece of information critically and decide if and how it fits into their overall comprehension. Students know that these early predictions may change as they read more. Other structures we use to orient students to the main idea include the following:

- Anticipation Guide (see chapter 5, page 86)
- Text Feature Walk (see chapter 2, page 40)
- Word Alert! (see chapter 5, page 91)
- Concept-Definition Sort (see below)
- Previewing, Predicting, and Learning From Text Features (see chapter 2, page 38)

Concept-Definition Sort

This activity, which asks students to match concepts with definitions, can help front-load concepts to be learned (Shwartz & Raphael, 1985). This activity can also be done in conjunction with the word splash lesson described later in this chapter. A concept-definition sort can help students clarify any words prior to the reading to enhance comprehension. As a stand-alone activity a concept-definition sort builds background knowledge and helps students make connections.

First, you must choose the important concepts that will be covered in the reading (see Figure 52) and write the concepts and definitions on separate slips of paper. Students, working in pairs or small groups, then discuss each concept and what they think they know about each. Then students read each definition and match it to the concept that they think goes with it.

FIGURE 52
Concept-Definition Sort for American Revolution

Debt	Money owed to another.
Tax	Money that the government collects from people.
Boycott	Refusing to buy or do something.
Patriots	Colonist soldiers who fought against British rule.
Loyalists	Colonists who supported the British.
Independence	Freedom.
Revolution	A sudden change in government.

Next, students read the text, looking for how the words connect to the main idea. After reading, they write a summary using all of the words from the concept sort. This can be done in pairs or individually.

I reflect on my prediction and either confirm or revise it.

In the prediction unit we taught students that they should revise or confirm their predictions as they read. This component reminds students that it is important to use this process on their main idea predictions as they read to help with summarizing, as well. If they do not revise incorrect predictions of the main idea as they read, their summaries will be inaccurate. An activity such as creating a prediction chart can help reinforce this component, as can all the previously mentioned summarizing activities.

I read the text features and think how they relate to the main idea.

Students should know that they continue to gain knowledge about the main idea the entire time they are reading. All text features in a well-crafted piece should serve to shed light on the central idea. Although you can acknowledge to students that this is not always so, you can guide them to focus on how all the pieces fit together. It is also important to choose very carefully the texts you ask students to summarize. Look for those in which the text features support the main idea, rather than illuminating a loosely related detail. As students become more proficient, you can choose texts less carefully and use those pieces that don't conform to launch teachable moments on what to do when you have to summarize an awkward selection. Activities you may want to use to teach this component include the following:

- Text Feature Walk (see chapter 2, page 40)
- Previewing, Predicting, and Learning From Text Features (see chapter 2, page 38)

I notice boldface and italic words and think how they relate to the main idea.

Knowing which words are critical to a text is a key component in comprehension. Students need to be aware of words that the author identifies as important, as well as be able to identify important words on their own. Students should also know that a strong summary should include the text's critical vocabulary. You can use the following activities to teach this component:

- Anticipation Guide Extension (see chapter 8, page 140)
- Word Splash (see page 163)
- Word Alert! Extension (see page 165)
- Knowledge Rating Scale (see page 165)
- Text Feature Walk (see chapter 2, page 40)
- Concept-Definition Sort (see this chapter, page 162)

Word Splash

For the word splash (see Figure 53) you will preselect vocabulary important to the text, including bold and italicized words. Students might be familiar with some, but not all, of the words. Arrange the words randomly ("splashed") on paper or a transparency and show to students. Help them read the words aloud, then ask them to predict what the piece they are about to read will be about. Encourage students to use these words in their predictions so that they develop an understanding of the words over the course of the discussion. Next, ask students to write a prediction summary of the text they are going to read using the words from the word splash. Students share their prediction summaries in pairs or in small groups.

After reading the text, students revisit their prediction summary and rewrite the summaries to reflect their understanding of the most important ideas in the text. They are often amazed at how close their original summaries come to the actual text.

FIGURE 53
Word Splash Example for American Revolution

Patriots
Loyalists
tax
revolution
boycott
debt
independence

Word Alert! Extension

We first introduced the Word Alert! in chapter 5 and have recommended it as an activity you can do for most of the strategy units. To use it with summarizing, students complete the first three columns of this think sheet. Afterward, ask students to write a predictive summary of what they think they are going to read and learn about (see Figure 54 for a student sample and Appendix B, page 201, for a reproducible). This activity is especially effective with content area studies. After reading and completing the last column of the Word Alert! chart students revisit their predictive summary. At this point you could have students edit their existing summary or rewrite it completely.

Knowledge Rating Scale

Similar to Word Splash, in this activity (adapted from Blachowicz & Fisher, 2006) you will preselect vocabulary words that are important to understanding the text, including bold and italicized words. Put the words in the first column on the Knowledge Rating Scale form (see Appendix B, page 218, for a reproducible) and photocopy it for each student. In the remaining columns, students will self-assess their knowledge of each word by indicating that they know it, have heard of it, or don't know it. The last column, "Why is it important?" is filled in after the reading. This column is specific to the content and desired knowledge. This activity causes students to pay attention to the vocabulary presented and gives them a purpose for the reading. Once they have filled in the last column, students can write a summary using the words from the knowledge rating form.

I read subheadings and titles and think how they relate to the main idea.

The titles and subheadings in a well-written piece should be a minisummary on their own. Again, not all text that you ask children to read will fit these criteria. Sometimes students will have to investigate and determine why a clever author titled a piece or section in a particular way. It is important for students to understand that the author chose to include and group information together for a reason and that the information in a section usually relates to the main idea in a similar way. The following activities can help make this point:

- Write a Better Heading (see below)
- Text Feature Walk (see chapter 2, page 40)

Write a Better Heading

In a perfect teaching world, all titles and section headings would clearly indicate what a text is about. We could simply teach students that the title and headings can always be used to make a skeleton summary. But because we use a variety of texts to engage our students, these access features are sometimes less than clear. One periodical we have

FIGURE 54
Word Alert! Extension and Predictive Summary About Rocks and Minerals—Student Sample

Title of Book **Rocks and Minerals**

Date 5/8/06

Name _____

Passage Critical Words	Is the word known? Y/N	How do I know the word? Definition/uses.	Check and highlight if unknown	Confirmation Definition Text evidence (page numbers)
mineral	Y	Some sort of vidimins.		a solid material that has the same repeating pattern or crystal C34
streak	Y	a wavy line.		the powder that is left behind when you rub it against a streakplate. C35
hardness	Y	How hard something is.		How good a mineral can resist a scratch. C35
luster	N		✓	The Luster is the reflection of the light on a mineral.
rock	Y	A hard form of Earth.		a rock is made up of one or more mineral. C40
igneous rock	N		✓	igneous rocks are formed when lava dries from a volcano eruption. C40
sedimentary rock	Y	Rock that can get eroded.		a sedimentary rock is formed when sediment is stuck together. C42
metamorphic rock	Y	Hard gems.		metamorphic rocks are formed when heat or pressure sticks rocks together.

Front Page

I think that the section of text is going to be about all different kinds of rocks and minerals. Also about how some might have streaks going through them, or the hardness of the rocks. What luster has to do with rocks. It also might talk about the different forms of rock like igneous, sedimentary, and metamorphic. Maybe it will talk about some rock formations that were formed by erosion. It also might talk about how the rock cycle forms rocks and how the weathering effects rocks.

Back Page

166

FIGURE 55
Write a Better Heading—Student Sample

Write a Better Heading: Aiding Summarization
Florida's Role in the American Revolution

Directions: Below are the sub-headings used by the author. Read each section of the text. After reading each section of the text write a better heading that gives the main idea.

Florida's Growing Up!

Lucky Pioneers Get Free land from England

Governor James Grant Gets Along With American Indians

Timbuc van indians are Peacful People

God, Save the King!

Florida loyal to the British

Patrick Tonyn—A Not-So-Nice Guy

Patrick Tonyon takes Grants office

Oh No! British Troops in Florida!

Non British People locked up.

The Spanish Are Always Getting Involved...When It Comes to Florida

Spain kicks out the British

The Outcome of the American Revolutionary War

British loyalists leave Florida

---

used with students is *Florida Studies Weekly*, which uses a newspaper format to teach students about their state. Using a periodical provides a way to step out of the textbook and teach important content as well as familiarize students with the newspaper genre. Unfortunately, the headings for each section tend to be ambiguous at best. We use this as an opportunity for students to write their own headings for the articles, effectively summarizing each piece.

Instruct students to predict what a newspaper, magazine, or textbook article is about, based on the headline or title and section headings. Next, they read a section at a time and rewrite the section's heading to be more direct and clear. Students share their new headings at the end of the session.

Another variation is to give students a copy of an article or section of text with the headings removed. Have students read, then write, headings that effectively summarize each section (see Figure 55 for a student sample).

I identify a section of text that I can read and remember.

Student learning is enhanced when the text is broken up into manageable chunks while reading (Wormeli, 2005). This is not always second nature. You must show students how to identify a portion of text they can read and remember, then have them practice as they read. The trick with this skill is reminding kids that the size of the chunk depends on the difficulty and complexity of the piece being read, as well as their interest in the topic. For instance, students might be able to read and remember an entire chapter of a self-selected fictional narrative because it interests them and because they're familiar with the genre, but only a few sentences from a section of their science textbook because the subject matter is not interesting. You can share examples from your own reading to substantiate this point. You could compare your experiences of reading a book for pleasure as compared with reading the manual that came with your new digital camcorder.

Students need to practice identifying how much of a text they can read before they need to pause and remember, also referred to as chunking text. They also need to know that it is not unusual for readers to forget when they read large chunks of difficult text—good readers use strategies, such as chunking and remembering text, to help make sense of it all. You can reinforce these ideas in whole-group and small-group lessons as well as reading conferences. Some of the activities to use to teach students to chunk text include the following:

- Chunking and Rereading Text (see below)
- Write a Better Heading (see this chapter, page 165)

Chunking and Rereading Text

This activity will require more modeling than the other activities in this chapter, but it is worth the extra time because it scaffolds the type of reading and summarizing students will most often do in secondary classrooms and beyond. Students use the Chunking and Rereading Text Think Sheet (see Appendix B, page 219, for a reproducible) as a note taking sheet, stopping after each page and reflecting on what they read to determine the big idea. They then write a sentence or two to capture their thinking. This continues throughout the reading until they are finished. What students are left with is a page of notes that contains the essence of the text. They use these notes to write a summary. This activity is especially helpful with textbook reading.

I stop at the end of a section of text to connect, visualize, or remember what I've read.

One problem we see in many young readers is that they don't remember what they have read, even right after they complete a piece. Stopping to connect, visualize, and re-member what's been read goes hand in hand with the previous component, identifying a piece of text that they can read and re-member. After students are able to identify a reasonable section of text that they can read and remember, they should stop and write a one-sentence summary in their own words. This is a good time, as well, to stop and visualize or connect what they are reading to a prior experience or another text. Teach students that this strategy is one way readers recall what they have read. It isn't something that occurs spontaneously at first, it must be practiced, but when students try to summarize what they have read, they will notice that they better understand and remember what they have read. The following activities may be helpful:

- Chunking and Rereading Text (see page 168)
- One-Sentence Summaries (see below)
- Write a Better Heading (see this chapter, page 165)
- Draw to Remember (see chapter 8, pages 144, 145, 151)

One-Sentence Summaries

From the beginning, we tell students that there are different levels of summarization. For example, they may be asked to give a thorough summary with the main idea and all the supporting details, or they may be asked to give a two-word summary that conveys the essence of the text. One-sentence summaries fall somewhere between the two extremes, and is just as it sounds: Ask students to summarize the main idea and any vital details in just one sentence. It is important to model this strategy, however, so you don't end up with a stack of three-paragraph, run-on sentences.

I answer questions I have asked.

The strategy of questioning is valuable only if we attempt to answer those questions as we read. Pausing to answer and rework the questions readers generate will help create deeper understanding, sustain interest, and ensure recall of important ideas. We want students to get in the habit of asking good questions, then searching for the answers as they read. The Questioning My Textbook activity (see chapter 7, page 126) may help reinforce this strategy component.

> Summarizing helps me with questioning because if I am asking a question and I find the answer in the book I might include it in my summary. —Andrea

I reread to verify important ideas.

You need to teach students the importance of checking their facts before committing their summaries to paper. Just like a reporter or editor ensures that all the information in a published work correctly conveys the topic, students must double-check to make sure they have highlighted the most important information. Remind students that a summary should not include any unimportant or incorrect facts, as this is a reflection of poor comprehension. The Summarizing Rubric (see page 161) can help reinforce this component.

I reread to clarify.

The difference between rereading to verify important ideas and rereading to clarify is subtle but important. Students reread to clarify when something they read just doesn't make sense. It can be anything from a word read incorrectly or omitted to an entire concept that has been misunderstood. When they reread to verify important ideas, on the other hand, students are gathering their thoughts for a summary, deciding which facts are important to include and which can be left out without losing the author's intended message. We've all seen students who, in the heat of the exercise, jump to some pretty wild conclusions based on a glimpse of a text feature or a single misread word. Sometimes these misconceptions rear their ugly heads in the summaries students write. Students need to double-check any facts that don't fit with the main idea or that seem a little odd, and referring to the Summarizing Rubric (see page 161) can help with clarifying.

I reread to choose supporting details and facts.

As students read, they should be mindful of the predicted main idea at all times. This awareness will help them read critically and understand why the author included each section of text. This will make the job of choosing supporting details and facts much easier. The test of whether a supporting detail should be included is simply answering the question "Could you fully understand the main idea without it?" You can scaffold this process as you model summary writing with the Question-and-Answer Book Writing activity that follows.

> Summarizing gets you to remember the important facts and details because you have to pick them to write your summary. —Bryce

Question-and-Answer Book Writing

After students have done an Expository Text Investigation (see chapter 5 and Appendix B, page 203) on question-and-answer (Q-and-A) books, they should be familiar with this type of text. Having them produce their own Q-and-A books that summarize a section of text is a great way to hone students' summarizing skills. It also reinforces what students know about text features and the organizational pattern of these types of books. Students must make use of content-critical vocabulary and carefully select the details they want to use.

For this writing assignment, students will first critically read a section of text that you want them to summarize. They should use all of their summarizing strategies before and during reading, and have a strong grasp of the content covered. Give students Q-and-A Planning Sheets (see Figure 56 for a student sample and Appendix B, page 220, for a reproducible) and instruct them to think of four big questions that were answered when they read. (Although this is an independent activity, depending on the level of scaffolding needed, you may have students generate a class list of big questions and allow them to choose from the list.) It is important to make sure students write questions that will allow them to effectively summarize the text, such as those focused on the main idea or important supporting details. Also, remind them that authors of Q-and-A books go beyond simply answering each question. Q-and-A book authors use each question as a heading for a broad category of related information. So, the questions students choose must be big enough to support a strong, paragraph-length answer.

After they write their questions, instruct students to choose carefully the vocabulary words they will include in their books. These words should go along with their selected questions and must be important to the main idea of the text. Students will then write four facts or details they want to include under each question and list a couple of possible text features to include on each page.

FIGURE 56
Q-and-A Planning Sheet—Student Sample

Topic or Title _The Earliest Floridians_   Name _____

Important vocabulary:

glacier, nomad, artifact, acheaogist , extinct, Ice age

Question 1:   What is a nomad?

Possible text features for Question 1: _picture and caption, timeline_

Fact 1: A nomad is a person who travels from place to place.

Fact 2: Nomads follow herds of animals so they can hunt them.

Fact 3: The people who came to North America the earliest were probably nomads.

Fact 4: Nomads might have also gathered plants to eat.

Question 2: What is a glaccier?

Possible text features for Question 2: Picture and caption map

Fact 1: A big, slow moving block of ice is a glacier.

Fact 2: During the last Ice age, glaciers covered a lot of the land.

Fact 3: With all the water in the glaciers, the water level dropped

Fact 4: When the water level dropped, a strip of dry land connected Russia and Alaska, which is probably how early floridians came here.

Question 3: What happened to the species of large animals long ago?

Possible text features for Question 3: _____

Fact 1: The large animals, like the mammoths, died out probably because of the the change of climate.

Fact 2: They also might have died out from being hunted

Fact 3: And their loss of habitat

Fact 4: Because of this, The early floridians had to hunt smaller animals

Question 4: What are Artifacts?

Possible text features for Question 4: picture and caption

Fact 1: Artifacts are any object made by a person long ago.

Fact 2: We know about the earliest Floridians by the artifacts they left behind.

Fact 3: Archaeologists find different things like hammers made of ribs and atlatls.

Fact 4: The early floridian had no written lauguage, so they could write stories to tell about their life.

After rereading their planning sheets and eliminating unimportant details, students can write a rough draft of their book. Final drafts must include a title, table of contents, glossary, and 7–10 text features. Students can refer to the Q-and-A Book Project Rubric for help (see Figure 57 and Appendix B, page 221). When students have completed their books, you can rest assured that they will have a much greater understanding of what was read, the structure of Q-and-A books, and nonfiction text features. Figure 58 shows an example of a student's Q-and-A book.

I eliminate unimportant details.

Before students turn in or share a summary, they should always go back over it to make sure all details are vital to the full understanding of the piece. Anything extraneous should be left out. Modeling is an effective way to teach students to eliminate nonessential information from their summaries. After reading a shared text while using other summarizing components (such as *Reading the Text Features and Predicting the Main Idea* and *Stopping at the End of a Section of Text to Connect, Visualize, and Remember What I've Read*) give students a copy of a summary you have prepared for the lesson. When you write the summary, be sure to include several extra, unimportant details. Have students work in pairs to highlight the details they identify as unimportant. Ask students to share and defend their deletions during a whole-class discussion. Using student suggestions, revise the summary together by removing unimportant details. Other activities that give students an opportunity to practice this skill include the following:

> I summarize when there is a special event and then I eliminate any bad facts and keep the good ones because the bad ones are not important. —Marshall

- Question-and-Answer Book Writing (see this chapter, page 170)
- Summarizing Rubric (see this chapter, page 161)

Self-Assessment and Goal-Setting

At this point in most of the other metacognitive units, students would be guided to record their strategy use on tally sheets during whole- and small-group lessons. Because we don't do formal summaries of students' self-selected reading, it is important to set aside time and provide appropriate materials for using the summarizing components. We like to use student periodicals (such as *Weekly Reader*) that address topics with which students are familiar. You could also have students read and summarize excerpts from their science or social studies textbooks while tallying the summarizing strategies they use. We set aside time at the end of these sessions for students to share the strategies they have used with this specific text.

After a few data gathering sessions, you can clean off the large class tally sheet and use it to collect class data on strategy use. Read each component and have students look at their own tally sheets to assess which components they have been using over the course of the unit. Then, with the help of a volunteer, tally the number of students who have been using each component regularly.

FIGURE 57
Q-and-A Book Project Rubric

Teacher Name:	_____			
Student Name:	_____			

CATEGORY	1	2	3	4
Content	Most of the material is not on topic or accurate. Answers have 1 fact and very little of the information necessary to understand the topic.	Some of the material is on topic and accurate. Answers have 2 facts and some of the information necessary to understand the topic.	Material is mostly on topic and accurate. Answers have at least 3 facts and all the information necessary to understand the topic.	Material is on topic and accurate. Answers have at least 4 facts and all the information necessary to understand the topic.
Format	The text is formatted with at least 1 question and answer. Questions are written correctly.	The text is formatted with at least 2 questions and answers. Questions are written correctly.	The text is formatted with at least 3 questions and answers. Questions are written correctly.	The text is formatted with at least 4 questions and answers. Questions are written correctly.
Text Features	There are at least 7 text features included. These features support the text and help the reader understand the answer. There is a title, a table of contents, and a glossary.	There are at least 8 text features included. These features support the text and help the reader understand the answers. There is a title, a table of contents, and a glossary.	There are at least 9 text features included. These features support the text and help the reader understand the answers. There is a title, a table of contents, and a glossary.	There are at least 10 text features included. These features support the text and help the reader understand the answer. There is a title, a table of contents, and a glossary.
Quality	Strong questions are not written. There are many errors in handwriting, grammar, spelling, and punctuation. The text features are not well done.	Some strong questions are written. There are some errors in handwriting, grammar, spelling, and punctuation. Some of the text features are well done.	Mostly strong questions are written. There are a few errors in handwriting, grammar, spelling, and punctuation. The text features are mostly well done.	Strong questions are written. The handwriting is legible, and correct grammar, spelling, and punctuation are used. The text features are well done.

F I G U R E   5 8
Q-and-A Book—Student Sample

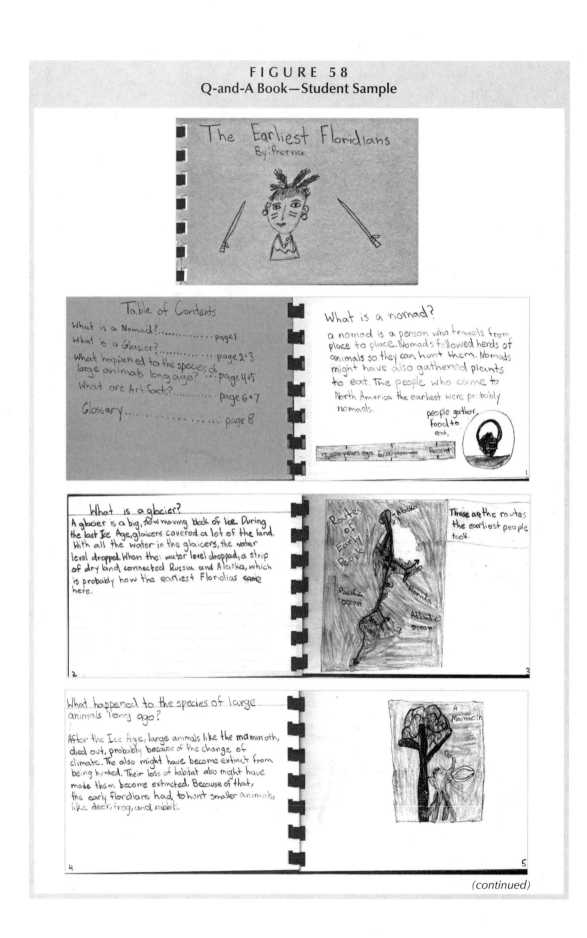

The Earliest Floridians
By: Prerna

Table of Contents

What is a nomad?

a nomad is a person who travels from place to place. Nomads followed herds of animals so they can hunt them. Nomads might have also gathered plants to eat. The people who came to North America the earliest were probably nomads.

people gather food to eat.

12,000 years ago   6,000 years ago   Present

What is a glacier?

A glacier is a big, slow moving block of ice. During the last Ice Age, glaciers covered a lot of the land. With all the water in the glaciers, the water level dropped. When the water level dropped, a strip of dry land connected Russia and Alaska, which is probably how the earliest Floridians came here.

Routes of Early People
Alaska
Pacific ocean
Florida
Atlantic ocean

These are the routes the earliest people took.

What happened to the species of large animals long ago?

After the Ice Age, large animals like the mammoth, died out, probably because of the change of climate. The also might have become extinct from being hunted. Their loss of habitat also might have made them become extincted. Because of that, the early floridians had to hunt smaller animals, like deer, frog, and rabbit.

A Mammoth

(continued)

FIGURE 58

Q-and-A Book—Student Sample (continued)

What are artifacts?

Artifacts are any object made by a person from long ago. The early Floridians had no written language, which means they couldn't write stories about their life. So we know about the earliest Floridians by the artifacts they left behind. Archaeologists find different things that help them learn about the earliest Floridians.

A Fish hook

6

Spear points

Atlatls helped hunters throw spears farther.

7

Glossary

Archaeologist - A person who studies artifact to about life long ago.
Artifact - a object made by a person long ago.
extinct - died out
glacier - a big, slow moving, block of ice.
nomad - a person who travels from place to place

8

Use this class data to model self-assessment and goal-setting. Then have students mimic your process with the Summarizing Tally Sheet and Thinking About My Reading: Summarizing—Self-Assessment and Goal-Setting Sheet to develop their own plans relevant to their data and needs. (See Figures 59 and 60 for student samples, and Appendix B, pages 216 and 222, for reproducibles.)

A good follow-up to the self-assessment and goal-setting lesson is to have students immediately use their plans with a short section of text. This way they can work out any kinks in their plans and get immediate practice while they are fresh in their minds. It also gives you time to circulate and skim through plans to identify any students who need help revising their plans and goals. Supply students with a text that lends itself to summarizing (such as a selection from a periodical or textbook), and give students time to read and use their summarizing plans. Remind them to really work their plan as they read the piece in order to fully understand what they read. After students are done reading and writing summaries, have them share with the class their summaries and how they used their plans. One note: Many times we ask students to summarize the books they read for literature circles when a unit is completed. You may want to focus

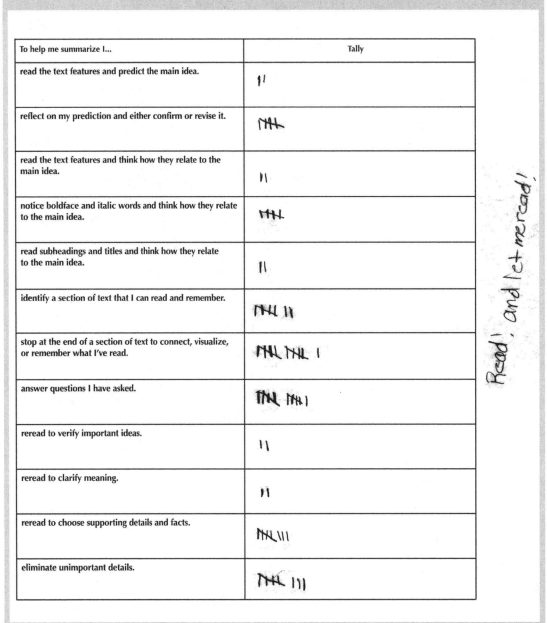

FIGURE 59
Summarizing Tally Sheet—Student Sample

To help me summarize I...	Tally
read the text features and predict the main idea.	1 I
reflect on my prediction and either confirm or revise it.	IIII
read the text features and think how they relate to the main idea.	I I
notice boldface and italic words and think how they relate to the main idea.	IIII
read subheadings and titles and think how they relate to the main idea.	II
identify a section of text that I can read and remember.	IIII II
stop at the end of a section of text to connect, visualize, or remember what I've read.	IIII IIII I
answer questions I have asked.	IIII IIII I
reread to verify important ideas.	II
reread to clarify meaning.	II
reread to choose supporting details and facts.	IIII III
eliminate unimportant details.	IIII III

Read! and let me read!

your choice on reading in literature circles rather than R[5] toward the end of this unit to provide more opportunities for summarizing practice.

Be sure to gather the plans and read through them so you can help those students who may need to make revisions. It also helps to meet with students in small groups and have them practice using their plans under your watchful eye. Again, have students share how they used their plans to help them summarize.

Name _____   Date _4/6/06_____

Directions: (1) Put a check mark by the things you do well as a reader when summarizing.
           (2) Highlight the things you think you need to work on to become a better reader.

- ☑ I read the text features and predict the main idea.
- ☑ I reflect on my prediction and either confirm or revise it.
- ☑ I read the text features and think how they relate to the main idea.
- ☑ I notice boldface and italic words and think how they relate to the main idea.
- ☐ I read subheadings and titles and think how they relate to the main idea.
- ☑ I identify a section of text that I can read and remember.
- ☑ I stop at the end of a section of text to connect, visualize, or remember what I've read.
- ☑ I answer questions I have asked.
- ☐ I reread to verify important ideas.
- ☑ I reread to clarify meaning.
- ☑ I reread to choose supporting details and facts.
- ☑ I eliminate unimportant details.

Choose one highlighted item to improve upon:

I reread to verify important ideas

Create a plan to improve upon this skill.

1. _Read any kind of text._
2. _Then write down on a post it what I thought was important_
3. _If something seems important to the story then go back and read it again_

Read ahead and find out if it is important to the main idea or plot.

Final Thoughts

We couldn't have said it better ourselves! We want kids to engage when they read, and summarizing ensures that they do. Our readers must tap into all of their reading strategies so they fully understand what is being read, then look back and evaluate as they write a summary. Summarizing helps students understand and remember what was important as well as assimilate new learning. Without the ability to effectively summarize, students are left thinking that comprehension is an all-or-nothing proposition—you either understand and remember everything you read, or you are left with just a few random ideas that don't serve much purpose. Being able to summarize (both in school and in life) serves us well as we encounter increasingly more complex texts and staggering amounts of information.

> Summarizing helps you remember, and it actually tests whether you're paying attention. You can't summarize something that you are just reading to get it over with. —Tyler

EPILOGUE

Teaching students how to use reading strategies is not enough. If we want our instructional time to be fruitful, we must teach and support students from the introduction of a strategy through to independence. The Metacognitive Teaching Framework (MTF) ensures that we do this. Just like the aspiring weavers of long ago who were apprenticed by master weavers, our students rely on the careful guidance and watchful eye of an expert reader to help them reach their reading potential. By breaking down each strategy and supporting our students as they assimilate these new skills—including their first faltering steps with independent use—we effectively change apprentices into masters. The focus on discussion helps make thinking more visible and allows us to monitor and support our kids more effectively. After all, comprehension shouldn't be silent.

The strategy units help make the MTF work. Without these units of study in cognition, students would not have the language and metacognitive skills to communicate effectively during literature circles, textbook circles, and R^5. The environment created through the MTF makes reading a thoughtful process that is not left inside one's head but shared in the classroom community. Throughout the MTF we take the silence out of reading by engaging students in meaningful talk that requires them to think about text as they construct meaning and motivates them to read.

Our students most likely won't become weavers when they grow up. In fact, many of the jobs they will hold may not yet be in existence. We can be sure, however, that our students will need to read and think critically to live full, rich lives. The time we spend teaching them to do so will reap productive, thoughtful, educated citizens and is well worth the extra effort.

Matrix of Activities for Teaching Metacognitive Strategies

Although these activities appear in specific strategy chapters, they can be used to help students improve in a broad range of cognitive skills.

	See page	Predicting	Making Connections	Questioning	Visualizing	Summarizing
Anticipation Guides	86	✓	✓	✓	✓	✓
Anticipation Guide Extension	140	✓				✓
Categorizing Questions	122			✓		
Character Quilt	142		✓	✓	✓	✓
Chunking and Rereading Text	168					✓
Common Senses	149	✓	✓		✓	
Concept-Definition Sort	162	✓	✓			✓
Connections Continuum	110		✓			
Cut-Up Story	96	✓	✓	✓		
Distinguishing Between Narrative and Expository Text	34	✓	✓			
Draw to Remember Events	144				✓	✓
Draw to Remember Setting	145				✓	✓
Draw to Remember Summaries	151				✓	✓
Expository Text Investigation (ETI)	94	✓	✓	✓		✓
Guided Reading Lesson	142	✓	✓	✓	✓	✓
Knowledge Rating Scale	165	✓	✓			✓
Noticing Text Features	86	✓				
One-Sentence Summaries	169					✓
Power of Words	90	✓		✓		✓
Preview, Read, Question	88	✓		✓		✓
Previewing, Predicting, and Learning From Text Features	38	✓			✓	✓

	See page	Predicting	Making Connections	Questioning	Visualizing	Summarizing
Question-and-Answer Book Writing	170	✓	✓	✓		✓
Questioning My Textbook	126			✓		✓
Scene It!	145				✓	✓
Setting Quilt	145				✓	✓
Sharing Visualizations in Think-Pair-Share	139				✓	
Sketch to Stretch	152				✓	✓
Sticky Note Questions	88	✓		✓		
Story Maps	93	✓	✓			✓
Summarizing Rubric	161					✓
Text Feature Walk	40	✓	✓	✓	✓	✓
Text Feature Wall	36	✓		✓		
Two-Column Charts	98	✓	✓	✓	✓	✓
Using a Picture Book With a Strong Character	143	✓	✓	✓	✓	
Using Text Features to Question	124	✓		✓		
Visual Timeline	144				✓	✓
Visualization Continuum	139				✓	
Visualizing During Shared Reading	138				✓	
Word Alert!	91	✓	✓	✓		✓
Word Alert! Extension	165	✓				✓
Word Splash	164	✓	✓			✓
Write a Better Heading	165					✓

Reproducible Forms, Templates, and Think Sheets

MTF Integrated Month-by-Month Planning Sheet

Time Frame	Metacognitive Focus	Activities	Texts for Think-Aloud, Shared Reading, Read-Aloud, and Small-Group Instruction	Writing Project
August–Mid-September	Define metacognition, self-monitoring, clarifying	Establish routines for R⁵, literature circles, Words Their Way, Soar to Success, writer's workshop, common language		
Mid-September–End of October	Prediction, with a special focus on text structure and features	Introduce metacognitive tally sheet, prediction indicators, prediction self-assessment and goal-setting sheet		
November–Mid-December		Introduce metacognitive tally sheet, making connections indicators, making connections self-assessment and goal-setting sheet		
January–Mid-February		Introduce metacognitive tally sheet, questioning indicators, questioning self-assessment and goal-setting sheet		
Mid-February–End of March		Introduce metacognitive tally sheet, visualizing indicators, visualizing self-assessment and goal-setting sheet		
April–Mid-May		Introduce metacognitive tally sheet, summarizing indicators, summarizing self-assessment and goal-setting sheet		

Silent Reading Behaviors Observation Checklist

Student	Out of seat	Looking around/ flipping pages/ not reading	Talking	Total # of off-task behaviors observed	Notes

Attitude and Metacognitive Survey

Student Name _____

1. Do you like reading? Circle yes or no. If yes, why do like to read? If no, why don't you like to read?

2. Where do you like to read?

3. Would you rather read alone or with a peer (friend)? Why?

4. Do you like when the teacher reads aloud? Why or why not?

5. If you are reading something and it doesn't make sense to you, what do you do?

6. When you come to a word you do not know, what do you do?

7. What strategies do you use while you read?

8. What do you think you do well as a reader?

9. What would you like to get better at in reading?

Interest and Wide Reading Inventory

1. If you could be anything in the world when you grow up, what would you be? Why? _____

_____

2. What are your hobbies? _____

3. If you could travel anywhere at all, where would you go? _____

_____

4. What do you like to do with your friends? _____

5. What is your favorite television show? Why? _____

6. What is your favorite animal? _____

7. What do you do when you have time to do what you want? _____

8. What subject or subjects do you like best in school? _____

9. What is the title of the last book you read? _____

10. What are you reading right now? _____

11. Put an X in the box that tells how you feel about reading each of the following:

Type of Text	I like it a lot.	I like it a little.	I don't like it.	I haven't tried it yet but would like to.	I don't know what it is.
Magazines					
Biography					
Science					
History					
Historical Fiction					
Adventure					
Romance					
Sports					
Comic Books					
Mysteries					
Science Fiction/Fantasy					
Realistic Fiction					
Horror					
Poetry					
Short Stories					
Picture Books					

Reprinted from Clausen-Grace, N., & Kelley, M. (2007).

Text Feature Hunt

Name _____

Date _____

Directions: Using the texts you have been given, identify which text features your books have and which text features they do not have. Place a "no" in a box if the text feature is not in the book. Write a page number if the book has the text feature. You need to give only one page number for each text feature. For example, if there are several photos in a book just put one of the page numbers (where the photo appears) in the box.

Title of Text	Table of Contents	Page Numbers	Pictures/ Captions	Cutaways/ Cross Sections	Maps	Diagrams	Glossary	Boldface	Index

Previewing, Predicting, and Learning From Text Features

Text Feature & Page	What does the text feature do?	What I learned from reading the text feature...

Literature Circles Training Template

Strategy	How I used this strategy...	Page number where I used this strategy
Connecting: I connected something in the text to something I've read about, seen, or experienced myself.		
Predicting: I used what I have read or what I know to make a prediction about the text.		
Questioning: I have a question about what I am reading or about ideas the text made me think about.		
Visualizing: I can see a clear picture of something in the text. Hint: You can write a description or draw a picture of what you see.		
Clarifying: I clarify vocabulary, an idea, or concept, or what has happened in the book.		
Writer's craft: I notice something unique or remarkable about the way the author wrote this text. Hint: This could include special words or phrases that really speak to you.		

Literature Circles Book

Literature Circles Conversation Starters

Literature Circles Conversation Starters	**Literature Circles Conversation Starters**		
Use these stems to help you start a conversation about your book.	Use these stems to help you start a conversation about your book.		
How come...	How come...	How come...	How come...
I don't understand...	I don't understand...	I don't understand...	I don't understand...
Did you know...	Did you know...	Did you know...	Did you know...
This reminds me of...	This reminds me of...	This reminds me of...	This reminds me of...
I can't believe...	I can't believe...	I can't believe...	I can't believe...
Can you imagine...	Can you imagine...	Can you imagine...	Can you imagine...
I can just picture...	I can just picture...	I can just picture...	I can just picture...
I had a question about...	I had a question about...	I had a question about...	I had a question about...
Do you think...	Do you think...	Do you think...	Do you think...
I read that...	I read that...	I read that...	I read that...
I think that ____ might be caused by ____...	I think that ____ might be caused by ____...	I think that ____ might be caused by ____...	I think that ____ might be caused by ____...
What does _____ mean?	What does _____ mean?	What does _____ mean?	What does _____ mean?
I love this part...	I love this part...	I love this part...	I love this part...

Literature Circles Bookmark Template (Back)

Literature Circles Conversation Continuers	**Literature Circles Conversation Continuers**	**Literature Circles Conversation Continuers**	**Literature Circles Conversation Continuers**
Use these stems to keep your conversation about the book going.	Use these stems to keep your conversation about the book going.	Use these stems to keep your conversation about the book going.	Use these stems to keep your conversation about the book going.
Are you sure...	Are you sure...	Are you sure...	Are you sure...
Can you show me in the text where it says that?	Can you show me in the text where it says that?	Can you show me in the text where it says that?	Can you show me in the text where it says that?
I thought that meant...	I thought that meant...	I thought that meant...	I thought that meant...
Have you ever seen anything like that before?	Have you ever seen anything like that before?	Have you ever seen anything like that before?	Have you ever seen anything like that before?
What do you think that looks (or smells, feels, sounds, or tastes) like?	What do you think that looks (or smells, feels, sounds, or tastes) like?	What do you think that looks (or smells, feels, sounds, or tastes) like?	What do you think that looks (or smells, feels, sounds, or tastes) like?
Why do you think the author chose to...	Why do you think the author chose to...	Why do you think the author chose to...	Why do you think the author chose to...
Let's get back on track...	Let's get back on track...	Let's get back on track...	Let's get back on track...

Five-Finger Test for Selecting Books

1. Read any passage or page from the book you want to read.

2. Hold up a finger for each word you do not know or cannot read.

3. Can you remember what you read? If not, put the book down and choose another.
   If you can remember, look at the number of fingers you have up.

4. Use the chart below to guide whether this book is right for you!

0–1 Fingers	Easy Book (I can read but not every time)
2–3 Fingers	OK Book
4–5 Fingers	Challenging Book (I may need to partner read)
More than 5 Fingers	Too Hard! (I might want to try again later)

Comprehension Shouldn't Be Silent: From Strategy Instruction to Student Independence by Michelle J. Kelley and Nicki Clausen-Grace. © 2007 International Reading Association. May be copied for classroom use.

Status-of-the-Class Sheet

Date	Student	Book/Page Number	Date	Book/Page Number	Date	Book/Page Number	Date	Book/Page Number

R⁵ Conference Form

Student: _____   Date: _____

Intervention (only if needed): ☐ Changing books ☐ Stuck in genre/series ☐ Books too difficult

1. Tell me a little about what you're reading. Title _____ Genre _____

2. Last time we met you were working on _____ (goal). Have you done this today?

   If yes,

   ☐ Able to give a specific example of strategy use from your current book.

   ☐ Able to give a specific example of strategy use from any text. (go to #3)

   If no,

   ☐ Example was nonspecific or invented.

   ☐ Unable to give an example of strategy use.

   Can you give me an example of a strategy you have used today?

   ☐ Connecting ☐ Predicting ☐ Questioning

   ☐ Visualizing ☐ Summarizing ☐ Other _____

   If needed, use probes on folded card to help students identify and/or better understand strategy use.

3. Let's look at your current self-assessment/goal-setting. Review plan:

   ☐ Plan is feasible. Have you been doing it? If yes, have student give example.

      If no, remind student to use plan, coach as needed.

   ☐ Plan is not feasible. Help student rewrite plan.

4. How can I help you become a better reader?

5. Goal for next conference:

Record of Conferences

Student Name	Aug.	Sept.	Oct.	Nov.	Dec.	Jan.	Feb.	Mar.	Apr.	May	June

Key: Use the code to identify conference

I-Intervention; P-Predicting; C-Connecting; Q-Questioning; S-Summarizing; V-Visualizing

✓-Need to check in with them again.

Vocabulary Bookmark

This **Vocabulary Bookmark** belongs to:

_____

List at least three new or unusual words from your reading. Include the page number where you found the word when you write it on your bookmark.

_____ page #_____

_____ page #_____

_____ page #_____

_____ page #_____

_____ page #_____

Good readers use **METACOGNITION** when they...

• make connections.

• predict.

• monitor their reading to make sure it makes sense.

• use fix-ups to get unstuck.

• visualize what they are reading about.

• form and answer questions as they are reading.

• summarize.

• reflect on (think about) what they are reading.

I AM A GOOD READER!

Independent Reading Log

Date	Title, Author	Genre	Response to What I Read: I'm wondering... I can see a clear picture of... I feel sorry for... I really liked it when... Can you believe... I made a connection to... WOW! Today in my story...	Strategy Used: Predicting, Connecting, Questioning, Visualizing, Summarizing

Preview, Read, Question Think Sheet

Before Reading: Preview the text, read the text features. Write 2–3 questions you expect to have answered as you read.	During Reading: What in your preview caused you to write the question? Cite any relevant page numbers.	After Reading: What was the answer to your question?

The Power of Words Think Sheet

Name _____ Title _____

1. What do you think this book will be about?

2. What important words would you expect to see in this text?

Important words I identified before reading... (while reading check mark any words you have written that have been important to the text)	Important words I added after reading...

Comprehension Shouldn't Be Silent, From Strategy Instruction to Student Independence, Michelle J. Kelley and Nicki Clausen-Grace

Word Alert! Think Sheet

Title of Book _____

Date _____ Name _____

Passage Critical Words	Is the word known? Y/N	How do I know the word? Definition/uses.	Check and highlight if unknown	Confirmation Definition Text evidence (page numbers)

Story Map Think Sheet

Main Characters

Other Characters

Story Map Think Sheet

Title & Author

Setting

Event 1:

Event 2:

Event 3:

Event 4:

Event 5:

Event 6:

Problem

Solution

Expository Text Investigation (ETI) Think Sheet

Researcher(s) _____

Title	Genre or Structure	Characteristics of this Book (What do we notice about how it is written?)

Predicting Tally Sheet

To predict, I...	Tally
use title and chapter headings.	
use the front and back cover.	
use pictures and captions.	
use questions that might be answered as I read.	
use what I already know about the topic, including vocabulary.	
use what I know about the author, genre, or series.	
use what I know about text organization and text structure.	
use what has happened so far in the book.	
use meaningful connections.	
use what I know about a character.	

Thinking About My Reading: Predicting—
Self-Assessment and Goal-Setting Sheet

Name _____   Date _____

Directions: (1) Put a check mark by the things you do well as a reader when making predictions.

(2) Highlight the things you think you need to work on to become a better reader.

- ☐ I use the title and chapter headings to predict.
- ☐ I use the front and back cover to predict.
- ☐ I use pictures and captions to predict.
- ☐ I use questions that might be answered as I read to predict.
- ☐ I use what I know about topic (including vocabulary) to predict.
- ☐ I use what I know about an author, genre, or series to predict.
- ☐ I use what I know about the text organization and text structure to predict.
- ☐ I use what has happened so far in the book to predict.
- ☐ I use meaningful connections to predict.
- ☐ I use what I know about a character to predict.

Choose one highlighted item to improve upon:

_____

_____

_____

Create a plan to improve upon this skill.

1. _____

2. _____

3. _____

4. _____

Making Meaningful Connections Think Sheet

Name _____

Connection	How does this connection help me understand the text better?

Making Connections Tally Sheet

I make connections...	Tally
to the characters.	
to the plot.	
to the setting or place.	
to visualize, taste, smell, feel, or hear the text.	
to predict or infer what will happen in the text.	
to what I know about a topic or word.	
to help me feel emotions related to the text.	
to what I know about the text organization and text structure.	

Thinking About My Reading: Making Connections—
Self-Assessment and Goal-Setting Sheet

Name _____   Date _____

Directions: (1) Put a check mark by the things you do well as a reader when making connections.
(2) Highlight the things you think you need to work on to become a better reader.

- ☐ I make connections to the characters.
- ☐ I make connections to the plot.
- ☐ I make connections to the setting or place.
- ☐ I make connections to visualize, taste, smell, feel, or hear the text.
- ☐ I make connections to predict or infer what will happen in the text.
- ☐ I make connections to what I know about a topic or word.
- ☐ I make connections to help me feel emotions related to the text.
- ☐ I make connections to what I know about the text organization and text structure.

Choose one highlighted item to improve upon:

_____

_____

_____

Create a plan to improve upon this skill.

1. _____

2. _____

3. _____

4. _____

Questioning Tally Sheet

I ask questions...	Tally
to clarify something in the text or a text feature.	
to help me understand vocabulary.	
to help me find specific information in the text.	
to help me connect to the ideas or characters in the text.	
to put myself in the text by using my senses (visualizing, tasting, smelling, and feeling).	
to understand choices the author made when writing the text.	
to help me understand the text organization and text structure.	
to summarize what I have read.	
to help me extend my learning beyond the text.	
to help me understand a character or an object.	
to help me predict.	

Using Text Features to Question Think Sheet

Text Feature Read	Question I have...
1.	1.
2.	2.
3.	3.
4.	4.
5.	5.
6.	6.
7.	7.
8.	8.
9.	9.
10.	10.

Questioning My Textbook Think Sheet

Name _____

Directions: Preview and read the text features for this section of text. Write two questions, not found in the book, that you expect to have answered as you read. During or after reading, write the answers to your two questions.

Question 1:_____

_____

Answer:_____

_____

Question 2:_____

_____

Answer:_____

_____

After reading, write two new questions (not in the textbook or above) that were also answered by the text. Write the answers to these questions as well.

Question 1:_____

_____

Answer:_____

_____

Question 2:_____

_____

Answer:_____

_____

Thinking About My Reading: Questioning— Self-Assessment and Goal-Setting Sheet

Name _____   Date _____

Directions: (1) Put a check mark by the things you do well as a reader when questioning.

(2) Highlight the things you think you need to work on to become a better reader.

☐ I ask questions to help me clarify something in the text or a text feature.

☐ I ask questions to help me understand vocabulary.

☐ I ask questions to find specific information in the text.

☐ I ask questions to help me connect to the ideas or characters in the text.

☐ I ask questions to put myself in the text by using my senses (visualizing, tasting, smelling, and feeling).

☐ I ask questions to understand choices the author made when writing the text.

☐ I ask questions to help me understand the text organization and text structure.

☐ I ask questions to summarize what I have read.

☐ I ask questions to extend my learning beyond the text.

☐ I ask questions to help me understand a character or an object.

☐ I ask questions to help me predict.

Choose one highlighted item to improve upon:

_____

_____

_____

Create a plan to improve upon this skill.

1. _____

2. _____

3. _____

4. _____

Making Meaningful Visualizations Think Sheet

Name_____

What I visualized...	How does this visualization help me understand the text better?

Visualizing Tally Sheet

I visualize...	Tally
to help me predict.	
to help me clarify something in the text.	
the characters, person, or creatures.	
the events.	
the setting or place.	
using my senses (smelling, tasting, hearing, or feeling).	
using a physical reaction (hot, cold, thirsty, upset stomach, etc.).	
using an emotional reaction (happy, sad, excited, lonely, etc.).	
using illustrations or text features in the text.	
to help me remember.	

Thinking About My Reading: Visualizing—
Self-Assessment and Goal-Setting Sheet

Name _____   Date _____

Directions: (1) Put a check mark by the things you do well as a reader when visualizing.

(2) Highlight the things you think you need to work on to become a better reader.

☐ I visualize to help me predict.

☐ I visualize to help me clarify something in the text.

☐ I visualize the characters, person, or creatures.

☐ I visualize the events.

☐ I visualize the setting or place.

☐ I visualize using my senses (smelling, tasting, hearing, or feeling).

☐ I visualize using a physical reaction (hot, cold, thirsty, upset stomach, etc.).

☐ I visualize using an emotional reaction (happy, sad, excited, lonely, etc.).

☐ I visualize using illustrations or text features in the text.

☐ I visualize to help me remember.

Choose one highlighted item to improve upon:

_____

_____

_____

Create a plan to improve upon this skill.

1. _____

2. _____

3. _____

4. _____

Summarizing Tally Sheet

To help me summarize I...	Tally
read the text features and predict the main idea.	
reflect on my prediction and either confirm or revise it.	
read the text features and think how they relate to the main idea.	
notice boldface and italic words and think how they relate to the main idea.	
read subheadings and titles and think how they relate to the main idea.	
identify a section of text that I can read and remember.	
stop at the end of a section of text to connect, visualize, or remember what I've read.	
answer questions I have asked.	
reread to verify important ideas.	
reread to clarify meaning.	
reread to choose supporting details and facts.	
eliminate unimportant details.	

Summarizing Rubric

Name: _____

CATEGORY	Intervention (D)	Instructional (C)	Independent (B)	Advanced (A)
Completeness	Included 1 or 2 facts, may include extra unimportant information	Partial summary with some important ideas, a few facts, may include extra unimportant information	Adequate summary with many important ideas, some details, facts and important vocabulary	Adept summary with most important ideas, details, facts, and important vocabulary
Correctness	Main idea is not expressed; it may include incorrect information	Main idea is partially expressed; it may include misinterpretation	Main idea is expressed; all facts included are correct	Main idea is clearly expressed; all facts included are correct
Quality of Writing	Written in own language or in copied text	Generally written in own language, may be presented as a list of disconnected ideas	Written in own language, generally flows from one idea to another	Written in own language, flows smoothly from one idea to another

Knowledge Rating Scale

Directions: Before reading the text read each term. Check whether you know it and can define it, have heard of it but can't define it, or do not know it. Read the text. In the next column, write why the term was important in the reading.

Term	Know It	Heard of It	Don't Know It	Why is it important?

Adapted from Blachowicz & Fisher, 2006.

Chunking and Rereading Text Think Sheet

Name _____   Text _____

Directions: Stop after each page you read and think about what was important. Reread to clarify what is the big idea on that page. Write the page number and your notes in the space below. Repeat. After reading the entire text, review your notes and write a summary that explains what you learned.

Page # _____   Notes _____

_____

Page # _____   Notes _____

_____

Page # _____   Notes _____

_____

Page # _____   Notes _____

_____

Page # _____   Notes _____

_____

Page # _____   Notes _____

_____

Page # _____   Notes _____

_____

Q-and-A Planning Sheet

Topic or Title _____   Name _____

Important vocabulary:

Question 1:
_____
_____

Possible text features for Question 1: _____
Fact 1: _____
Fact 2: _____
Fact 3: _____
Fact 4: _____

Question 2:
_____
_____

Possible text features for Question 2: _____
Fact 1: _____
Fact 2: _____
Fact 3: _____
Fact 4: _____

Question 3:
_____
_____

Possible text features for Question 3: _____
Fact 1: _____
Fact 2: _____
Fact 3: _____
Fact 4: _____

Question 4:
_____
_____

Possible text features for Question 4: _____
Fact 1: _____
Fact 2: _____
Fact 3: _____
Fact 4: _____

Q-and-A Book Project Rubric

Teacher Name: _____

Student Name: _____

CATEGORY	1	2	3	4
Content	Most of the material is not on topic or accurate. Answers have 1 fact and very little of the information necessary to understand the topic.	Some of the material is on topic and accurate. Answers have 2 facts and some of the information necessary to understand the topic.	Material is mostly on topic and accurate. Answers have at least 3 facts and all the information necessary to understand the topic.	Material is on topic and accurate. Answers have at least 4 facts and all the information necessary to understand the topic.
Format	The text is formatted with at least 1 question and answer. Questions are written correctly.	The text is formatted with at least 2 questions and answers. Questions are written correctly.	The text is formatted with at least 3 questions and answers. Questions are written correctly.	The text is formatted with at least 4 questions and answers. Questions are written correctly.
Text Features	There are at least 7 text features included. These features support the text and help the reader understand the answer. There is a title, a table of contents, and a glossary.	There are at least 8 text features included. These features support the text and help the reader understand the answers. There is a title, a table of contents, and a glossary.	There are at least 9 text features included. These features support the text and help the reader understand the answers. There is a title, a table of contents, and a glossary.	There are at least 10 text features included. These features support the text and help the reader understand the answer. There is a title, a table of contents, and a glossary.
Quality	Strong questions are not written. There are many errors in handwriting, grammar, spelling, and punctuation. The text features are not well done.	Some strong questions are written. There are some errors in handwriting, grammar, spelling, and punctuation. Some of the text features are well done.	Mostly strong questions are written. There are a few errors in handwriting, grammar, spelling, and punctuation. The text features are mostly well done.	Strong questions are written. The handwriting is legible, and correct grammar, spelling, and punctuation are used. The text features are well done.

Thinking About My Reading: Summarizing—
Self-Assessment and Goal-Setting Sheet

Name _____   Date _____

Directions: (1) Put a check mark by the things you do well as a reader when summarizing.

(2) Highlight the things you think you need to work on to become a better reader.

☐ I read the text features and predict the main idea.

☐ I reflect on my prediction and either confirm or revise it.

☐ I read the text features and think how they relate to the main idea.

☐ I notice boldface and italic words and think how they relate to the main idea.

☐ I read subheadings and titles and think how they relate to the main idea.

☐ I identify a section of text that I can read and remember.

☐ I stop at the end of a section of text to connect, visualize, or remember what I've read.

☐ I answer questions I have asked.

☐ I reread to verify important ideas.

☐ I reread to clarify meaning.

☐ I reread to choose supporting details and facts.

☐ I eliminate unimportant details.

Choose one highlighted item to improve upon:

_____

_____

_____

Create a plan to improve upon this skill.

1. _____

2. _____

3. _____

REFERENCES

Allington, R.L. (2006). *What really matters for struggling readers: Designing research-based programs*. Boston: Pearson.

Anderson, R.C. (1996). Research foundations to support wide reading. In V. Greaney (Ed.), *Promoting reading in developing countries* (pp. 55–77). Newark, DE: International Reading Association.

Anderson, R.C., & Nagy, W.E. (1992). The vocabulary conundrum. *American Educator, 16*(4), 14–18, 44–47.

Anderson, R.C., Wilson, P.T., & Fielding, L.G. (1988). Growth in reading and how children spend their time outside of school. *Reading Research Quarterly, 23*, 285–303.

Armbruster, B.B. (1988). *Why some children have trouble reading content area textbooks* (Tech. Rep. No. 432). Champaign, IL: Center for the Study of Reading.

Armbruster, B.B., Lehr, F., & Osborn, J. (2003). *Put reading first: The research building blocks for teaching children to read*. Jessup, MD: National Institute for Literacy.

Atwell, N. (1990). *Coming to know: Writing to learn in the intermediate grades*. Portsmouth, NH: Heinemann.

Atwell, N. (1998). *In the middle: New understandings about writing, reading, and learning* (2nd ed.). Portsmouth, NH: Heinemann.

Beaver, J.M., & Carter, M.A. (2000). Developmental reading assessment: DRA 4–8. Parsippany, NJ: Pearson Learning Group.

Beers, K. (2003). *When kids can't read: What teachers can do: A guide for teachers 6–12*. Portsmouth, NH: Heinemann.

Blachowicz, C., & Fisher, P. J. (2006). *Teaching vocabulary in all classrooms* (3rd ed.). Upper Saddle River, NJ: Pearson.

Bransford, J.D., Brown, A.L., & Cocking, R.R. (Eds.). (2000). *How people learn: Brain, mind, experience, and school*. Washington, DC: National Academy Press.

Calkins, L.M. (1986). *The art of teaching writing*. Portsmouth, NH: Heinemann.

Calkins, L.M. (2001). *The art of teaching reading*. Portsmouth, NH: Heinemann.

Chall, J., Jacobs, V., & Baldwin, L. (1990). *The reading crisis: Why poor children fall behind*. Cambridge, MA: Harvard University Press.

Clausen-Grace, N., & Kelley, M. (2007). You can't hide in R[5]: Restructuring independent reading to be more strategic and engaging. *Voices From the Middle. 14*(3), 38–49.

Cunningham, A.E., & Stanovich, K.E. (1997). Early reading acquisition and its relation to reading experience and ability 10 years later. *Developmental Psychology, 33*, 934–945.

Daniels, H. (2002). *Literature circles: Voice and choice in book clubs & reading groups*. Portland, ME: Stenhouse.

Daniels, H., & Zemelman, S. (2004). *Subjects matter: Every teacher's guide to content-area reading*. Portsmouth, NH: Heinemann.

Darling-Hammond, L. (2000). *Teacher quality and student achievement: A review of state policy evidence*. Retrieved August 8, 2006, from http://epaa.asu.edu/epaa/v8n1/

Davidson, J., & Koppenhaver, D. (1993). *Adolescent literacy: What works and why*. New York: Garland.

Diehl, H. (2005). Snapshots of our journey to thoughtful literacy. *The Reading Teacher, 59*, 56–69.

Donahue, P., Voelkl, K., Campbell, J., & Mazzeo, J. (1999). *NAEP 1998 reading report card for the nation and states*. Washington, DC: U.S. Department of Education, Office of Educational Research and Improvement.

Duke, N.K. (2004). The case for informational text. *Educational Leadership, 61*(6), 40–44.

Durkin, D. (1993). *Teaching them to read* (6th ed.). Boston: Allyn & Bacon.

Feitelson, D., & Goldstein, Z. (1986). Patterns of book ownership and reading to young children in Israeli school-oriented and nonschool-oriented families. *The Reading Teacher, 39*, 924–930.

Flavell, J.H. (1987). Speculations about the nature and development of metacognition. In F.E. Weinert & R.H. Kluwe (Eds.), *Metacognition, motivation, and understanding* (pp. 21–29). Hillsdale, NJ: Erlbaum.

Fountas, I.C., & Pinnell, G.S. (2001). *Guiding readers and writers grades 3–6: Teaching comprehension, genre, and content literacy.* Portsmouth, NH: Heinemann.

Gambrell, L.B., & Almasi, J.F. (1996). *Lively discussions! Fostering engaged reading.* Newark, DE: International Reading Association.

Gambrell, L.B., & Bales, R.J. (1986). Mental imagery and the comprehension-monitoring performance of fourth- and fifth-grade poor readers. *Reading Research Quarterly, 21,* 454–464.

Gillet, J.W., & Temple, C. (1994). *Understanding reading problems: Assessment and instruction* (4th ed.). New York: HarperCollins.

Good, T.L., & Brophy, J.E. (1997). *Looking in classrooms* (7th ed.) New York: Longman.

Gottfried, A.E. (1990). Academic intrinsic motivation in young elementary school children. *Journal of Educational Psychology, 82,* 525–538.

Graves, D.H. (1983). *Writing: Teachers & children at work.* Portsmouth, NH: Heinemann.

Graves, M.F., & Graves, B.B. (2003). *Scaffolding reading experience: Designs for student success* (2nd ed.). Norwood, MA: Christopher-Gordon.

Gunning, T.G. (2003). *Building literacy in the content areas.* Boston: Pearson.

Guthrie, J.T., & Wigfield, A. (2000). Engagement and motivation in reading. In M.L. Kamil, P. Mosenthal, P.D. Pearson, & R. Barr (Eds.), *Handbook of reading research* (Vol. 3, pp. 403–422). Mahwah, NJ: Erlbaum.

Guthrie, J.T., Wigfield, A., Metsala, J.L., & Cox, K.E. (1999). Motivational and cognitive predictors of text comprehension and reading amount. *Scientific Studies of Reading, 3,* 231–256.

Harris, T.L., & Hodges, R.E. (Eds.). (1995). *The literacy dictionary: The vocabulary of reading and writing.* Newark, DE: International Reading Association.

Harvey, S., & Goudvis, A. (2000). *Strategies that work: Teaching comprehension to enhance understanding.* York, ME: Stenhouse.

Hibbing, A.N., & Rankin-Erickson, J.L. (2003). A picture is worth a thousand words: Using visual images to improve comprehension for middle school struggling readers. *The Reading Teacher, 56,* 758–770.

Honig, B., Diamond, L., & Gutlohn, L. (2000). *Teaching reading: Sourcebook for kindergarten through eighth grade.* Novato, CA: CORE.

Irvin, J.L. (1998). *Reading and the middle school students: Strategies to enhance literacy.* Boston: Allyn & Bacon.

Jerry, L., & Lutkus, A. (2003). *The nation's report card: State reading 2002, Report for Nebraska.* Princeton, NJ: Center for Education Statistics (ED), Washington, DC.

Kaufman, D. (2000). *Conferences & conversations: Listening to the literate classroom.* Portsmouth, NH: Heinemann.

Keene, E.O. (2002). From good to memorable: Characteristics of highly effective comprehension teaching. In C.C. Block, L.B. Gambrell, & M. Pressley (Eds.), *Improving comprehension instruction: Rethinking research, theory, and classroom practice* (pp. 80–105). San Francisco: Jossey-Bass.

Keene, E.O., & Zimmermann, S. (1997). *Mosaic of thought: Teaching comprehension in a reader's workshop.* Portsmouth, NH: Heinemann.

Kelley, M., & Clausen-Grace, N. (2006). R[5]: The Sustained Silent Reading makeover that transformed readers. *The Reading Teacher, 60,* 148–156.

Klingner, J., Vaughn, S., & Schumann, J. (1998). Collaborative strategic reading during social studies in heterogeneous fourth-grade classrooms. *Elementary School Journal, 99,* 3–22.

Krashen, S. (1988). Do we learn to read by reading? The relationship between free reading and reading ability. In D. Tannen (Ed.), *Linguistics in context: Connecting observation and understanding* (pp. 269–298). Norwood, NJ: Ablex.

Kristo, J.V., & Bamford, R.A. (2004). *Nonfiction in focus: A comprehensive framework for helping students become independent readers and writers of nonfiction, K–6.* New York: Scholastic.

Langer, J., & Close, E. (2001). *Improving literary understanding through classroom conversation.* Albany, NY: National Research Center on English Learning and Achievement.

Lubliner, S. (2001). *A practical guide to reciprocal teaching.* Bothell, WA: Wright Group/McGraw-Hill.

Marshall, J.C. (2002). *Are they really reading? Expanding SSR in the middle grades.* Portland, ME: Stenhouse.

Marzano, R.J., Pickering, D.J., & Pollock, J.E. (2001). *Classroom instruction that works: Research-based strategies for increasing student achievement.* Alexandria, VA: Association for Supervision and Curriculum Development.

McQuillan, J. (1998). *The literacy crisis: False claims, real solutions.* Portsmouth, NH: Heinemann.

Miller, D. (2002). *Reading with meaning: Teaching comprehension in the primary grades.* Portland, ME: Stenhouse.

National Assessment of Educational Progress. (1988). *NAEP reading report card for the nation.* Washington, DC: National Assessment of Educational Progress.

National Institute of Child Health and Human Development. (2000). *Report of the National Reading Panel. Teaching children to read: An evidence-based assessment of scientific research literature on reading and its implications for reading instruction* (NIH Publication No. 00-4769). Washington, DC: U.S. Government Printing Office.

Neumann, S.B. (2000). *The importance of classroom libraries.* New York: Scholastic.

Nichols, M. (2006). *Comprehension through conversation: The power of purposeful talk in the reading workshop.* Portsmouth, NH: Heinemann.

Ogle, D.M. (1986). K-W-L: A teaching model that develops active reading of expository text. *The Reading Teacher, 39,* 564–570.

Pearson, P.D. (1985). Changing the face of reading comprehension instruction. *The Reading Teacher, 38,* 724–738.

Pearson, P.D., & Gallagher, M. (1983). The instruction of reading comprehension. *Contemporary Educational Psychology, 8,* 317–344.

Pellegrino, J.W., Chudowsky, N., & Glaser, R. (2001). *Knowing what students know: The science and design of educational assessment.* Washington, DC: National Academy Press.

Perkins, D. (1992). *Smart schools: Better thinking and learning for every child.* New York: Free Press.

Perkins, D. (1995). *Outsmarting IQ: The emerging science of learnable intelligence.* New York: Simon & Schuster.

Pilgreen, J. (2000). *The SSR handbook: How to organize and manage a sustained silent reading program.* Portsmouth, NH: Heinemann.

Pilgreen, J., & Krashen, S. (1993). Sustained silent reading with English as a second language high school students: Impact on reading comprehension, reading frequency, and reading enjoyment. *School Library Media Quarterly, 22*(1), 21–33.

Pressley, M. (1977). Imagery and children's learning: Putting the picture in developmental perspective. *Review of Educational Research, 47,* 585–622.

Purcell-Gates, V., Duke, N.K., Hall, L., & Tower, C. (2002, December). Text purposes and text use: A case from elementary science instruction. In W.H. Teale (Chair), *Relationships between text and instruction: Evidence from three studies.* Paper presented at the annual meeting of the National Reading Council, Miami, FL.

Raphael, T. (1982). Question-answering strategies for children. *The Reading Teacher, 36,* 186–190.

Readence, J.E., Bean, T.W., & Baldwin, R.S. (1995). *Content area reading: An integrated approach* (5th ed.). Dubuque, IA: Kendall/Hunt.

Recht, D.R., & Leslie, L. (1988). Effect of prior knowledge on good and poor readers' memory of text. *Journal of Educational Psychology, 80,* 16–20.

Reutzel, D.R., & Fawson, P.C. (2002). *Your classroom library: New ways to give it more teaching power.* New York: Scholastic.

Robb, L. (2003). *Teaching reading in social studies, science, and math: Practical ways to weave comprehension strategies into your content teaching.* New York: Scholastic.

Rosenblatt, L.M. (1978). *The reader, the text, the poem: The transactional theory of literary work.* Carbondale: Southern Illinois University Press.

Routman, R. (2000). *Conversations: Strategies for teaching, learning, and evaluating.* Portsmouth, NH: Heinemann

Routman, R. (2003). *Reading essentials: The specifics you need to teach reading well.* Portsmouth, NH: Heinemann.

Santa, C.M., Havens, L.T., & Vadles, B.J. (2004). *Project CRISS: Creating independence through student-owned strategies* (3rd ed.). Dubuque, Iowa: Kendall/Hunt.

Short, K.G., Harste, J.C., & Burke, C. (1996). *Creating classrooms for authors and inquirers.* Portsmouth, NH: Heinemann.

Shwartz, R., & Raphael, T. (1985). Concept of definition: A key to improving students' vocabulary. *The Reading Teacher, 39,* 190–205.

Simpson, M.L., & Nist, S.L. (2000). An update on strategic learning: It's more than textbook reading strategies. *Journal of Adolescent & Adult Literacy, 43,* 528–541.

Sousa, D.A. (2004). *How the brain learns: A classroom teachers guide* (2nd ed.). Thousand Oaks, CA: Corwin Press.

Spencer, B.H. (2003). Text maps: Helping students navigate informational texts. *The Reading Teacher, 56,* 752–756.

Stien, D., & Beed, P.L. (2004). Bridging the gap between fiction and nonfiction in the literature circle setting. *The Reading Teacher, 57,* 510–518.

Stronge, J.H. (2002). *Qualities of effective teachers.* Alexandria, VA: Association for Supervision and Curriculum Development.

Sweet, A., Guthrie, J.T., & Ng, M. (1998). Teacher perceptions and student reading motivation. *Journal of Educational Psychology, 90,* 210–223.

Tierney, R.J., & Readence, J.E. (2005). *Reading strategies and practices: A compendium* (6th ed.). Boston: Pearson.

Tovani, C. (2000). *I read, but I don't get it: Comprehension strategies for adolescent readers.* Portland, ME: Stenhouse.

Vygotsky, L. (1978). *Mind in society: The development of higher psychological processes* (M. Cole, V. John-Steiner, S. Scribner, & E. Souberman, Eds. & Trans.). Cambridge, MA: Harvard University Press. (Original work published 1934)

Wang, M., Haertel, G.D., & Walberg, H. (1993). What helps students learn? *Educational Leadership, 51*(4), 74–79.

White, B.Y., & Frederickson, J.R. (1998). Inquiry, modeling, and metacognition: Making science accessible to all students. *Cognition and Instruction, 16,* 3–118.

Wilhelm, J. (2001). *Improving comprehension with think-aloud strategies: Modeling what good readers do.* New York: Scholastic.

Wolfe, P. (2001). *Brain matters: Translating research into classroom practice.* Alexandria, VA: Association for Supervision and Curriculum Development.

Wormeli, R. (2005). *Summarization in any subject: 50 techniques to improve student learning.* Alexandria, VA: Association for Supervision and Curriculum Development.

Yopp, R.H., & Yopp, H.K. (2000). Sharing informational text with young children. *The Reading Teacher, 53,* 410–423.

LITERATURE CITED

Individual Titles

Abbott, T. (1999). *The secrets of Droon: Journey to the volcano palace*. New York: Scholastic.

Avi. (2002). *Crispin: The crown of lead*. New York: Hyperion.

Berger, M. (1993). *Wild weather*. North Borough, MA: Newbridge Communications.

Berger, M., & Berger, A. (1999). *Can it rain cats and dogs?* New York: Scholastic.

Birney, B.G. (2004). *The world according to Humphrey*. New York: Putnam.

Bloor, E. (1997). *Tangerine*. New York: Scholastic.

Bray-Moffatt, N. (2003). *Disney princess essential guide*. New York: Dorling Kindersley.

Capriani, N. (1996). *The encyclopedia of rocks and minerals*. New York: Barnes & Noble.

Clements, A. (2003). *A week in the woods*. New York: Scholastic.

Collins, S. (2003). *Gregor the overlander*. New York: Scholastic.

Cooper, K. (2001). *What a girl wants: The ultimate survival guide for beauty, health, and happiness*. New York: Scholastic.

Cowley, J. (1997). *Bow down, Shadrach*. Bothell, WA: Wright Group.

Creech, S. (2003). *Granny Torrelli makes soup*. New York: Scholastic.

DiCamillo, K. (2000). *Because of Winn-Dixie*. Cambridge, MA: Candlewick.

DiCamillo, K. (2001). *The tiger rising*. Cambridge, MA: Candlewick.

Donkin, A. (2000). *Bermuda Triangle*. New York: Dorling Kindersley.

Drake, E. (2005). *The dragonology handbook: A practical course in dragons*. Cambridge, MA: Candlewick.

Farley, W. (1941). *The black stallion*. New York: Random House.

Fisch, S. (2000). *Batman beyond: No place like home*. New York: Random House.

Fletcher, R.J. (1996). *A writer's notebook: Unlocking the writer within you*. New York: Avon.

Fletcher, R.J. (2000). *Flying solo*. New York: Dell Yearling.

Forney, M. (2000). *Oonawassee summer*. Poulsbo, WA: Barker Creek.

Fuerst, J. (2005). *A guide to rocks and minerals*. Parsippany, NJ: Celebration Press.

Funke, C.C. (2003). *Inkheart*. New York: Scholastic.

George, J.C. (1987). *The talking earth*. New York: HarperTrophy.

Haddix, M.P. (1998). *Among the hidden*. New York: Simon & Schuster.

Henkes, K. (2003). *Olive's ocean*. New York: Greenwillow.

Hiaasen, C. (2002). *Hoot*. New York: Knopf.

Hiaasen, C. (2005). *Flush*. New York: Knopf.

Horowitz, A. (2005). *Raven's gate*. New York: Scholastic.

Jennings, P. (1998). *Listen ear and other stories to shock you silly!* New York: Puffin.

Kehret, P. (2003). *Escaping the giant wave*. New York: Simon & Schuster.

Lewis, C.S. (1950). *The lion, the witch and the wardrobe*. New York: HarperCollins.

Martin, A.M. (1988). *Dawn and the impossible three*. Lakeville, CT: Grey Castle.

Martin, A.M. (1988). *The truth about Stacey*. Lakeville, CT: Grey Castle.

Martin, A.M. (2005). *A dog's life: The autobiography of a stray*. New York: Scholastic.

Martin, R., & Shannon, D. (1992). *The rough-faced girl*. New York: G.P. Putnam's Sons.

McElroy, L. (2006). *Drake & Josh: Blues brothers*. New York: Scholastic.

McLerran, A. (1991). *Roxaboxen*. New York: HarperCollins.

Melville, H. (1986). *Moby Dick*. New York: Chelsea House.

Paolini, C. (2003). *Eragon*. New York: Knopf/Random House.

Paulsen, G. (1987). *Hatchet*. New York: Atheneum.

Paulsen, G. (2003). *Brian's hunt*. New York: Scholastic.

Pearson, R. (2005). *The kingdom keepers: Disney after dark*. New York: Disney Editions.

Philbrick, W.R. (2005). *The young man and the sea*. New York: Scholastic.

Platt, R. (2004). *D-day landings: The story of the Allied invasion*. New York: Dorling Kindersley.

Ryan, B. (2004). *The legend of Holly Claus*. New York: HarperCollins Children's Books.

Rylant, C. (1986). *Night in the country*. New York: Bradbury Press.

Sachar, L. (1998). *Holes*. New York: Farrar, Straus and Giroux.

Sanderson, J. (1993). *Dog to the rescue: Seventeen true tales of dog heroism*. New York: Apple.

Sanderson, J. (1995). *Dog to the rescue II: Seventeen more true tales of dog heroism*. New York: Scholastic.

Sewell, A. (1989). *Black beauty*. New York: Waldman.

Simon, S. (2003). *Hurricanes*. New York: HarperCollins.

Snicket, L. (2000). *A series of unfortunate events: The reptile room*. New York: Scholastic.

Wallace, B. (1980). *A dog called Kitty*. New York: Holiday House.

Wang, M.L. (1989). *The ant and the dove*. Chicago: Children's Press.

Werther, S.P. (2002). *The Donner Party*. Chicago: Children's Press.

Yep, L. (1995). *Hiroshima*. New York: Scholastic.

Series

Berger, M., & Berger, G. Scholastic question & answer series. New York: Scholastic.

Haddix, M.P. Shadow children. New York: Scholastic.

Korman, G. On the run. New York: Scholastic.

Martin, A. The baby-sitters club. New York: Scholastic.

Nix, G. The seventh tower. New York: Scholastic.

Roy, R. The A to Z mysteries. New York: Random House.

Snicket, L. A series of unfortunate events. New York: HarperCollins.

Favorite Authors

DiCamillo, Kate. http://katedicamillo.com/

Hiaason, Carl. http://www.carlhiaason.com/

Paulsen, Gary. http://www.randomhouse.com/features/garypaulsen/about.html

INDEX

Note: Page numbers followed by *f* or *r* indicate figures and reproducibles, respectively.